Forward-Looking Conservatism:

A Renegade Sociologist Speaks Out

Melvyn L. Fein

The Social Individualism Foundation

2 Forward-Looking Conservatism

Cover Photo: Linda Treiber

Cover Design, Kathryn Siggelko, Shari Sheridan

Other Books by Melvyn L. Fein:

Role Change
Race and Morality
Human Hierarchies
The Limits of Idealism
Post-Liberalism
The Great Middle Class Revolution
Evolution versus Revolution
Unlocking you Inner Courage

Contents

I. Introduction..5

II. A Nation In Crisis...19

III. Principled Change..42

IV. Liberal Failures...66

V. The Neo-Marxist Connection..99

VI. The Assault on Our Social Integrity............................125

VII. Traditional Values—Updated.....................................157

VIII. The Mis-Education of Our Youth..............................196

IX. Forward-Looking Conservatism..................................235

X. Some Final Thoughts...278

4 Forward-Looking Conservatism

Chapter I

INTRODUCTION

A Renegade Sociologist

Let me start by explaining my sub-title. Why do I describe myself as a renegade sociologist? Is there some virtue with being out of step with the vast majority of my academic colleagues? It should be no secret that sociology is a remarkably liberal discipline. For years, it has been duking it out with English Literature and Anthropology to see which could be more left-wing. Surveys show that at least ninety present of scholastic sociologists identify as liberal or some version of neo-Marxist. They may call themselves progress-ives or moderates, but an examination of their beliefs demonstrates socialist inclinations. Indeed, a few decades ago, when I asked a prominent member in the field whether it were possible to be a sociologist without being a socialist, after a moments hesitation he replied in the negative. No, he responded; the two go together and always had. To believe in the importance of social causes, he opined, obviously required social solutions.

The same surveys that reveal the leftward tilt of sociologists, suggest that no more the three percent consider themselves conservatives and of these nearly half identify as religious conservatives. As a secular conservative, I therefore belong to a very small fraternity. A friend of mine, who is a libertarian economist, set out to find out just how many. Nation-wide, he found no more than a dozen. The authors of the book *Passing on the Right,* in their research on how conservatives survive in a university setting, identified nine. No wonder that I feel isolated when I attend sociological conferences. No wonder that I seldom find colleagues who agree with my political sentiments or concur with my analyses of social events.

Yet the situation is worse than that. I am routinely excoriated for my views. More than once, I have literally been told to shut up when expressing standpoints inconsistent with those around me. Furthermore, I have been vigorously lectured on the correct positions. There was no balanced dialogue. There was no scientific interchange designed to ferret out the truth. Since the truth was believed to be known, it was my job to fall into line. Nor was I allowed to write about my deviant conclusions. Journal articles were rejected even though they were described as "elegantly written and elegantly argued." They were, I was informed, out of the mainstream that consequently of no interest to the periodical's readers. An editor even refused to publish a piece of mine for the newsletter of an organization to which I belonged. Although I had organized several conferences that yielded thousands of dollars for the association, he disapproved of my sentiments and hence would not let them see the light of day. They might, heaven forefend, corrupt those who read them.

Worse yet, after I began contributing columns to the *Marietta Daily Journal*, the husband of a close colleague *ordered* me to desist. In front of a room filled with other sociologists, he demanded that I stop writing such trash. My pieces were, he insisted, not sociological. It was therefore unethical for me to represent myself as a sociologist. It did not matter that I had a Ph.D. in sociology. Nor did it count that I had written a dozen books on the subject and was a tenured full professor at a sizeable university. Because my views were inconsistent with his, as well as those he considered valid representatives of the discipline, I was misrepresenting the truth. This was intolerable and an insult. It was time to bring my distortions to an end.

For my own part, I still regard myself as a scientist. The truth is not something inscribed in an official document. It is not something that a majority of academics happen to believe at a single moment in time. To the contrary, it is something to be sought and verified by disciplined observation. Science is not a catalog of approved facts. It is a process. It is a means of getting closer to the truth by using empirical tools to corroborate what appears to be the case. Disinterested investigations of the real world are to enable us to discover when we are in error and point the way to closer approximations of reality. Yes, some scientists will defend the received wisdom, but they are also obligated to let it be challenged. They must be sufficiently open-minded to admit they might be wrong. Moreover, if their views are subsequently found to be wanting, they are obliged to admit this fact. They must swallow hard and accept newly established findings.

On these grounds, I have found much of contemporary sociology to be defective. Ever since the mid-twentieth century, the field has been taken over by neo-Marxists. These academics may call themselves "conflict theorists," but they are died in the wool adherents of Karl Marx. As apologists for their master's suppositions, they agree with him that his postulates were completely scientific. For this reason, his claims are treated as immutable. Like all good Marxists, these scholars dedicate themselves to promoting an orthodoxy—his. Disagreements are not tolerated, while dissent brings quick retribu-tion. Where once sociologists tolerated diversity, this has been replaced by self-righteous conformity. Although scientific rigor is preached, in practice it is suppressed by a dreary recitation of official dogmas.

Sociology has, in essence, been swallowed by identity politics. In the name of promoting the universal cooperation, which is the supposed endpoint for mainstream Marxism, they divide people into competing camps. Women are pitted against men; blacks are urged to protest against whites; gays are encouraged to be hostile toward straights. Although this policy is portrayed as advancing a healthy diversity, it, in fact, permits so-called "progressives" to reward their allies, thereby cultivating support for their hegemony. This is a power play, not a scientific ploy. It is a form of bullying, not collaborating. It is why sociology is nowadays swamped by advocacy research. The goal of this counterfeit practice is not to learn new things, but to solidify the status of conclusions that sustain the leftist agenda. As a result, sociology has become utterly predictable. Outsiders do not have to study its tenets in order to forecast the assertions of its adherents. Nor can conservatives expect encourage-ment from these conclusions. What is broadcast to the world is always the same. It persistently identifies members of a selfish elite as exploiting the weak and continuously recommends that the villains be overthrown so that their victims are able to occupy their well-deserved place in the sun. This strategy is called "social justice" and is regarded as the inexorable culmination of history. What is more, the alternative is assumed to be malicious and anti-intellectual and thus beyond the civilized pale.

So where did I go wrong? Why do I find that I have more in common with conservatives than liberals? How, despite decades of pressure to conform, did I manage to retain my intellectual independence? If I am now happy to characterize myself as a "renegade," what drove me to defect from the established verities? It was not always this way. I was not always out of synch with leftist canons. When I was much younger—before I became a sociologist—I considered myself an ardent socialist. During my Brooklyn youth, I am not sure I ever met anyone who considered him or herself a conservative. Everyone I knew voted Democratic. Everyone with whom I had political discussions expressed a devotion to leftwing causes. I even had an uncle who, as a teenager, belonged to the Communist Party. He was a beloved uncle and I deeply sympathized with him when he feared that McCarthyism might deprive him of the opportunity to

8 Forward-Looking Conservatism

obtain a city job. Nor did I have teachers who advocated capitalism. Instead I heard quite a bit about the virtues of the New Deal. Although it was acknowledged to have been a failure, the reason for this was plainly that it was "too little, too late." If only Franklin Roosevelt had been bolder. If only he had been more socialistic in his policies, our nation would have prospered. More complete government control of the economy would have delivered the fairness and affluence he promised.

So far as I was then concerned, conservatives were ignorant and selfish. They were obviously not smart enough to understand that when people cooperated with one another everyone flourished. Because they wanted more than they deserved, they were prepared to deprive others of what they had rightfully earned. These troglodytes did not read books; they did not write books. They were far too preoccupied with plotting how to steal resources from the vulnerable. In short, capitalism was a hoax. It was an excuse for theft and oppression. No good person could possibly support such an agenda. No human being, with an ounce of decency, would stand by and allow it to prevail. I, of course, was one of the good guys. I would fight for truth and justice. As a bright student, I would use my abilities to further the socialist cause. Just as my teachers urged, I would use my talents to strengthen the government so that it could better provide ordinary people with what they needed. Rather than innovate for the sake of enhancing private profit, I would develop new ways to make public entities more efficient. This would be my contribution to saving the world.

But, as they say, a funny thing happened on the way to this idealistic conclusion. Initially I was not so much mugged by reality as shaken into a reconsideration of my beliefs by two close friends. When I entered college, my goal was to be a physicist. I wanted to be the next Albert Einstein. The trouble was, as I quickly realized, that I hated physics and calculus. For a while, I was distraught. Then I discovered philosophy. It would teach me why the world was they way it was and how I ought to lead my life. Happily, I also developed relationships with a couple of fellow students who initially shared this orientation. They were smart and committed, and thus a pleasure to debate. This was at Brooklyn College and so you may rest assured that these disputes were vigorous.

Then something unexpected intervened. My friends switched out of philosophy and into economics. Moreover, in doing so, they became conservative. Eventually, after we graduated and shared an apartment, our disputes stretched into the wee hour of the morning. I retained my socialist inclinations, while they challenged these at every turn. One of our major areas of contention was rent control. Did the government, in freezing rents in place, benefit ordinary folks. I said yes. This prevented rapacious landlords from gouging their tenants. They said no. It actually reduced the housing stock because owners could not afford to repair their properties when their receipts were kept artificially low. They pointed to the destruction in the South Bronx as evidence of what occurred. Houses literally tumbled to the ground when those with title to them had no incentive to protect their value.

One of my friends, Walter Block, became enamored of Ayn Rand and her objectivist movement. Nathanial Brandon, then Rand's primary acolyte, spent a great deal of time seeking converts at Brooklyn College. Walt was impressed. He enjoyed debating Brandon and visiting Rand in her apartment. Eventually he obtained his doctorate from Columbia University and became a nationally recognized advocate of libertarian principles. As of this writing, he is a distinguished professor of economics at Loyola University in New Orleans and the author of many monographs on the importance of personal liberty.

My other friend, Benjamin Klein, got his Ph.D. in economics from the University of Chicago. Since I was, at the same time, attending the University of Wisconsin in Madison, I got to visit him on several occasions. On one of these, I had the privilege of sitting in on a class given by Milton Friedman. He was discussing the effects of monetary policy on economic expansion. This was an eye-opener. Whatever else he was, Friedman was no dummy. He was no hack who was simply repeating the shibboleths of long dead sages. It was thus no longer possible for me to believe that liberals had a monopoly on intelligence or innovative ideas. Ben, who absorbed these lessons, later went on became a noted professor of economics at UCLA. There he developed into a internationally recognized expert on contractual arrangements and economic competition. More recently he joined the consulting firm of Compass Lexicon as a senior fellow.

These friendships provided a window on a world that had previously been closed to me. While they did not result in an immediate switch to the dark side, they gave me something to think about. Names such as Friedrich Hayek and Edmund Burke now became familiar. So, decades later, did that of Thomas Sowell, who had been a student at Chicago at the same time as Ben. In fact, I began to resent my earlier education. Why had my teachers failed to mention that there were respectable thinkers on the right? Why did they imply that there was but one side to the story? The more I read, the broader the context I could bring to bear on my own conclusions.

Intellectual conversions are major events. People seldom change their minds about fundamental questions without undergoing what amounts to a mental and emotional earthquake. To go from liberal to conservative represented a betrayal of my family and ethnic tradition. Previously, I had regarded socialism as part of my Jewish heritage. How could I abandon it without abandoning those I loved? A decade was therefore required for me to decide there was more truth on the side of the conservatives. This entailed rethinking a host of commitments and reorganizing the way I thought about the future. If I was going to save the world, it was not going to be by participating in a Marxist revolution. If I was going to be a truly moral person, it was not because I strengthened the role of government. These, I had come to regard, as impediments to genuine progress.

The years after I dropped out of the philosophy program in Wisconsin were therefore ones of turmoil. Where formerly I assumed I would become a college professor, now my future was in flux. Aside from reconsidering my political allegiances, I did not know where to turn. First, I served a stint in the military as an artillery mechanic, then I stumbled through a series of jobs that included being a caseworker for the New York City Welfare Department, a cabdriver, a reporter for a New Jersey Newspaper, a market researcher, and even a temp in a mailroom. None of these positions, however, satisfied my need to do something important. They did, nonetheless provide me with an education in unfamiliar aspects of the world. Gradually I began to leave some of my naiveté behind. I also spent six years in psychotherapy exploring my inner life. In both individual and group therapy, I became better acquainted with my unconscious motives. This developed into a classic period of "finding myself." And, oh yes, for a while I got into a live-in relationship with a woman I knew was not going to be my wife. She was very much the hippy and not an intellectual, but she introduced me to the mysteries of sex and heterosexual intimacy. While these experiences were not always pleasurable, and I was not proud of my irresponsibility and egotism, I kept bouncing from one unanticipated encounter to another.

In due course, I found myself working as a counselor at a methadone program. Because my self-image remained fragile, I assumed that the only thing I had to offer others was my dedicated assistance. This much of my liberal orientation remained. Moreover, I became skilled at working with damaged human beings. I genuinely cared about their welfare and hence was able to establish supportive relationships. Nonetheless, much of what they were experiencing was a mystery to me. I had never lived in a ghetto. I had never been addicted to a potent drug or been dependent on public transfer payments. What then did I know of the challenges my clients faced? It was at this point I resolved to become more professional. I would return to graduate school, but in which discipline? For a while, I debated between psychology and sociology. The former was the more traditional route, but the latter held the promise of introducing me to lifestyles outside my experience. Although I had had but a single undergraduate course in sociology—in which I got a C—I took the plunge. I enrolled in the sociology program at the Graduate Center of the City University of New York.

Although I was aware of sociology's reputation for being ultra-liberal, my aim was not to be a renegade. I hoped to be authentically scientific and so my focus was on learning as much as I could. By my estimate, about a third of my academic cohort was Marxist, but I chalked this up to residing in New York. In fact, this was at the height of the battles between conflict theorists and functionalists. The former were winning, but had not yet assigned their foes to perdition. In any event, my specialties were socialization, education, and complex organizations; none of which was overtly political. This kept me out of the line of fire. Besides, I was playing catch-up. If I was going to be a first-rate sociologist, I had some reading to do. There were literally hundreds of books to devour before I could feel confident in my mastery of the field. On top of this, I hoped to contribute to the development of clinical sociology. If I were successful, I would take the knowledge accumulated by over a century of sociologists and apply it to solving the personal problems of needy clients.

Nonetheless, once I finished my course work, I was still too insecure to seek an academic position. Instead I found work as a state employment agency where I was at first out-stationed in a psychiatric hospital and then in a community mental health center. While this had not been planned, there could scarcely have been a better situation in which to pursue my clinical ambitions. Working as a rehabilitation counselor was not a theoretical endeavor. The clients I served were real people with real difficulties. As a consequence, I could not count myself as successful if all I did was write papers about what I observed. Those I served needed to make concrete progress or I was evidently kidding myself. A failure to achieve what I intended indicated that I probably did not understand what was going on. This removed me from the mindset of scholastic sociology. My accomplishments would not be measured by the opinions of other Ph.D.'s, but the outcomes of my daily efforts. Here and now realism, not disembodied concepts, had to be the touchstone of my exertions.

On the other hand, I loved ideas and reveled into converting these into actualities. My father had been a man of action. As a practicing engineer, he was suspicious of ungrounded philosophies. From his point of view, all I had thus far mastered was book learning. When I was young, the two of us accordingly fought about which was more important— theory or experience. Now as a practicing quasi-therapist, I concluded that the interaction between the two was best. Theory should guide practice, whereas practice could bring theory down to earth. It was this attitude that I brought to developing my ideas about *Resocialization*. This sociological re-interpretation of psychotherapy was to be an improvement upon what psychologists and psychiatrists did in that it highlighted the impact of social relationships on individual travails. In this, it would explicate what actually happened when people confronted their personal demons. As such, it would enable practitioners to improve clinical outcomes.

It was at this point that I completed my first two books about individual change. They put the process of relinquishing dysfunctional personal roles in social perspective. This achievement finally gave me the confidence to seek academic employment. Now I believed that I had learned enough to merit sharing my insights with others. To this end, I applied for an assistant professor position at Kennesaw State University. My future colleagues were looking for someone to create a program in clinical sociology and hence I fit the bill. Once more, politics was not the issue. Shortly thereafter, I moved to an unfamiliar part of the country. Although I had never previously lived in the South, residing some forty miles north of Atlanta was to prove a salutary learning experience. The distorted fantasies I had acquired up North would melt away as I interacted with my new neighbors. They were not as vicious or backward as I had previously assumed. If anything, I found their conservative attitudes congenial.

As for my attempts to set up a program in clinical sociology, they quickly foundered. The Dean of our college would not allow them to move forward. Instead I had to shift my area of concentration. Soon I would be teaching courses on race relations and social class. More significantly, I would also be teaching one on the nature of social change. At first, this was a disaster. My former expertise was in personal, not social, transformations. Sadly, the two did not seem to jibe. While I had read far more history than most sociologists, I did not know how to make this fit with my new assignment. Slowly, however, a new way of looking at things emerged. I began to realize the limits of my own idealism as I struggled to integrate the enormous amounts of data relevant to explaining the modern age. This included understanding how morality and social hierarchies functioned—which eventuated in recognizing that our nation was in the midst of a middle class revolution. The realization was an eye-opener. As such, it helped me diagnose the significance of professionalization and self-direction. I could now begin to appreciate why liberalism had failed. As crucially, it pointed the way to recognizing that a new way of comprehending how society was evolving was imperative.

Over the years, and during the course of writing a dozen more books, my ideas about forward-looking conservatism emerged. Subsequent to my conversion away from liberalism, I began to realize how temperamentally conservative I was. Like most folks on the right, I believed in the value of a smaller government. Years of first-hand experience demonstrated the limitations of massive bureaucracies. Ever since my debates with Walt and Ben, I also acknowledged the virtues of a market economy. If my commitments to liberty, a strong military, and sturdy families were added to this, I possessed the core of what Barry Goldwater termed the "conscience of a conservative." What is more, I was not opposed to tradition. While I did not want to be trapped in the past, I appreciated the merits of respecting the achievements of my predecessors. Hence, although I was a non-practicing Jew, I was never tempted to deny my heritage. It was part of who I was. As if this were not enough to seal my right wing identity, I finally got married, which further stabilized my attitudes and personal wellbeing. Having a wife taught me many things about the essence of the human situation that could not have been acquired elsewhere. It internalized crucial emotional understand-ings that made them more salient.

Even so, I had never been conservative in the sense of resisting change. My childhood desire to make a better world still burned in my chest. There was nevertheless an important shift. Mine was now a more realistic, as opposed to, a romantic idealism. I wanted to build on tradition, not repudiate it. Long gone were fantasies about constructing a society without limitations. I had discovered too much about my personal shortcomings, and the roadblocks thrown up by an intransigent world, to believe in miracles. Some people become embittered by life's frustrations. I had not. As importantly, at no point in my convoluted history had I sold out. I always maintained my integrity. What was more, I was now happy. I loved college teaching. I loved my wife. I was comfortable where we lived and proud of the intellectual advances I had made. True, I had not found a warm welcome in my academic discipline. On the other hand, I had discovered one in my home department. This amiability did not come without a struggle. When I had initially gone up for tenure, my then chair sought to deny it. There next followed a three-year battle that ended in my complete victory. Not only was I granted tenure, but I helped establish a new department. I was thus professionally safe. Because of this, I could think and write as a wanted, despite being surrounded by professors who cast a wary eye on my opinions. My brand of conservatism might not have been appreciated, but I could uphold it without experiencing daily opposition.

Which brings me to the columns collected in the ensuing chapters. I did not begin composing them by design. The original impetus came almost a decade ago when I was lobbying for additional funds for my university. The state was then on a belt-tightening binge, the effects of which I opposed. When I had, years earlier, worked as an apprentice journalist, I contemplated a career as a columnist. Nothing came of this because I had nothing noteworthy to say. This time was different. After complaining that our college was underfunded, I became aware that the editors of the Marietta Daily Journal were prepared to print my pieces. At first, these efforts were sporadic. When a particular issue demanded attention, I expressed my reaction on the editorial page. Soon the essays became bi-weekly and then morphed into a weekly feature. As quickly became evident, I had a talent for short essays. Not only did I relish writing them, but reader feedback indicated that many agreed with my opinions. Some, of course, were hostile. This was consistent with my classroom encount-ers. I was a polarizing figure. People seemed either to love or hate me. When I was a teenager, and longed for universal admiration, this reaction would have been horrifying. Now, as an established professor, who had survived countless wounds, I did not care. My ambition was to do for sociology what Sowell did for economics. As an avid reader of his columns, I admired the way he customized information that laymen considered dull. I would attempt to do the same for my discipline.

A similar outlook infuses to the following compilation, which includes 140 odd out of the more than 500 pieces I have penned (see *professionalized.blogspot.com* for the others). Selecting them turned out to be more difficult than I imagined. My goal was to tell a cohesive story that illuminated forward-looking conservatism. The idea was to make independently conceived essays coalesce into a persuasive whole. This meant that there would be some repetition and some choices out of context. Some would also contain conclusions that I no longer support. Nor are they always in chronological order. It also necessitated eliminating many of my most political pieces. I had, for instance, written more about the Obama presidency and political campaigns than appears on these pages. The same goes for my columns on race and gender. Nonetheless, I hope that readers will find what remains stimulating. First and foremost, I sought to be honest. As a result, much of what ensues may be controversial.

These are trying times. The following chapter therefore sets up the central problems we today confront. We are, at the moment, trapped in an ideological crisis. The fundamental conceptual tools we use to make sense of a puzzling universe have let us down. This requires that we step back and take fresh look at the larger picture. To me, it is clear that the neo-Marxist hegemony, which in recent years has dominated the intellectual and political scene, is a disaster. It has totally misconstrued the nature of the difficulties we face and thus led us astray. Our present national malaise results, in large part, from the failure of this "social justice" agenda to fulfill its promises. Americans on the left and the right are frustrated by high hopes dashed by unforeseen reality checks. The question is why have things gone wrong and what can be done about it? Is there a way out of our cul-de-sac? Can we truly make changes for the better?

If we are to find a viable way forward, we must eschew romantic idealism in favor of principled realism. Rather than pursue liberal versions of neo-Marxism, we have to understand the complexities of the mass techno-commercial in which we are immersed. This requires that instead of being saved by government interventions, we learn to save ourselves. In order to do so, we have to become more professionalized. Many more of us must learn to be self-motivated experts who can make sound independent choices. The answer, it seems to me, is "social individualism." We must become emotionally and intellectually mature enough to make competent decisions. This entails appreciating our personal and social limitations. This is not easy. Nor are big changes made quickly. Nevertheless, abandoning ourselves to the tender mercies of a bloated government is far more dangerous.

Liberalism has failed. The tortured politics we are currently experiencing result from this historic collapse. For the better part of a century, Americans accepted the progressive dream of total equality and universal niceness as sponsored by a benevolent federal government. We were promised so much that we expected near heaven on earth. Then this prophecy crashed and burned. The economy faltered and social tensions rose. Instead of admitting this, however, liberals added further promises. With this came additional disappointments—such as ObamaCare—that subsequently needed to be defended with a fortress of myths. In any event, as the Bible teaches, progressivism ought to be known by its fruits. PC fatigue has consequently set in. Liberal arrogance can no longer be concealed. The self-deceptions, the intellectual bankruptcy, and the false pretense of niceness are there for all to see. So are the counterfeit compassion, phony tolerance, and fake integrity. Liberals are, in fact, world-class haters. They espouse love, but do not display it. Disagree with them and they go straight for the jugular. We must instead return to common sense. We need to deal with reality as it is—not as we would like it to be.

Whatever its affectations, liberalism is a form of neo-Marxism. Despite a century of strenuous denial, it is a watered down variation on the socialist theme. Whereas progressives have the identical intellectual pretensions as traditional Marxists, they are also tied to its sorry record of malfunctions. Unfortunately, these dogmatic frauds have infiltrated into the heart of our culture. They have captured the media, our educational system, and the entertainment industry. From these perches, they perverted our traditional beliefs. In their place, they substituted identity politics. Social justice has accordingly become a scam that can only be excised by major surgery. Just as Ronald Reagan argued, swollen government is now the enemy. Its bureaucratic mentality fosters inefficiency and organizational paralysis. Sadly, the Democratic Party endorses further bureaucratize-tion. Its minions have burrowed their way into the entrails of government agencies and sought to expand their control.

The upshot has been moral collapse. Corruption is nowadays rife, while immorality regularly masquerades as morality. Americans have been seduced into supporting vice. Their moral compass has gone askew. Rather than recognize that "moral is as moral does," they allowed themselves to be misled by Barack Obama's transparent dishonesty. Swarms of "noble lies" convinced them that all politicians lie, but that this deception might be for our own good. They, for example, accepted the perverted notion that social justice requires coerced equality. And so hordes of falsehoods have flourished. Amazingly, an industry to manufacturing them developed. Being truthful, personally responsible, or socially fair thus went out of fashion. Honor and justice were likewise eschewed. Even worse, millions of Americans were prepared to deny that this perversion was occurring. They stridently insisted that they were fighting for truth and righteousness.

Much of this tragedy has been perpetuated by the mis-education of our youth. From kindergarten through college, they are indoctrinated in neo-Marxist fabrications. As a college professor, I have been immersed in this calamity. Daily, I watch, as students are shoved ahead without learning what makes our country great. In particular, I stand by as students, who are not equipped for higher education, struggle and fail. College is not for everyone, but because liberals pretend it is, we are creating a bubble. By trying to force everyone into the same mold, while simultaneously promoting social justice, we have produced a generation of snowflakes. Liberty and a diversity of opinions are under assault. Students say they don't want to be offended. And so, they refuse to be exposed to conservative attitudes. The result is that they never learn what they ought to learn. Many faculty members are appalled by this development, but these traditionalists have been marginalized. Rampant bureaucratization has insisted on uniformity, as opposed to individuality. This amounts to academic suicide, yet meaningless courses and vapid online programs proliferate. Rather than produce the self-direction necessary for professionalization, colleges currently hand out worthless credentials like party favors.

What might be construed as *trickle-down corruption* is undermining our traditional values. The glue essential for holding our complex and diverse society together is consequently being eaten away. Morality is not obsolete, but it needs to be updated to deal with unanticipated difficulties. Forward-looking conservatism must therefore confront unpleasant truths. Unlike liberalism, I ought not invent fresh moral entitlements out of whole cloth. Liberals have been shameless and self-righteous. Nonetheless, good people need to recognize evil when they encounter it. They should not engage in unconditional moral surrender just because they have been falsely rebuked as extremists. Human nature must be respected and absolute power not allowed to perpetuate itself. To this end, we may require a secular Great Awakening. We need to think ahead to avoid the perfection trap. Principles suitable for our times ought to be embraced. Not total equality, but universalism, i.e., the same rules for everybody, needs to be sought. Courage, emotional maturity, and genuine compassion have to be nurtured.

Although mistakes are inevitable, we must promote the self-discipline essential for making appropriate moral choices.

Social change is upon us, whether we like it or not. Conservatives cannot afford to ignore it. They must, for that reason, be forward-looking. As our world becomes more professionalized, they have to take the lead in this unfolding social awareness. To begin with, they must avoid the liberal's most egregious mistake. We will never become one huge, loving family. There are simply too many of us for that to occur. Fortunately, contemporary conservatives are not really conservative. If anything, it is liberals who are backward looking. This enables conservatives to be the ones who tackle today's problems. Perhaps the most serious of these is the upsurge in unwed parenthood. Cohabitation and divorce have convinced many people that marriage is outdated. It is not. Although radical feminists pervert its depiction, matrimony is essential for promoting adult intimacy and childhood socialization. The traditional gender division of labor clearly needs to be revised, but this is doable. How we deal with the poor ought similarly be amended. We are a hierarchical species and therefore complete equality is not possible. Still, widespread opportunity is feasible, as long as people are encouraged to develop the appropriate orientations. Everyone, including the poor, must abide by suitable rules. Affirmative action alone cannot do the job. No society can hold itself together if it depends on a plethora of strong-arm tactics to maintain its standards. Once more, social individualism is essential. But this orientation must be within the confines of a balanced society. Emotionally mature and socially enlightened individuals need to function as the fulcrum upon which this equilibrium is achieved.

As I see it, this adds up to *forward-looking conservatism*. This updated way of looking at what is needed appreciates the core objectives of historical conservatism, namely smaller government, democracy, personal liberty, the free market, and family values, but adjusts these to meet emerging challenges. Tradition ought to be respected, but amplified by being made consistent with contemporary needs. Nowadays, many Americans fear that our political conflicts are intractable. They despair for the future of our nation. Nonetheless, the Gordian knot can be cut. Social individualism, combined with principled realism, point to a way out. General Electric once bragged that, "progress is its most important product." This needs to remain a national goal. But it must not be progress as defined by "progressives." It has to be the genuine article, not a neo-Marxist fantasy!

Chapter II

A Nation In Crisis

What Went Wrong?

I love America. This is a constant refrain in my columns. I believe that it is the greatest nation on earth and should continue to lead the way into an enhanced future. The late Seymour Martin Lipset, a sociologist I admire, often wrote about American exceptionalism. He too believed that we were special and had achieved a unique level of freedom, democracy, and prosperity. In short, there was an American Dream, which we had gone a long way to realizing. Nonetheless, a large proportion of our fellow citizens have doubts. A pall has settled over the nation. This has produced a sour atmosphere and internecine warfare. Something evidently went wrong, although we are not sure what.

Liberals, in particular, have come to rue our heritage. They bemoan what they incessantly describe as our historical racism, sexism, and classism. From our colonial roots onward, we are described as a collection of selfish exploiters who were determined to rape the environment, enslave less powerful humans, and suppress women. Our sacred institutions, far from promoting fairness or decency, were designed to keep a minority of self-satisfied Northern European males in power. It is therefore time that we recognized this reality and seek to change it. Indeed, only a version of socialism can cultivate the social justice we require. In other words, only if we work together under the aegis of a benevolent government can we reverse capitalist rapacity.

Naturally, both religious and economic conservatives object—as do I. They fail to see the virtues of a Neo-Marxist agenda, nor do they appreciate the implied rejection of their prior achievements. As a result, we have entered a cycle of recriminations and counter-recriminations. Each side identifies the inadequacies of the other and blames it for the present impasse. Neither faction, however, has developed a workable solution. They tend instead to double down on their historical agendas; even though these have proven deficient. As a consequence, pessimism has become rampant. Where once the American Dream seemed destined to trend ever upward and conquer the world, misgivings crept in. Millions of Americans suspect something is amiss, although—apart from repeating the claims of vapid politicians—they do not know what. They may hate the current incivility, but are unsure of the way out, which serves only to increase their unease.

In the following essays, I address these growing apprehensions. My preliminary aim is to trace these developments and put them in perspective. What has happened? Why do we believe that our upward march stalled? Did something identifiable precipitate this change in our collective mood? After all, we remain the wealthiest and most potent nation the world has ever produced. Our personal comforts have never been greater, while our military prowess is unmatched. On these grounds alone, we should be savoring our success. We should be awash in self-congratulatory sentiments and an expectation of further gains. Except that we are not. Our progress has apparently come to a standstill, while our economic and military preeminence did not convert our personal lives into havens of love and happiness. We want more, but are not sure of what.

Few would disagree that our collective optimism has eroded. But are there persuasive explanations for these reservations? Why have we lost our way? If we no longer retain confidence in our shared fortunes, what is the cause? In this chapter, I inaugurate an explanation that will be fleshed out in subsequent chapters. We are, in my estimation, in the midst of an ideological crisis. The intellectual systems we have hitherto used to make sense of the world and provide a guide to the future hit a roadblock. Events outpaced the conceptual tools we inherited from our ancestors. Neither religious conservatism, nor libertarianism, nor liberalism has demonstrated an ability to deal with the complexities of our post-modern age. All were developed under conditions very different from our own and hence are incapable of dealing with a mass techno-commercial society. Each, it its own way, simplifies the unprecedented conundrums we must now solve. But because we don't possess a viable alternative, we cling to theories that have collapsed or are in the process of collapsing. To put the matter succinctly: we are confused. Drowning is a sea of uncertain-ties; we lash out at others who dare to disagree with us.

The good news is that once we understand a problem, we are in a better position to deal with it. First, however, we must sketch out the dimensions of our dilemma. This is what the ensuing essays attempt. They therefore start out with a prospect that frightens many of us. Will we emulate the Romans or ancient Greeks? Will the institutions that we established over the last several centuries prove incapable of overcoming the challenges that these very organizations introduced? In short, are we too destined for decadence and devastation? Or is there a way out of this ideological emergency? In my columns, I use the difficulties of the moment to illustrate our sense of alarm. Because most of them were written during the Obama era, he figures prominently in my messaging. As the reader will quickly become aware, I was no fan. Time and again, he chose what I regard-ed as the wrong path. Even so, his actions were more sign of the times than their foundation. Himself a product of our slide to neo-Marxism, he believed he was advancing our civilization. Larger forces were, in fact, operating to sabotage our society. These were laying the groundwork for our present anxieties. The important issue, of course, is figuring out what went wrong so that it can be remedied.

My Efforts to Figure It Out

American Decadence

During the heyday of the Roman Republic, ordinary citizens took up arms to protect it from invaders. Heroes, such as Cincinnatus, left their farms to battle the foe and then returned to the plow once victory was achieved. Their patriotism, their willingness to make personal sacrifices, eventuated in a great empire.

But once the empire was securely in place, once the riches of the orient and slaves from central Europe began pouring in, ordinary Romans lost interest in joining the legions. They preferred to stay home and enjoy the bread and circuses that had been bought by the blood of their ancestors.

Instead they began to hire barbarians to stand guard on the borders. German and Hunnish mercenaries now fought their battles. That is, until these non-Romans decided to march on Rome. It was then that this great empire fell.

For a while the Romans were able to buy off their enemies, but ultimately their reluctance to defend themselves spelled their doom. Are we now witnessing the same decline of the American hegemony? Have we too grown so decadent that we are unwilling to protect our interests?

Barack Obama tells us that he has no intension of putting boots on the ground in the Middle East. He likewise sought to buy off the Iranians with a craven quasi-treaty. As for the Russians and the Chinese, he merely tells them they are on the wrong side of history. This magical incantation will no doubt bring them to their senses.

Meanwhile closer to home, rioters are calmed by allowing them free reign of our inner cities, while protesters are assured that their demands are in the vanguard of social justice. All we need do to bring peace to our streets is to confiscate the resources of the wealthy and shovel them toward the poor.

The home of the brave and the land of the free are a distant memory. Our forebears may have battled to protect their frontiers and establish great industries, but all we need to do is live off the affluence they created.

Politicians declare that we can become great again, but how is that possible when so many of us are unwilling to exert ourselves? How is it feasible when we embrace the fictions we hear in school and the media? Can a people intoxicated by entitlements ever stand up for themselves?

Nowadays we tell children that if they are bullied, they must immediately appeal to an adult for relief. They are advised *not* to stand up for themselves. How is this supposed to instill courage or personal resolve?

Schools are likewise swept up in a vortex of grade inflation. Students expect to be at the top of their class even if they learn nothing. They also expect trophies merely for participating in little leagues games.

Americans may be awash with self-esteem, but they are living in a fool's paradise. As the clichéd observation has it, they were born on third base, yet are convinced that they hit a triple.

Nor are we alone in our decadence. The people of Western Europe are also so self-satisfied that they too have forgotten how to protect themselves. Somehow they cannot say no to importing millions of foreigners who are intent on destroying their civilization.

Wealth and power are apparently enervating. They draw the courage and motivation out of people. So intent are these folks on dining on peacock's tongues and playing their lyres that they do not notice when they are in danger.

The national debt may be unsustainable, but the economy has not yet collapsed. Our military is in decline, but it remains strong. American families are disintegrating as we speak, but children are not starving in back alleys. Thus, why should we worry when the temple still stands?

Decadence is a fatal condition. If it is not recognized; if it is not stemmed, it is lethal. Will this be our fate? Will we passively allow it?

Has America Become Decadent?

Once Rome was the glory of the Western World. It created the largest and most prosperous empire Europe has ever seen. But then Rome fell. After centuries of decline, it was over-run by barbarian invaders and so thoroughly dismantled that it took over a millennium for the continent to recover.

For many years, historians contended that the cause of this debacle was "decadence." They argued that the Roman people had abandoned their moral core and hence were unable to muster the resolve to fend off disaster. Sadly, there is much truth to this verdict.

In the case of Rome, the Republican virtues of steadfastness, patriotism, and honesty were forsaken in favor of luxury and selfishness. Rather than lead the legions to victory, its patricians preferred to recline on couches sipping wine and noshing on peacock's tongues. Meanwhile, the plebeians were content to live off the dole, biding their time in a haze of free bread and circuses.

The question we must now face is has the United States come to this same pass? Have we too, after a century of political and economic dominance, succumbed to a similarly fatal decadence? The end is not yet upon us, but are the barbarians knocking at a gate that is no longer being defended?

It is certainly true that many Americans no longer subscribe to the values that made our nation great. They—especially the liberals—believe that our democracy is bankrupt and that our market system is inherently unfair. Instead, they would like us to emulate the West Europeans and embrace what they call "social democracy."

To see what is happening, we need look no further than the last line of our national anthem. It proclaims that America is "the land of the free and the home of the brave." But is this true? Are we as a people still living up to these values?

Our recent election argues otherwise. Thus, a majority of Americans voted for a president who rarely praises the virtues of liberty. To the contrary, he prefers to fly the standard of "social justice." By this he means that our federal government has a duty to enforce his version of fairness.

Barack Obama and his supporters believe that the federal government must be our keepers. They are convinced that the rest of us cannot make good decisions unless they (our liberal leaders) guide us in the proper direction. This, of course, translates into ever more regulations and a larger burden of taxes.

The bottom line is that in exchange for safety ordinary citizens are asked cede their personal freedoms. Genuine freedom, it is assumed, inevitably leads to mistakes and unfairness, and therefore cannot be tolerated.

As to demonstrating courage, what greater failure of nerve can there be than voluntarily surrendering one's right to decide to a bevy of strangers who insincerely claim to have our interests at heart? Free peoples do make mistakes, but they also have the intestinal fortitude to correct these without resorting childish helplessness.

Thankfully our military has not yet gone spineless. The bravery our soldiers and sailors have shown in defense of our liberties has been exemplary. And yet we have an administration intent on hollowing out our armed forces. Yes, there are words in tribute to their heroism, but then comes the budgetary ax.

A truly brave people, a truly free people, would be up in arms at these trends. They would be outraged by the lies they have been told and by the diminution in personal and national power they have suffered.

But no, many Americans are evidently more worried that the federal government has yet to provide them with free contraceptives. Nor were they willing to celebrate the business success of the truly good man who sought to lead them.

Amazingly, citizens who continue to assume that they are the hope of the free world have opted to be led by the nose by a false prophet and his ignoble disciples.

Catastrophe

The wheels have been coming off the Obama administration. Domestically and internationally, policy failures abound. At home, the IRS, VA, Immigration, and Obamacare debacles linger. Abroad, ISIS, the Ukraine, and China present challenges that our president and his minions do not know how to address.

But things are worse than that. Unless corrections are made, over a hundred thousand Americans will lose their employer-based medical insurance, the national debt will rise to unsustainable proportions, Social Security, Medicare and Medicaid will go broke, a roaring inflation will erupt and the economy will continue to limp along.

How bad do things have to get before people realize that we require major fixes? The president and his allies are in a deep state of denial. They have become so adept at rationalizing their mistakes that they have come to believe their cover stories. They genuinely consider others to be at fault.

A couple of weeks ago, I read a book by Hugh Trevor-Roper about seventeenth century Europe, which got me thinking. This was the period during which the Counter-Reformation was tearing the continent apart. What struck me is that people back then did not make significant changes until a catastrophe was upon them—and sometimes not even then.

Thus while England was going through the paroxysms of its Civil War thereby reforming its central government, Spain circled the wagons to preserve the indefensible excesses of its monarchy. As a consequence England prospered, while Spain declined.

Sometimes a catastrophe can be swift and wrenching. A disaster, such as Germany's total defeat during World War II, can be so unsettling that people are prepared to accept something new. Sometimes if can take centuries of humiliation, as with China, before its leaders contemplate significant correctives.

What will be the case with the United States? We have become so fat and happy, that we assume our position as the dominant super-power is preordained. We also seem to believe that we do not have to improve on our institutions because they are nearly perfect.

Sadly, most Americas do not even pay attention to the news. Many are content to collect their transfer payments from the federal government without straining their mental faculties to recognize that the wolf is at the door.

My father used to tell me that I should learn from his mistakes. I was asked to heed his warnings and mend my ways. Years of hard experience, however, taught me that almost no one follows such advice. It is only when we ourselves encounter substantial difficulties that we are prepared to consider real alternatives.

To what extent is this liable to be true for our nation? Will we be like the junky who becomes so addicted to heroin that he dies of an overdose before he can kick the habit? Or will we be like the pothead who gradually gives up the weed as he matures?

In other words, will the binge we are presently on inflict so many wounds that a recovery is not possible? Will we spend so much—so foolishly—that the capital needed to rebuild our economy will have been squandered? Will we so weaken our military that small threats accumulate into insurmountable ones?

The process of turning our ship of state around is bound to be slow and laborious. Nonetheless, the sort of instant gratification to which we have become accustomed is not in the cards. Significant changes in cultures and institutions are always difficult.

The question that I earlier asked can thus be put another way. Do we have the moral fiber to pursue so challenging a mission? Has our pioneering spirit so completely eroded that we cannot tear ourselves away from our video games, Reality TV, and Caribbean vacations?

I hope so, but I am not sure. Things are bad and getting worse, but can we stop our slide before the catastrophe is fully upon us. The choice is, as usual, up to us.

Pogo: We Have Met The Enemy
During the Viet Nam War, the political cartoonist Walt Kelly neatly captured the attitude of those who opposed the conflict. As his character Pogo opined, "We have met the enemy and he is us." In other words, we Americans were responsible for inflicting death and destruction.

Nowadays this characterization needs to be updated. It should be the mantra of contemporary liberals. If anyone has been intent upon destroying our nation, it is them. Although they routinely accuse others of malice, they are currently the most dangerous foe of the American Dream.

Liberals hate America. They may swear up and down that they are trying to change us because they love us, but when the transformations insisted upon are too dramatic, they demonstrate revulsion. Its like saying we love the way you look; nonetheless we require you to undergo radical plastic surgery.

Citizens of the United States have been proud of their freedoms, but the liberals are dedicated to stripping these away. Progressives are always prepared to impose new governmental regulations so that people behave in a way leftists believe they should.

Freedom has historically included freedom of speech, but political correctness has invaded almost all aspects of life. People now tremble that they might be accused of sexism or racism. They worry that this could cost them their jobs.

Liberals also hate the family. They claim they are only trying to liberate women, whereas they are undermining heterosexual trust. This places children in jeopardy, as witnessed by the growing number of out-of-wedlock births. Yet the progressives do not care. They just re-label this shambles "diversity."

Liberals also hate our culture. They are therefore willing to admit millions of illegal aliens who do not share our values—and do not intend to. So far as liberals are concerned, if some immigrants wish to impose Sharia law upon us, this is their prerogative.

This lack of concern for our institutions also extends to our personal safety. Liberals do not wish to vet potential terrorists. Neither do they want to deport criminal aliens. They are even prepared to allow gang members to run rampant on the streets of Chicago.

We are also seeing this mentality affect Congress. For years, Democrats complained that Republicans were obstructionists. After all, conservatives voted against reducing the size of the military and for dismantling Obamacare. They even sought to thwart Obama's Iran deal.

In this, the liberals confused resistance with obstruction. They were utterly uncomfortable with the idea of a loyal opposition. Instead of seeking common ground where they agreed to some conservative demands, they wanted things their way—or no way.

Barack Obama often spoke about the need for compromise. Nonetheless, by compromise he meant that those who disagreed with him must eventually come around to realizing he was right. He never understood that mutual concessions were part of what made our democracy work.

Now that Trump has taken power, the extent of the anti-democratic impulses of Democrats has been revealed. They have openly proclaimed that they will obstruct the new president in everything they can. Thus, they slowed his cabinet appointments and plan to oppose any health care reforms or tax reductions.

At the height of the Cold War, many Republicans accused Democrats of being "knee-jerk" liberals. Whatever issue came up, the first left-wing response was to suggest a new federal regulation or program. At the moment, we are seeing knee-jerk obstructionism.

Some of this has been ludicrous. The malfeasance with which many Trump nominees have been charged is absurd. To blame Tom Price of a conflict of interest because his broker purchased stocks without Price's knowledge was silly. To say that the Statue of Liberty is crying because terrorists would be denied admission into the country was harebrained.

This is not the way we—together—will make America great. Liberals may still be in mourning because they lost the election, but this does not give them the right to lose their heads. Political disagreements are fine: sabotaging our political system is not!

America: Be Not Proud!
Many words have been spoken and a lot of ink spilled decrying Barack Obama's admonition that Christians and Jews should get off their "high horse." Muslims, we are told, are merely following in the footsteps of our misdeeds; hence we must understand.

If Muslims are now killing people in the name of their religion, so once did we. Who then are we to judge? Our pride should not motivate us to assume we are better than them. Besides, ISIS is not really Islamic.

The question is: Do we have a right to be judgmental? Can we look upon rape, mass murder, beheadings, and immolation and declare these barbaric? Are our hands so bloody that we must hang our heads in shame rather than identify the religious affiliation of the perpetrators?

As many commentators have observed, the crusades, Inquisition, slavery, and Jim Crow are behind us. We are not perfect. We never were and never will be. But should that prevent us from making comparisons? Must we agree that everyone is exceptional and therefore we cannot claim to be better than them?

This is absurd! To be thoroughly non-judgmental is to have no standards. Utter amorality is, in fact, immoral. We do not have to be perfect in order to condemn savagery. Were this a requirement for enforcing values, morality would be impossible.

So why does Barack Obama imply something so ridiculous? The answer—the only one that makes sense—is that he does not love the United States or take pride in its accomplishments. He does not want us to defeat ISIS, or any other global opponent—because we do not merit victory.

At this point, we must think the unthinkable. People have been scratching their heads trying to explain Obama's foreign policy. Why does he routinely reward our enemies and punish our friends? Why, for that matter, has he kept our economy enfeebled?

Consider the evidence. It is overwhelming. Barack hates Israel, but loves Iran. He likewise pretends to be fighting back against ISIS, but does the minimum he can. Obama knows this is a losing strategy. Our president is a smart man. He must know! He just doesn't care.

Obama has also refused to help the Ukraine resist Russian aggression. This threatens to destabilize Europe, but all he sends the Ukrainians is Meals Ready to Eat. Why? He doesn't care. He is per-fectly happy to see the Russian Bear regain preeminence.

Obama told us he would never allow Iran to obtain a nuclear weapon. But isn't that what he is doing? Aren't his negotiations with the Iranians slow-walking us to this conclusion? Israel and the United States are in mortal danger if the Middle East explodes. But he doesn't care. If we are harmed, our arrogance deserves to be tempered.

Or think about the Keystone pipeline. The argument that this will destroy the environment has been debunked—even by the State Department. Nonetheless Obama keeps finding excuses to stop it. Our economy is being harmed and Canada alienated, but who cares?

Now we have a newly stated national strategic policy and what are its priorities? Amazingly, fighting global warming ranks higher than confronting radical Islam. Can this be serious? Is this *strategic patience* or a decision to do nothing to defend us from genuine threats?

Neither ISIS nor Russia is about to overrun our homeland. In this sense, they are not "existential" challenges. But who knows what they will develop into if these festering sores are not addressed. Can passivity in the face of aggression and barbarism be truly wise?

Or is it a prescription for losing? Our president evidently believes that we are greedy racists. We are depicted as innately unfair, insufferably smug, and too powerful for our own good. Ergo, we need to be taken down a peg!

But I love America and am proud of it! I do not want to see us lose. I hope enough Americans feel the same.

Who Won the Culture Wars?

A few weeks ago I participated in a panel sponsored by the Cherokee County Republican Assembly. The question was: Did the Conservatives lose the culture war? According to businessman Alex Gimenez, they did. Given that liberals have captured the media and schools, he identified these folks as setting our cultural agenda.

Matthew Perdie, a documentary moviemaker, disagreed. He argued that Donald Trump's electoral victory demonstrates that political correctness is on the wane. As for Catherine Bernard, a lawyer, she was more equivocal. She suggested that conservatives should be more tolerant of minorities.

In my opinion, however, nobody won the culture wars. Liberals, conservatives, and libertarians alike were losers. Each faction promoted a program that is now in tatters. All made promises that were not kept. The result is a stalemate in which each side still expects to claim victory.

The reason that none will is because they are out of date. All three endorse ideas created hundreds or thousands of years ago. None was specifically designed to address the problems we currently experience.

Thus many conservatives urge us to embrace religious verities. They tell us that if we recommit to laws handed down by a merciful God, we will regain his favor. We must therefore love one another. We are to treat each other essentially as siblings so as to safeguard our collective welfare.

This strategy will not work because too many Americans are secular. They refuse to embrace the old-time religion. Nor can three hundred and thirty million people truly love one another. Although they may behave decently toward strangers, they are not, and never will be, kin.

As for the libertarians, they advise us to become entrepreneurs. If we are free to pursue our private interests in an unfettered marketplace, we will all be better off. The problem with this approach is twofold. First, we are not equally talented or aggressive. Second, this leaves love entirely out of the equation.

Although the liberals have been dominant for about a century, they too aspire to the untenable. They tell us to turn to the government for salvation. If we allow its experts to make decisions we are incapable of making for ourselves, we will prosper as never before.

The liberals call this social justice and explain that a fully democratic regime will create complete equality. Once it controls the means of production, it will ensure that everyone receives a fair share. With greed having been suppressed by a myriad of regulations and affirmative action empowering the least formidable among us, the playing field will finally be level.

Except that we have now had some experience with residing under a bureaucratic yoke. Government experts turn out to be at least as corrupt as the industrial moguls who preceded them. Their version of political correctness pits minority groups against one another such that it is the politicians who enrich themselves.

No one is happy with the current situation because no one has obtained the alleged benefits. As it happens, we have developed into a mass techno-commercial society. This ushered in undreamt of wealth and a myriad of choices. But it also introduced unprecedented in-securities.

With so much power at our disposal, we are today capable of big mistakes. The traditional ideologies guarded against these. Religion gave us divinely inspired answers. The marketplace stimulated a multitude of technical and political innovations. As for the progressives, they offered relief from frightening choices by making these for us.

The alternative to these failed worldviews is for us to take care of ourselves. If we become emotionally mature grown-ups who understand the problems before us, we can individually determine what is best for us personally and collectively. As self-motivated experts, we ought to learn from the traditional philosophies so as to take charge of our destinies.

The problem with this option, however, is that it thrusts the responsibility upon us. Aside from the hard work it takes to master contemporary complexities, if things go wrong, we will be to blame. This prospect has already stimulated a flight from freedom and reanimated cultural solutions that have hitherto demonstrated major limitations.

The Great Middle Class Revolution

When I first moved to Georgia, one of my colleagues at Kennesaw State University explained how her ancestors acquired land in Cherokee county. They won it in the lottery associated with the Trail of Tears. This story brought home to me how recently Georgia had been on the frontier.

It was, in fact, not that long ago that our ancestors were pioneers. Whether they braved the hazards of the trek west or confronted the dangers of taking a sailing ship across the Atlantic, they voluntarily accepted the risks of dealing with the unknown.

Today we are infinitely more prosperous than our forebears. We do not dread Indian attacks or need to obtain work in sweatshops. We might occasionally have to put up with a natural disaster, but we know that relief will be coming. There will surely be enough to eat and drink—and it won't be long before the electricity is restored.

Nonetheless, we too are pioneers. We have also entered unfamiliar territory. The world is changing around us—and changing radically. We are participants in a great middle class revolution. This is new! No other peoples have ever had to deal with the challenges we are experiencing.

Because we are in the midst of it, we seldom realize that ours is the first predominately middle class nation in all of history. Never before have so many individuals been in the middle class. Never before have these middling level folks exercised so much power.

The question is what to do with this good fortune. We are no longer farmers. Most of us are not even factory workers. Instead of laboring with our hands, we are more likely to work with our heads. Many more of us have thus become professionalized or semi-professionalized. We have been transformed into self-motivated experts in complex activities.

Ours is a mass techno-commercial society. We are surrounded by millions of diverse strangers upon whom we depend for survival. They feed us; they clothe us; they build our homes. Were their services erratic, we would be in serious jeopardy.

What is more, because the tasks they perform are often technological, they must master complicated skills. They must also acquire the social aptitudes to cooperate with people very different from themselves. This requires that they be educated far beyond what was demanded of their ancestors.

Today we must cope with the uncertainties of selecting and preparing for an occupation. We will not simply do what our parents did. We must instead choose from a panoply of possibilities that we do not fully comprehend. What is available and what will we be good at?

Today marriage and family have also become optional. If we decide to take a spouse, who will it be? And if we make such a commitment, can we be sure it will not end in divorce? Isolated as we are in separate nuclear households, it is up to us to make our intimate relationships work.

Today we must likewise decide whether we will have children. But if we have them, how will we raise them? Which techniques must we employ to prepare them for a successful middle class adulthood? The old practice of demanding that the young be seen and not heard is no longer appropriate.

And how about politics? Once city hall seemed so far away that fighting it was inconceivable. Today we are so affluent and well-educated that more of us participate in self-governance. But how are we to do this? The split between conservatives and liberals is evidence that we fiercely disagree.

Our grandparents might have been wonderful people, but they are not adequate role models for what we need. Like it or not, we must figure out new ways to do many things. While we can learn from the past, we must also innovate. This ensures we will make mistakes that require flexibility to rectify.

Despite the sense of entitlement that many young people feel, nothing about our future is preordained. Unless we make suitable choices, our good luck could run out. Unless we are responsible, and intelligent, and hard-working, the progress we nowadays expect could come to a screeching halt.

An Ideological Crisis

Why are we at a political impasse? Why has it proven so difficult for politicians to arrive at a viable consensus? Part of the reason, I submit, is that we are in the midst of an ideological crisis. Our ideas about where society is headed are seriously out of whack.

Think about it. All of the theories guiding our political decisions were created centuries ago. None of our current ways of understanding our problems were developed in our times, for our times.

Liberalism is at least two hundred years old. Even in its Marxist formulation, it is one hundred and fifty years old. Developed in opposition to the Industrial Revolution, it aims to return us to the rural villages in which our medieval ancestors once lived.

Thus liberals expect us to know and care about each other as if we were intimately acquainted. Unfortunately we are not. Because our society numbers in the hundreds of millions, most of us are, and will remain, strangers to one another.

Meanwhile conservatism is about as old. In its economic guise it celebrates the advent of capitalism. Conservatives want to promote economic progress, but often in a manor that was appropriate when most businesses were small.

Actually, in its religious guise, conservatism is far older. In this, it asks us to return to a social condition that is millennia old. We are essentially being requested to join a single family of humankind, despite the fact that families are emotionally close, whereas strangers are not.

Even the libertarians have a hoary lineage. Their idea of freedom is grounded in a marketplace composed of independent com-petitors. Massive corporations and representative democracy are therefore not part of their calculations.

But we are not returning to village life, or Mom and Pop storefronts, or an old-time religion. These are nostalgic fantasies that have nothing to do with how we live or are going to live. They cannot guide us in making political choices because the problems we face are very different from the ones they address.

And so we are adrift. Cast at sea, unsure of what is happening, we cling to that which is familiar. Although we are secular, not religious; urban, not rural; and specialists, not generalists, we pretend that we are simple folk, who, if we only make the right choices, will return to a virtual Garden of Eden.

But guess what, complete equality is not in the cards. Nor is complete liberty. Our mass techno-commercial society demands much more of us than that we hold hands and sing Kumbaya. At the very least, we must be honest about our situation.

Here, however, is the tricky part. A new, more appropriate, ideology will not be found in a box of Cracker-Jacks. Social ideas do not appear fully formed as enunciated by a charismatic leader. They evolve. They emerge slowly from our combined social experience.

In this regard, our current gridlock is part of the learning curve. Sometimes people have to experience discomfort before they are motivated to seek an alternative. Sometimes things must go seriously wrong before they are prepared to contemplate a novel answer.

What that answer is, is a good question. While I suspect that we are on course to become a more professionalized society, I do not control events any more than does anyone else. This no doubt is scary, but then again life is scary. There are risks we must take merely because we are human.

I know, however, where we must begin. We must start with courage. We must first admit that we are confused about our situation. Instead of following ideologues who insist that they know the answers, we must accept reality for what it is. We have to be candid about our problems.

Then we must accept the fact that no solutions will be perfect. We are human and human societies are always fraught with complications. To imagine otherwise only confuses an already diffi-cult task.

The Three Cornered War

This electoral cycle has been a study in catastrophe. Almost no one is happy with the emerging results. People are slowly adjusting to the potential choices, but they wish they had an alternative. The problem is that we are in the midst of a three-cornered war that all sides are destined to lose.

Conservatives have clearly suffered a major setback. Donald Trump is not one of them and they know it. Many are coming around to the need to support him because they fear that if Hillary wins, their cause will experience a greater defeat. They know this is bad news, but don't know what to do about it.

Meanwhile, the liberals are not faring much better. They have had one of their own in the White House, but are not satisfied that he has delivered hope and change. And so many of them have decided to become more extreme—that is, more idealistic. They have kicked over the traces and embraced a socialist.

As for the libertarians, they have become an asterisk in this melee. Their candidates have disappeared from sight. The diehards remain—especially among the young—but the cooler heads know that this will not be their year.

Indeed, Hillary and Trump represent the triumph of crass pragmatism over ideological purity. Both are perceived as people who can get things done. The conservative, liberal, and libertarian doctrines have been found so devoid of practical results that voters are willing to settle for problem-solvers.

If we redefine the three chief ideologies that have been contesting for power, we may begin to see why we are at this impasse. Conservatism, at least of the traditional sort, may be thought of as spiritual collectivism; libertarianism as market individualism; and liberalism as bureaucratic collectivism.

Each of these philosophies is, unfortunately, built around a cosmological myth. They tell us that our social world is constructed in ways that it is not. As a consequence, the solutions they propose to our dilemmas cannot work. This leaves people frustrated and angrily howling at the moon.

First, the spiritual collectivists assume that we must one day become one huge family in which we all protect each other's interests. For the religious among them, this will occur under the stewardship of God. Nonetheless, the central element in their ideology is universal love.

Second, the market individualists believe that if the economic marketplace is liberated from external constraints, people will make good decisions. Each of us will pursue our own needs and negotiate with others such that all are better off. The central element of their ideology is therefore universal freedom.

(Note: Contemporary conservatism is often a blend of spiritual collectivism and market individualism,)

Third, the bureaucratic collectivists agree with the tradi-tionalists that we should become one big loving family, but they believe this is best accomplished under the tutelage of the government. In a democracy, this means that everyone's interests will be protected. Their touchstone is thus universal equality—which is also described as social justice.

Nonetheless, universal love, universal freedom, and universal equality are all unattainable. They are myths! They are idealistic fairytales that cannot be converted into reality. As long as human beings remain human, these can never come to fruition.

We humans are incapable of loving all other humans. As social creatures, we are likewise incapable of granting each other complete autonomy. Lastly, as hierarchical animals total parity is utterly unattainable.

Our love is always circumscribed, our freedoms are always limited by a need to recognize the rights of others, and our equality is undermined by our personal ambitions. All of us want to be special and in the process we compete with one another for love, power, and respect.

Is there an answer to this dilemma? In one sense: No. The visions of perfection that we sometimes entertain can never be consummated. On the other hand, we can be more realistic. We can recognize our limitations and work within them.

Why We Lost Our Way

In *Through the Looking Glass*, Alice says "Why, sometimes I believe as many as six impossible things before breakfast." Yet American voters have made her look like a piker. They are determined to believe in hundreds of impossible things before they head to the polls to choose a president.

It is not as if most of them do not know that the candidates are over-promising. They have been along this path before. They have witnessed countless grandiose pledges crumble to dust once their favorites got into office.

But still they believe. How can this be? Why do so many otherwise intelligent people remain willfully ignorant? Can't they see that in deciding to bust the budget, or gut the military, or start a trade war, we will all ultimately suffer? The idea that the politicians can rescue us from our current anxieties may sound plausible, but it is a myth.

And yet millions believe. The reason is that the world is so complicated that we require a roadmap in order to find our way around. In order to be useful, however, this map must simplify the terrain. If it corresponded one-to-one with reality, it would be just as confusing as reality.

Nonetheless, in simplifying, these maps distort. They leave out important factors, while over-emphasizing others. This can prompt us to take the wrong turns in moments of doubt. That, in fact, is where we today find ourselves.

What are these roadmaps? They are our ideologies. These idea systems tell us how the world is constructed and therefore what we should do in order to get where we want to go. They help us make sense of facts that are, in their absence, too complex to grasp.

The problem is that our current ideologies are out of whack. They have deviated so far from reality that they often encourage us to go astray. It is as if we were trying to circumnavigate the planet by consulting a chart that was drawn up when people believed the earth was flat.

What are these out-of-date ideologies? They are none other than the current liberal and conservative catechisms. The ideals these espouse may seem beyond question—at least to their adherents—and yet the policies they promote are frequently defective.

Take liberalism. It is often conflated with being "progress-ive." Liberals believe they are on the cutting edge of a brave new world. As they see it, they are rationally seeking to reconstruct the world along egalitarian lines. In other words, they are for social justice, whereas their foes are not.

But liberalism is not progressive. Its central ideas are at least two centuries old. They go back to Jean-Jacques Rousseau and Karl Marx. Ideas, such as the "general will" and a proletarian revolution, color their vision of ideal social arrangements.

But in truth, there is no general will and the proletarian revolution fizzled. The notion that we will all eventually be equal is likewise fanciful. It is a pipe dream that is in the process of being converted into a nightmare. Robbing the rich to give to the poor is a recipe for reducing everyone to poverty and oppression.

Unfortunately some conservative visions are little better. They too were formulated hundreds, if not thousands, of years ago. Consider the libertarian utopia. It is derived from the Enlightenment observations of Adam Smith. He noted, with some justification, that an invisible hand regulates the economy.

And yet the libertarians have turned this into a call for dismantling the government. While it is certainly true that liberals promote too much government, too little is also dangerous. Nor are we solely economic animals. Our family life, for instance, cannot prosper in a totally laissez-faire environment.

Ours is a new world that confronts us with challenges our ancestors could have not imagined. Doubtless, they were smart people. There is unquestionably much we can learn from them. Nonetheless, if we bind ourselves too tightly to their beliefs, we are bound to stumble.

What Do We Do Now?

One summer, while I was in college, I sold encyclopedias door to door. My territory was in the south Bronx. This was why I was walking along the Grand Concourse, not far from Yankee stadium. It was, therefore, where I encountered my first face-to-face death.

The concourse is a broad, multi-lane boulevard. On this day the traffic was about as usual. Therefore I don't know why it caught my attention, but I noticed a woman driving by with her two young sons playing in the back seat.

Then all of a sudden the back door flung open and a preschooler came tumbling out. At this point, his mother panicked. For some reason, she threw the vehicle into reverse. And then she drove backwards trapping the boy under the car.

To this day I can call up the image of the child bouncing up and down like a sack of potatoes between the tarmac and the undercarriage of the sedan. I am not sure that this killed him, but it is difficult to imagine how he survived.

In any event, I froze in my tracks. My horror was such that I did not know what to do. I did not run toward the vehicle because I was too terrified of what I might find. Instead I ran into a nearby apartment building to call the police—who in short order arrived.

Nowadays I have experienced much the same feeling in witnessing the car wreck that has been the Republican primary process. That Donald Trump has emerged as the nominee designate strikes me as unbelievable. So unexpected—and unwelcome—is this outcome that I do not know what comes next.

Donald Trump is not a conservative. He never was, and I don't believe ever will be. That voters, who are unhappy with their party because it is insufficiently conservative, should have selected a man who is mildly liberal makes no sense.

Over the last few weeks I have participated in intense conversations with several Trump supporters. In each case, I was amazed at how indifferent these folks were to the facts. All of them liked the Donald because they perceived him to be honest and strong. None were concerned with his political convictions.

For me, this is one more piece of evidence that we are in the midst of an ideological crisis. Many people, who describe themselves as conservative, care precious little about the goals promoted by conservatism. Either they do not understand these—or they don't give a darn.

Something similar seems to be true on the Democratic side of the ledger. The enthusiasm, such as it is, is on the side of Bernie Sanders and not Hillary Clinton. Bernie is liked, whereas Hillary is distrusted.

Evidently many Democratic voters do not care that until recently Sanders was no more a member of their party than Trump was of the Republicans. He was, and is, a declared socialist—a man who honeymooned in the Soviet Union.

In other words, Sanders represents mainstream liberalism no better than Trump represents mainstream conservatism. And yet people are unconcerned. It is enough that Sanders is regarded as honest and authentic.

Let's put this into perspective. The two major parties are supposed to champion conflicting political agendas. They are ostensibly distinguished by the clear-cut doctrines to which their partisans subscribe.

And yet their supporters don't subscribe to these ideologies. Perhaps this is because they have lost faith in them. The Republicans have come to see establishment politicians as RINOs (Republicans in name only) who have not delivered on their promises to roll back Obama's programs.

Meanwhile, the Democrats have also lost faith in their establishment figures. However much they defend Obama, they know that he has not produced "hope and change." In short, they too are disillusioned.

Can it be that neither conservatism nor liberalism is capable of fulfilling its promises? Perhaps these ideologies have become hollow dreams. They may not deliver because they are unable to deliver.

The Glory That Was Greece

My wife Linda and I recently returned from a magnificent cruise through the Greek isles. This was one of the most enjoyable vacations we have experienced, as well as one of the most enlightening.

Few people—least of all the Greeks—are unaware of the economic and political crisis gripping their nation. With unemployment at record levels and chaos periodically clogging their streets, it would be difficult to overlook the fact that something is wrong.

Nonetheless, from a tourist's point of view, much remains business as usual. The Parthenon still stands there in all of its tumbledown glory, while the merchants in the Plaka continue to be as aggressive in marketing their baubles.

Yet for those who look, there is ample evidence of why Greece is no longer the cutting-edge force it was. This came to my attention during a long conversation with owner of a jewelry story chain. Upon learning that I was an American college professor, he was eager put his country's plight in perspective.

Soon our tête-à-tête ranged candidly across the historical and the contemporary landscape. Thus, we agreed that the ancient Athenians had laid the foundation for modern Western civilization, whereas today's Greeks have accomplished little of which to boast.

The question was why? The Greeks are surely as intelligent and vibrant as ever. They are also as desirous of success. The problem is that many are not as entrepreneurial as their forebears. Oh yes, the shopkeepers in the market remain assertive, but where (save for a few shipping magnates) are the large-scale operators? They are largely absent.

Where then are today's Greek men (and some women) to be found. By late morning it is plain that they are sipping coffee at street side cafes and arguing about everything—especially politics. Their ancestors, to be sure, were likewise a talkative bunch—think of Socrates or Plato—but they were also out scouring the Mediterranean seeking their main chance.

Nowadays many Greeks must leave home to improve their lot. Vassili Economopoulos, a buddy of mine at Kennesaw State University (sadly no longer with us) epitomized this dilemma. He migrated to the United States to obtain his Ph.D., then stayed because this is where the opportunities were.

As Vassili explained, Greece is a poor country, more mountain and rock than arable land. With a topography good for growing olive trees, grape vines and little else, its people long ago learned to convert these into oil and wine. Next they went into the business of selling these to all and sundry.

The difference between then and now is that the ancients thought big and exploited trade however they could. Indeed, it was their commercial dynamism that produced the glories of the Hellenic city-states. Their fleets of hard-hitting merchants financed the arts and architecture we still admire; their agoras teaming with innovative artisans created the democratic politics we continue to venerate.

The direction of causality has not changed. Free and dynamic citizens individually in pursuit of economic success are the ones who generate governments "of, by, and for the people." It is not governments that create their wealth, sophistication, or freedom, but the other way around.

The Greek merchant with whom I discussed these matters understood this. As a result, he and I were distressed that many of his countrymen do not. We also agreed that many Americans are oblivious of this nexus. They too appear to be looking to politicians, not businesspersons, for salvation.

Lest we forget: Greece fell when its people could not unite to defend their institutions. Its glory did not last forever. Yet neither may the eminence of United States if its people cannot coalesce to defend the free marketplace and decentralized politics that made it great.

Glory and freedom go only to those who possess the confidence to protect their traditions. So we must ask: Do we have this spirit? Do we have what the Greeks lacked? Time will tell.

Chapter III

Principled Change

Idealism versus Realism

Who doesn't want to make the world a better place? Who does not want to believe that he or she is on the side of the angels? The trouble is that when things go wrong, we do not always know the best way forward. Nor are we always sure about how to initiate change. The next set of essays deal with these difficulties. They ask us where we want to go and what might be the best way to get there. Instead of being naively idealistic, they recommend that we be realistic. If we are in the bowels of a middle class revolution, what do we have to do to make this come out right? If we are becoming a more "professionalized" society in which we require self-motivated experts to deal with increasing complexities, why do we ask so many people to abdicate their personal responsibilities? Do we really want to fight the old wars? This would be a foolish strategy because recycling past solutions is unlikely to lead us to a better future.

What we need is, in fact, social individualism. If we, in this way, accurately understand the nature of the challenges we confront, we will be more effective in surmounting them. Yet this also requires that we, as individuals, become stronger and more independent. In other words, we have to save ourselves. Instead of looking to others to rescue us, we need to do the rescuing. This, however, is a daunting prospect. Enduring it will not be easy. Neither will it be quick. Major changes—of the sort that appear necessary—are never achieved over night. They are never the result of something like a Marxist revolution. They must also, as I will later insist, be principled. Unless they are constrained by well-founded moral boundaries, they will produce more damage than good.

Marxism is a failed paradigm. In its pure form, it is quixotic fantasy. As modified by liberalism, it is merely an excuse for excessive government control. Donald Trump may not have answers to our political impasse, but that does not validate the progressive agenda. As an ideological pipe dream, it eschews crucial principles in favor of false promises. The reality is that a childish idealism, whether of the left or the right, cannot solve adult problems. That is why a social individualism perspective deserves serious consideration. This is also why we must be prepared for the long haul. If we are to rescue ourselves from the doldrums into which we have fallen, we must be patient. The work that needs to be done demands a clear head and a willingness to exert disciplined effort.

A Way Forward

Quo Vadis

Quo Vadis was one of the blockbuster movies of the 1950's. Its title derived from an apocryphal story told about when Saint Peter was fleeing Rome in order to avoid crucifixion. On his way, he encountered Jesus who asked "Quo vadis?" Where are you going? It was then that Peter returned to meet his fate.

Today we must also ask, where are we going? Peter was guided by his faith, but where are we to find the guideposts needed to direct our way? As I have previously written, we are experiencing an ideological crisis. The belief systems that once steered our course have let us down.

Actually, I have been struggling to find a way to demonstrate why relevant ideologies are vital. These may seem to be mere "as if" stories, yet they enable us to make sense out of a world that would otherwise be too confusing to navigate.

So let me tell a story. When I was in my early twenties, I decided it was time to learn how to drive a car. Even though I was living in New York City, I craved greater mobility. Nevertheless, my father refused to teach me. He feared that this would raise his insurance premiums.

Instead I turned to my uncle Milton. He was a bus driver and a very nice person. Happily, he agreed to help me out. As a consequence, I met him when he finished his route so that we could ride home together. Then, once we arrived in Queens, he turned the wheel over to me.

Milton assumed that I knew more about driving than I did. Perhaps I had exaggerated the skills I acquired by driving a friend's car around a parking lot. In any event, I was terrified when I venturing onto the Queensboro Boulevard. At first, I did not know where to look.

This thoroughfare had three lanes in each direction, with side lanes to boot. There were thus automobiles and trucks everywhere. They were in front of me, behind me, and on both sides of me. It felt as if any one of them could veer into me at any moment.

Although I managed to keep from hitting anything, my panic was evident. This was when my uncle asked me to pull over so that he could resume control.

To this day, I remember how relieved I was. The thought of having to endure my terror for several more miles was overwhelming.

Nowadays, of course, the situation is different. I routinely drive on the interstates without a moment's hesitation. What has changed is that during the interim I accumulated hundreds of thousands of hours on the road. As importantly, I built up a mental frame of reference in the process.

I now know that I do not have to keep track of every vehicle around me. I have, in essence, become aware of what is normal and what is anomalous. My attention is therefore drawn to the unusual. I am even able to anticipate when a driver is liable to do something amiss—such as changing lanes without signaling.

A few hours driving around a parking lot could never have provided the guidance to handle I 75 where it widens to eight lanes. By the same token, centuries of living in a preindustrial society did not furnish the insights needed to manage in a post-industrial civilization. Countless experiences in the former are simply not applicable in the latter.

This, in fact, is the circumstance we currently find ourselves. Our ideological frameworks developed in eras long preceding our own. The liberal, conservative, and libertarian perspectives all evolved during periods extremely different from our own.

As a result, they often steer us wrong. The upshot is that what we seek frequently does not bring us satisfaction. This is one of the reasons for our present political impasse. Voters are frustrated by broken promises. Yet these promises are broken because those making them are following inappropriate guideposts.

The Wrong Side of History

By now you have heard it many times. The Russians are going to be rolled back in the Ukraine and in Syria because they are on the wrong side of history. The same goes for ISIS in its quest to revive the Caliphate. It is even true of Republicans when they resist gun control.

In each of these instances, when asked to explain his policy, Barack Obama has resorted to this argument. His listeners are routinely assured that everything will eventually be well because things are destined to work out favorably. All we need to do is be patient.

The question is where did Obama dredge up this thesis? In fact, it is good old-fashioned Marxism. Karl Marx insisted that he knew the direction of history.

His "scientific" study of dialectical materialism led him to the conclusion that a proletarian revolution was inevitable.

Marx further believed that the progression from socialism through to communism could not be prevented. Whoever sought to stand in its way would be rolled over by the steamroller of its inexorableness. It was, therefore, wise to step aside and allow his supporters to take over.

This did not mean, however, that Marx was passive. He passionately inveighed in favor of the coming revolution. "Workers of the work unite. You have nothing to lose, but your chains." And then he participated in organizing conventions in order to consolidate the troops.

Barack Obama's approach is a bit different. He believes that the inevitability of his progressive agenda requires him to do nothing to advance his cause on the international stage. He must merely stand back and allow the Russians, the Iranians, and the Chinese to implode.

The trouble with this strategy was revealed long ago. Edmund Burke told us that the only thing necessary for evil to succeed is for good people to do nothing. It follows from this that unless we protect freedom and democracy, their enemies will fill the void.

Meanwhile on the domestic front, Obama has decided to act on his own. He is going to pretend that the Republican "obstructionists" in congress don't exist. Rather than follow the constitution, he will simply do what is going to happen anyway.

Obama is so sure he is correct that he does not have to convince others of his wisdom. If the congress or the American people disagree, he must nonetheless do what is in their interest. Because he knows best, he must not allow their reservations to get in the way of historical necessity.

Here the difficulty is that Obama is not as brilliant, or perceptive, as he believes. Time and again, his "common sense" strategies have little to do with common sense. Time and again, they have failed to achieve the objectives he solemnly pledged. No doubt it would be the same with gun control.

Of course, Marx's predictions did not turn out well either. The western European revolution he expected never occurred, while the Russian and Chinese Revolutions delivered tyranny and privation. The brotherhood supposedly inherent in communism clearly did not arise.

As an aside, isn't it interesting how much progressive liberalism has in common with socialism? For years Democrats bridled at being labeled socialists. Thus, they howled like stuck pigs when ObamaCare was described in this way.

But now that Bernie Sanders, and avowed Democratic Socialist, is running for their presidential nomination, they have mellowed. Somehow neither Hillary Clinton, nor Debbie Wasserman Schultz, chair of the Democratic National Committee, will define, or renounce, socialism.

The fact is that socialist principles are in their blood. Liberalism is socialism light. It, therefore, affects the mindset of adherents like Barack Obama. But, worse still, it influences their policies. They really believe the collectivist dogmas, which have repeatedly been disconfirmed, are unimpeachably correct.

It is time for the rest of us to wake up to what is actually happening—before we march off the cliff to which they are leading us.

What Do We Do Now?

One summer, while I was in college, I sold encyclopedias door to door. My territory was in the south Bronx. This was why I was walking along the Grand Concourse, not far from Yankee stadium. It was, therefore, where I encountered my first face-to-face death.

The concourse is a broad, multi-lane boulevard. On this day the traffic was about as usual. Therefore I don't know why it caught my attention, but I noticed a woman driving by with her two young sons playing in the back seat.

Then all of a sudden the back door flung open and a preschooler came tumbling out. At this point, his mother panicked. For some reason, she threw the vehicle into reverse. And then she drove backwards trapping the boy under the car.

To this day I can call up the image of the child bouncing up and down like a sack of potatoes between the tarmac and the undercarriage of the sedan. I am not sure that this killed him, but it is difficult to imagine how he survived.

In any event, I froze in my tracks. My horror was such that I did not know what to do. I did not run toward the vehicle because I was too terrified of what I might find. Instead I ran into a nearby apartment building to call the police—who in short order arrived.

Nowadays I have experienced much the same feeling in witnessing the car wreck that has been the Republican primary process. That Donald Trump has emerged as the nominee designate strikes me as unbelievable. So unexpected—and unwelcome—is this outcome that I do not know what comes next.

Donald Trump is not a conservative. He never was, and I don't believe ever will be. That voters, who are unhappy with their party because it is insufficiently conservative, should have selected a man who is mildly liberal makes no sense.

Over the last few weeks I have participated in intense conversations with several Trump supporters. In each case, I was amazed at how indifferent these folks were to the facts. All of them liked the Donald because they perceived him to be honest and strong. None were concerned with his political convictions.

For me, this is one more piece of evidence that we are in the midst of an ideological crisis. Many people, who describe themselves as conservative, care precious little about the goals promoted by conservatism. Either they do not understand these—or they don't give a darn.

Something similar seems to be true on the Democratic side of the ledger. The enthusiasm, such as it is, is on the side of Bernie Sanders and not Hillary Clinton. Bernie is liked, whereas Hillary is distrusted.

Evidently many Democratic voters do not care that until recently Sanders was no more a member of their party than Trump was of the Republicans. He was, and is, a declared socialist—a man who honeymooned in the Soviet Union.

In other words, Sanders represents mainstream liberalism no better than Trump represents mainstream conservatism. And yet people are unconcerned. It is enough that Sanders is regarded as honest and authentic.

Let's put this into perspective. The two major parties are supposed to champion conflicting political agendas. They are ostensibly distinguished by the clear-cut doctrines to which their partisans subscribe.

And yet their supporters don't subscribe to these ideologies. Perhaps this is because they have lost faith in them. The Republicans have come to see establishment politicians as RINOs (Republicans in name only) who have not delivered on their promises to roll back Obama's programs.

Meanwhile, the Democrats have also lost faith in their establishment figures. However much they defend Obama, they know that he has not produced "hope and change." In short, they too are disillusioned.

Can it be that neither conservatism nor liberalism is capable of fulfilling its promises? Perhaps these ideologies have become hollow dreams. They may not deliver because they are unable to deliver.

Ideology versus Principles

Liberals are ideologues. They have a simplified view of what the world is and should be. As they see it, if we were all nice to each other and treated each other as complete equals, the government, which they will control, would provide everything we need in order to be happy.

As "progressives," they consider it inevitable that a compassionate bureaucracy will one day furnish everyone with free health care, free higher education, and comfortable living conditions, without anyone having to work for these. Much as Henry VIII of England once looted the monasteries to finance his lavish lifestyle, they will take from the rich to give to the poor.

The problem is that in order to realize this fairytale, they have had to jettison their moral principles. Liberals have few ethical standards because they assume their limitless kindness makes canons of decency unnecessary. Thanks to their unparalleled intelligence and good intentions, they will always do what's best.

Liberals tell us that we must be non-judgmental and are as good as their word. They have, in fact, abandoned all pretenses of reasonable judgment. When it comes to distinguishing right from wrong, they can no longer tell the difference.

Liberals do not believe in honesty, or personal responsibility, or elementary fairness, or family commitments, or individual liberty. Although they sometimes pay verbal deference to these values, their actions reveal an underlying conviction that these are outmoded.

Thus the left-wing idealists, who dominate the mainstream press, consider it their duty to distort what conservatives believe. They would rather cut off a right arm than give Donald Trump credit for anything. To this end, they omit information that might cast him in a favorable light and egregiously misread the import of his policies.

By the same token, political agitators campaign against public safety. They do not believe it is the government's responsibility to protect its citizens or theirs to respect the free speech of those with whom they disagree. Others may have such duties, but they have only rights.

As for fairness, they routinely condemn double standards when these are applied to them, but eagerly use them against their foes. Hence Trump is vilified for his alleged exploitation of women, whereas we were asked to "move on" with respect to Bill Clinton's sexual misdeeds,

Meanwhile, liberal feminists disparage the family. Men are portrayed as serial rapists; while women are assured that they do not need to marry and will not benefit from the assistance of a husband. Children, of course, are depicted as dead weight that prevent women from realizing their potential.

Finally, liberty is dismissed as a rationalization for exploitation. Liberals believe that a multitude of statutes must prohibit people from making dire mistakes. Only government experts are capable of determining how many carbonated drinks people should be allowed or whether a mud puddle on a family farm endangers planetary climate.

What liberals fail to understand is that when they undermine basic moral principles, they also undermine their ability to deliver the benefits they promise. No large-scale society can function without broadly held, and consistently enforced, interpersonal rules.

We humans are a contentious species. We want what we want when we want it. We are also a dangerous species. We—all of us—are capable of injuring others. Given the availability of the proper weapons, no one is invariably safe from anyone else.

These hazards are magnified in massive communities where millions of strangers need to cooperate if they are to prosper. People, who depend upon each other, but do not know one another, must be constrained by internalized principles. Love is not enough to render them selfless when they are not bound by personal attachments.

Ideological fairytales are no substitute for a conscience or shared commitments. Visions of what would happen if we were a different sort of creature, cannot constrain people if they do not possess internal limitations.

We currently see what happens when principles are absent. People engage in riots, vulgarly insult their foes, and misrepresent facts. Moreover, they do so with a clear conscience. Like contemporary liberals, they are self-congratulatory, even as they slander others.

The Perils of Naïve Idealism

This is the best-educated generation of Americans—ever! And yet it is also one that has made a host of foolish choices. How does this compute? How can superior knowledge and rash irresponsibility so routinely track together?

Politicians have always made absurd promises. They have always told voters that they would deliver more than is humanly possible. These assurances were nonetheless often believed because the average citizen did not have enough information to evaluate the validity of such claims.

I have recently been watching the PBS special on the Great War. One of its highpoints is an emphasis on how President Woodrow Wilson explained the need for the United States to enter this conflict. It was, he asserted, essential that we "make the world safe for democracy."

For Wilson, this was to be the war to end all wars. It would enshrine democratic principles around the globe such that no one would be motivated to resort to combat. We, of course, know how this turned out. The Second World War was even more ferocious than the First.

In 1917, most Americans did not have a high school education. Most were farmers or laborers. They knew little about history, and less about international politics. Although they did not want war, they could be persuaded that its outcome might be glorious.

Americans have long been idealists. They still are. They want peace and prosperity. They also want a world that is fair and forward-looking. But why do they believe society can be perfected? Hasn't experience taught them that there are limitations to what can be accomplished?

Consider two related examples. The current generation of college students is clamoring for socialism *and* social justice. Many of them want the federal government to provide all manner of free stuff, e.g., healthcare and higher education. They also want everyone to be made exactly equal.

So what have these aspirations given us? On the one hand, they busted the federal budget such that the nation will go broke in little more than a decade. On the other, they enshrined political correctness so firmly that free speech has become a quaint oddity.

These trends are unmistakable. Why then have so many of the best and brightest embraced rank impossibilities. Don't they realize that no socialist government has ever worked to the extent it promised? Aren't they aware that compete equality has likewise never been achieved at any time, anywhere?

The fact is that many cotemporaries, it their hopefulness, do not want to admit these truths. They prefer to demand ever more services, while at the same time silencing folks who disagree with them. In the name of compassion and justice, they literally punch people in the nose and/or put them out of business.

The contradiction between what "reformers" advocate and produce is thus blatant. Yet they refuse to see it. This, however, is more than selective perception. It is a consequence of our becoming a nation of naive idealists. Many people now want what they want when they want it, whether or not this is reasonable.

An extended period of unprecedented prosperity, coupled with unparalleled international power convinced millions of Americans that anything is possible. A century of success also insulated them from the negative consequences of their innocence and selfishness.

Whatever goes wrong, these romantics expect to land on their feet. They always have and so they imagine they always will. Besides, don't they deserve to be winners? They do not need to work very hard in order to merit the best that the world has to offer.

Nonetheless, optimism must be tempered. Neither affluence nor safety is guaranteed. Both require effort and intelligence to obtain and preserve. They also cry out for an awareness of the limitations imposed by an occasionally hostile universe.

Unfortunately naïve idealists seldom acknowledge limits. They refuse to concede the importance of exertion, knowledge, and emotional maturity in achieving what they desire. Unbounded niceness, however, is not enough. If we are to succeed in making the world a better place, we also require a fair amount of toughness.

Idealism from Hell

Many young people are idealists. They believe in social purity. As a consequence, millions of them intend to be warriors dedi-cated to pursuing public perfection. They hope to rescue the world from the mess bequeathed them by a bitter elder generation.

We encounter this attitude in the enthusiasm of the college students at Bernie Sanders rallies. They cheerfully regard themselves as socialists. The way they see it is if the government can provide a safety net, it should be allowed to save us from *every* other peril.

We observe it in a competing set of college students who are enthralled by Rand Paul. These undergraduates are ardent libertarians. The way they understand things is that if the free marketplace can provide economic prosperity, it ought to be allowed to confer *every* other benefit of freedom.

Unfortunately, the world is a bit more complicated. It regularly confronts us with problems that are not solved by ideological purity. The young, however, don't know this. In their inexperience and ignorance, they seek a golden key that will unlock every social mystery.

The young people of Germany did the same almost a century ago. Their nation had lost the First World War, been devastated by a roaring inflation, and was mired in an economic depression. They, therefore, wanted it to be great again. The result was youthful communists battling youthful Nazis on the streets.

While the young can be forgiven their penchant for idealistic extremism, what are we to make of the empty headed extremists who are coming out for Trump rallies? Don't they know better than to indulge his muddle-headed call for greatness?

Trump is not usually associated with idealism. He and his followers are generally regarded as hardheaded realists. They expect his business acumen to rescue us from the throes of an Obama induced lethargy. He will obviously point us in the right direction to recapture our national glory.

How is this idealism? The answer is simple. Trump's alleged ability to provide magical answers lies in his "outsider" status. Because he has not been a politician, he is presumably untainted by the corruption that abounds in Washington. He therefore sees what jaded members of the establishment cannot.

But do you remember another idealistic outsider. As I recall, his name was Barack Obama. He was a community organizer from Chicago who was going to bring hope and change to the nation's capital. He too was going to cut the Gordian knot of official ineptitude.

Nonetheless, the notion that outsiders are somehow purer than insiders is regularly belied by history. Hitler was an outsider. So was Mussolini. For that matter, so were Lenin, Mao, and Castro. All of these proto-saviors claimed to be uncorrupted by the political chaos that preceded them.

Or how about Ross Perot? This other businessman was going to reform our tax code, but he instead allowed Bill Clinton to eject George Bush the elder from the presidency. After all, the only things that Bush had accomplished were winning the Gulf War and presiding over an orderly conclusion to the Cold War.

The question should not be who is an insider and who an outsider. It ought to be who has the character and the skills to deal with the very real difficulties our nation is facing. Who knows how to get the economy moving again and possesses the foreign policy expertise to contend with Russian, Chinese, Iranian, and Caliphate ambitions?

We are living in dangerous times. A squishy idealism will only make things worse. I submit that Donald Trump's qualifications for our highest office are slim to non-existent. His sole political policy is unbridled narcissism, while his favorite political tactic is the *ad hominem* attack.

This is not the stuff of which statesmen are made. It is thus time for voters to grow up. They must put away the idealistic play-things of their youth and get down to the serious business of evaluating the candidates for president.

Realistic Idealism

Do you remember the jokes the late-night comedians would make at the expense of George Bush the elder? He was regularly pilloried for being stogy and out of touch. One of their favorite zingers was to imitate him saying, "It wouldn't be prudent."

Well, the Republicans have become the party of prudence, whereas the Democrats have been the party of inspiration. While Republicans keep telling us that we are spending too much and will go broke if we do not mend our ways, Democrats promise to educate our children and create a pollution-free world.

As for me, I am all for prudence; yet look at the results of the last two presidential elections. It seems clear that young people, women, and minorities opted for inspiration over prudence. They did not want to hear establishment types talking about preserving the constitution or paying down the national debt.

My conclusion is that if Republicans are to become electorally competitive, they too must be inspirational. But that does not mean they should try to out-promise Obama. No one can do that. Nor does it mean they should abandon the constitution. Its stability is too important to our joint well being.

No, I am suggesting something different. It seems that important constituencies demand national leaders who are "idealistic." So I say, conservatives should give it to them. A shell-shocked GOP has been casting around for a winning strategy and this may be it.

Nevertheless, Republicans must be wary of a "romantic idealism." If they, like the Democrats, make promises they cannot redeem, they will be found out. The young and naïve often live with their heads in the clouds, yet they too eventually turn against leaders who do not deliver.

In my book *The Limits of Idealism* I argued that the young are idealistic because they are both moral and inexperienced. They fall for the simplified ideas of moral extremists because they have not yet learned the limitations of what is possible. They, for instance, believe it when told anyone can become president.

Sober heads that wish to sustain our nation must consequently avoid this trap. Nonetheless they should not avoid moralism. The trick is to be morally stirring without being foolishly saccharin or demagogically misleading. Moral goals can be promoted in ways that actually work.

As I have previously written, I believe there are five moral objectives to which Americans of all stripes can subscribe. These are *honesty, responsibility, fairness, family* and *liberty*. If they are presented vigorously and realistically they can serve as a corrective to the moral quagmire we have entered.

Consider the example of Jimmy Carter. Although he began his political career in obscurity, he captured the nation's imagination by promising that he would never lie to the public. Many people had qualms about his religious fervor, but they were eager to move past the Watergate scandal.

I submit that many Americans will soon be ready to move past the Obama quagmire. Four years of economic stagnation were not enough to disabuse them of their hero's virtues, but maybe eight will be. The same applies to ObamaCare. Maybe its implementation will convince them it was a mistake.

In the meantime, our president continues his cavalcade of distortion and deception. He tells us the world will end when sequestration kicks in, and then he acknowledges that perhaps it won't. He asserts that these cuts were not his idea, but then this spokesman grudgingly admits that maybe they were. And so it goes.

It is this sort of flim-flammery Republicans must eschew. They must tell the American people over and over again that they stand for honesty; then they must be honest. They need to appeal to better instincts of the young and of women so that they too appreciate this objective.

People want a better world, but a better world can only be a more moral one. So let those who wish to be elected shout this from the rooftops!

The Case for Principled Realism

Several years ago I came to the conclusion that we were in the midst of an ideological crisis. Liberalism was clearly not working, but there did not seem to be a practical substitute. Few Americans were prepared to resurrect laissez-faire capitalism or to embrace a Judeo-Christian theocracy.

So what was the alternative? My sociological analysis convinced me that we were headed toward "social individualism." As our society grew more affluent and complex, there were more personal decisions to make. Yet unless these were based on what was possible, they were apt to backfire.

Liberalism was grounded in a troika of fantasies. Progress-ives told us that social justice depended on universal love, interpersonal equality, and sexual androgyny. Yet I knew these were fairytales. A sustainable social order depended upon being more realistic about the sort of creatures we are and the challenges we confront.

So when I began writing about these issues, I talked about social realism. We were social creatures so we would have to start by understanding our social nature. Love was important, but it was directed toward people we knew well, not strangers. We were also hierarchical creatures. That is, everyone wanted to be special. Lastly there are genuine differences between men and women.

I had also come to believe that in our mass techno-commercial society, more of us would need to be professionalized. We would have to become self-motivated experts in the tasks we performed. Both on the job and at home, we would have to base our decisions on what achieved our aims.

And yet, there was nothing sexy about professionalization, or for the matter social realism. These were not inspirational concepts. Not many people were going to wake up in the morning breathlessly eager to become more professional or socially sophisticated.

Liberalism might be dying, but people crave hope. They need a goal that promises to make life better. Moreover, this goal needs to be easy to grasp. It has to intuitively provide a noble reason for living.

Then it hit me, why not call what I was after "progressive-conservatism." The liberals had appropriated their current label from folks who today would be called libertarians. Turn about was fair play, and progressivism had a ring of inexorable improvement.

Besides, I liked the idea of calling myself a "pro-con." A colleague, however, threw cold water on this by pointing out that conservatism continues to suggest a retrograde orientation. This sent me back to the drawing board.

It was at this point that the notion of "principled realism" dawned on me. Being in tune with reality was not enough. Our shared aspirations had to be in accord with standards that reduced interpersonal conflict. Unless we respected each other's ambitions, we could not cooperate in saving the world.

Then when president Trump gave his speech to Islamic leaders in Saudi Arabia, my hunch was confirmed after he used this very phrase. Trump was referring to political reforms. He wanted to bring contrasting civilizations together to fight a common threat.

But why couldn't a renewed practicality also apply to our personal lives? Why couldn't it relate to strengthening our marriages and reducing social tensions? We have jointly been fed so many myths about gender, race, and social class that might not a dose of truth prove a sovereign corrective?

Reality is a hard taskmaster, but fairytales are more dangerous. Sooner or later, they entice us to place our fate in the hands of monsters. Moral principles too can be demanding. They often require us to sacrifice beguiling dreams for the sake of the common good.

As I write this, I fear that I may be sounding like the college professor that I am. Nonetheless, it seems imperative to me that we as a society wake up from the angry nightmares we have conjointly created. Our unprecedented prosperity will mean nothing if we do not deal with the world as it is.

If we don't recognize our individual and collective limitations, we will not be able to take advantage of our individual and collective opportunities. Life can be difficult, but it is much more difficult with our heads buried in the sand and our hearts dedicated to selfish pursuits.

Fighting the Last War

Generals are notorious for fighting the last war. They go into battle assuming that they are pitted against an enemy just like the last one and therefore that they must employ the same weapons and tactics as before. Only bitter experience forces them to alter their plans.

I am not talking about the war against ISIS or Radical Islam. While we have been slow to adjust to their challenge, I am referring to a domestic problem. The warriors looking backwards nowadays are the Liberal/Progressives.

Over a hundred years ago, the Progressives took aim at the abuses of laissez-faire capitalism. With the acceleration of the Industrial Revolution, trusts were then growing at an alarming rate. These precursors to the modern corporation had unexpectedly consolidated into monopolistic giants.

Thus, John D. Rockefeller towered over the oil industry. For years, he had been forcing his smaller competitors out of business. If this entailed underselling them or compelling railroads to charge them higher rates, he did what was necessary. This included bribing politicians to protect his interests.

Yet Rockefeller was not a bad man. He was a power hungry person who was determined to consolidate his success so that he would never have to re-experience the insecurities of his youth. In fact, his quest for efficiency reduced the price Americans spent on kerosene.

Meanwhile J.P. Morgan towered over the finance industry. Never as wealthy as Rockefeller, his preeminence as a banker bestowed enormous power. Determined to rationalize commerce, he brought steel companies together under the aegis of U.S. Steel—and soon tried to do the same for railroads.

Morgan too was not a bad man. It simply made no sense to him that railroads should waste money building parallel tracks. If there was only one line, it could obviously charge less. He also, virtually singlehandedly, prevented two financial panics—because this too was good for business.

The problem with the robber barons was not that they were thieves. The problem was that they could have been had they been less scrupulous. Their empires were so vast that no competitor could challenge them—no matter how vile their behavior.

As a result, the Progressives sought to use government as a counterweight. Only it had the power to break up these monopolies. When backed by the demands of an outraged public, it could reduce corruption and bring the tycoons to heal.

Today the problem is big government. Over the last hundred years, its scope has so increased that its functionaries have their fingers in everyone's business. There is scarcely a corner of life that escapes its oversight and regulation.

Big government, however, is dominated, not by tycoons, but bureaucrats. Not single individuals, but battalions of faceless officials, now exercise unrestrained power. These too are not bad people, yet collectively they are as arrogant as any capitalist mogul. They too have the power to ride roughshod over opposition.

This then is today's battle. While big business still needs to be regulated, so does big government. Where once the muckrakers mobilized public opinion to reign in overzealous corporations, ordinary Americans must now be mobilized to demand that the federal government be curbed.

We do not have to rid ourselves of big government any more than we had to rid ourselves of big business. The issue is control, not elimination. We must thus reduce its excesses, rather than agitate for chaos. We still, for instance, need a government-sponsored safety net.

But we do not need an iron cage built by the government any more than we needed one built by Rockefeller or Morgan. An unfettered marketplace provided an invitation for abuse. So does an unfettered government.

The current political wars should therefore not be between Progressives and Nineteenth century conservatives. It should be between ordinary Americans who hope to retain control over their lives and Bureaucrats who are as overbearing as any tin pot dictator.

A Professionalized Society: Our Real Future

When I asked my wife, she suggested that most people do not want to become professionals in the sociological sense. She was not even sure that a majority of persons are capable of it.

When I brought the subject up with Dan Papp, President of Kennesaw State University, he replied that he thought a great many people did aspire to become professionals. That's why they came to college.

When my literary agent referred my manuscript "A Professionalized Society: Our Real Future" to a publisher, she wrote back that she didn't believe there was a market for the work. According to her, it was "too intelligent."

As for myself, I remain convinced that we are headed toward a more professionalized society. We may be getting there slowly— at an almost glacial pace—but I think we are inexorably moving in this direction.

Professionals are "self-motivated experts". Almost everyone agrees that doctors fit this definition. They spend many years learning how the human body works and studying what is needed to fix it when it stops functioning. But more than this; when they apply their knowledge, they are expected to do so of their own accord.

When a physician arrives at a diagnosis, he or she is supposed to get it right because he or she is personally committed to helping patients. Doing so to please a supervisor would be considered a dereliction of duty. So would prescribing a particular treatment merely because this is demanded by an insurance company.

Doctors are supposed to pursue competence because they care—and by and large they do. To engage in shoddy work, or to make a particular choice solely because they were ordered to, would violate their sense of professional integrity. It would reduce them to the level of a manual laborer, which would cancel out the many years of effort expended to achieve their exalted status.

Nowadays, this attitude also extends to nurses. Where once they were the dutiful handmaidens of physicians, they have risen to become semi-independent practitioners. Although still less prestigious than doctors, they are often delegated tasks that require both substantial competence and personal responsibility.

To illustrate, last year I suffered a lung infection that required the insertion of a PICC line (that is, a peripherally inserted central catheter). This thin plastic tube was introduced into a vein in my upper right arm and then threaded down into the center of my chest. The procedure, though delicate, was entirely entrusted to two nurses.

Fortunately, the nurses who attended me were experts in what they did. At no time did they require a physician to directly supervise their activities. Moreover, they were professionally dedicated to getting the procedure done correctly—which they did.

This greater professionalization of nurses is reflected in the training they receive at colleges such as Kennesaw State University. Before being accepted to one of these programs, they must demonstrate academic abilities and a personal maturity much in excess of the average student.

So challenging is KSU's nursing program that, as with physicians, our graduates take pride in their accomplishments. They feel like professionals because they have indeed become self-motivated experts; experts who are perfectly capable of independent courses of action.

I contend that this is becoming more the norm for business managers, accountants, police officers, architects, air conditioner technicians, engineers, educators, computer programmers, and social workers. All have become more professionalized and therefore more capable of supervising their own work.

If this is true, then we as a society are becoming more capable of true democracy. We can literally be more self-governing in our daily activities because we are better able to make high-quality choices—for ourselves and others.

The "Social Individualism" Solution

I have been arguing for some time that liberalism is dying. I have written about this in my columns; I have explained why in greater specificity in my book *Post-Liberalism: The Death of a Dream*. I have not, however, presented a viable alternative; at least, not in sufficient detail. This column is dedicated to beginning this process.

Liberalism is clearly falling apart. The debris of failed governmental programs and the conflicts inherent in political fraud surround us. Unless we find an alternative, violence and tyranny will soon beset us. The question is what can we do that provides social justice, while maintaining our freedom and prosperity?

Old-time conservatism will not do. Laissez-faire capitalism has been found wanting. By concentrating wealth in a few hands, it endangered the wellbeing of millions. Its focus on greed and economics also underestimated our need for love and steadfast families.

Nor will old-time religion do. It cannot provide us with the scientific advances necessary to sustain a mass techno-commercial society. Besides, its dependence on faith ensures the persistence of countervailing beliefs that cannot be reconciled.

We plainly need something different; something new. There has to be a way to organize our civilization that protects our rights, while providing an opportunity for political, economic, and personal progress. I submit that that form of organization is "social individualism."

Yes, I know that this sounds like an oxymoron. Isn't there a contradiction between being social and individualistic? How can we be both *for* ourselves, but also *for* others? The fact is that there is a tension between these two; a tension but not a logical inconsistency.

The Rabbi Hillel put this difficulty well two millennia ago. He asked, "If I am not for myself, who will be? And if not now, then when? But if I am only for myself, what am I?"

We can be for ourselves *and* others. We just need to know how. In fact, we cannot be for ourselves, if we do not know how to deal with other humans. We are social creatures. We have individual brains and personal feelings, but these, of necessity, function within a social context.

As social individualists, we must therefore make private choices that mesh with the private choices of many others. We are not monads, entirely separate from our fellows. But neither are we ants bound together by rigid genetic mechanisms.

What is more, our need to make good personal choices has been amplified by our prosperity. With so many more options now available to us, it is easy to go off on tangents that produce grave injuries. Indeed, the effects of bad decisions, such as chemical addiction and ideological warfare, currently besiege us.

Nevertheless, making good decisions entails three prerequisites. First, we must be realistic. We need to understand our personal and social abilities, as well as our limitations. If we are trapped in utopian fantasies, as is the case with liberalism, we are doomed to fail.

Second, we must be emotionally mature. We have to be grown-ups who can deal with our fears and stresses. We must also be able to cope with love, sadness, and anger. These biologically constrained passions need to be tamed so that they generate sensible conclusions. If not, we can expect a host of unintended and unwelcome consequences.

Third, we must be principled. We need shared social stand-ards, lest our conflicts get out of hand. We must internalize these, but also enforce them. As I have previously contended, these have to include honesty, personal responsibility, fairness defined as universality, liberty, and family values. Without these, we are destined for a Hobbesian war of all against all.

These preconditions are, to be sure, difficult to implement. We humans are frail beings who are easily led astray by our desires and social pressures. Indeed, perfection is unattainable. This being so, no form of social organization will completely solve the problem of living together in contented harmony.

Even so, social individualism can bring us closer to what is needed. It can free us from the toxic fantasies, at present, tearing us apart. By being truthful about the challenges we face and aiming at what is achievable, it can bring about the progress to which so many of us aspire.

Saving Ourselves

Decades ago, when I worked as a clinician, I learned an important lesson. I had begun under the assumption that it was my job to save people from the catastrophes in which they were enmeshed. I needed to be wise enough to point them in the right direction and strong enough to make sure they heeded my instructions.

It soon became apparent, however, that I had neither the knowledge nor the power to rescue my clients. Whether they were drug addicts, mentally ill, or normal folks who were unhappy with their lives, their success depended more on them than me.

The problem was not my inadequacies—which were many—but that humans are not puppets. As virtually all helping professionals discover, people must save themselves. A helper can provide assistance, but unless these folks do the hard work, it will not get done.

It is the same with society at large. Unless ordinary people address their personal issues, they will not be solved. Looking to others to do the heavy lifting, in fact, impedes progress. No matter how gifted or well-intentioned prospective helpers, they cannot do what people can only do for themselves.

Some eight years ago, millions of Americans fervently believed that Barack Obama would rescue them from the doldrums. The hope and change he promised would produce social justice and economic prosperity of unprecedented proportions.

Yet this was not how things turned out. Many liberals assume that this failure was attributable to the reactionary scoundrels who sabotaged their savior. Had these selfish individuals not stood in his way, equality and interpersonal devotion would have become the norm.

Now many conservatives imagine that Donald Trump will perform comparable miracles—from the opposite side of the political spectrum. He will repeal and replace ObamaCare and reform the tax code to such an extent that almost everyone will prosper.

Trump, to be sure, does not possess the messianic aura of Obama. He nonetheless makes extraordinary promises. His are so big that, as both his supporters and foes realize, they were not immed-iately realized.

The truth is that politicians cannot work magic. Although they can remove some of the obstacles to personal success, they are unable to create jobs, or strengthen marriages, or ensure personal happiness. These are up to us—individually and in conjunction with our role partners.

Principled realism begins with being realistic about what is possible. This starts with the realization that we are a hierarchical species and therefore will never be completely equal. Some folks will always be more powerful than others. Some will also grow richer than their peers.

The government can help level the playing field, but it cannot play the game for the participants. Thus, if they do not develop their skills or put in the effort to become winners, they will not be.

Whether we are loved is also within our purview. To begin with, universal love of every person for every other person is absurd. Genuine love depends on the creation of an emotional bond between individuals who know each other very well. It is therefore limited in scope.

Love is consequently something that persons must procure for themselves. They have to develop the emotional maturity to enter intimate collaborations. They must make commitments to other humans who reciprocate their dedication. This can be extraordinarily difficult, nevertheless only those involved can achieve it.

Government officials may promise us success and yet they are too far away and too emotionally detached to make much of a difference. As it happens, they are capable of less assistance than are professional helpers. Why? Because they neither understand, nor care about, the complications in actual human lives.

If this is true, then looking to Washington to underwrite our success on the job or in our homes is feckless. In abdicating our personal responsibilities, we would lay the groundwork for disillusionment. Although politicians share some of the blame by making pledges they cannot fulfill, we would be at fault for believing them.

Human perfection is not possible and in this sense neither is unqualified salvation. Even so, improvements are feasible. We can consummate these as long as we realize that we must begin by helping ourselves.

Major Changes Always Take Time

When I was in my twenties, I knew that I did not want to be like my father. Although he was a very smart man, with good intentions, he had an explosive temper that undermined his efforts to be successful. I intended to be different, but was not sure how.

Eventually, upon the advice of the college professor I considered my men-tor, I entered psychotherapy. For the next six years, I struggled to remake myself. Even after this, however, I remained a work in progress. Indeed, I am still laboring to become the person I hope to be.

Personal change, I learned, is difficult to come by. Our emotions, many of which are unconscious, often sabotage our efforts. Deeply embedded fears and intemperate anger prevent us from letting go of the past and moving on to something better.

Nowadays, as a professor of sociology, I teach about social change. I try to help students understand how this occurs and why it is more difficult than they suppose. As idealists, these young folks typically want immediate reforms.

Acutely aware of some of what has gone wrong, they see no reason why it should persist.

In this, they are not alone. The public at large regularly demands instantaneous action. When politicians promise dramatic changes, they clamor for even greater ones. Why should they settle for half a loaf when the whole loaf would be so much better?

And so what do we get? If we are lucky, we get a few crumbs. Obama, for instance, was going to remake Washington. But did this happen? He was also going to bring the nation together. In fact, we are now further apart than we were when he became president.

When these sorts of thing happen, we blame the politicians. We accuse them of failing to keep their promises. Thus, if we are Democrats, we rail at the conservatism of the Republicans. Or, if we are Republicans, we blame the irresponsibility of the liberals. Seldom, however, do we blame ourselves.

Yet this is where a substantial portion of the onus lies. If we did not assume that extraordinary changes can occur almost overnight, we would not demand them. If we were not convinced these were possible, we would not be disappointed when they do not arrive on schedule.

Nonetheless, big changes always take place slowly. They are evolutionary rather than revolutionary. Although small changes are possible in the short run, major ones take decades, centuries and sometimes millennia to be realized.

And why not? If personal changes are hard to implement, why would social changes be less difficult? If individuals can take years to remake who they are, why would millions of individuals require less time? Is it because millions of people are less emotional than a single person?

Consider the Black Lives Matter movement. Its advocates insist on an immediate overhaul of every police department. But how probable is this? They also want racism to disappear instantaneously. Yet is this in the cards? These activists may be angry, but can anger redo the world?

Not only is what they demand impossible to provide on their timetable, but the way they demand it alienates many people. When folks feel attacked, they get their backs up. Instead of doing what is asked, they do the opposite. If so, change is slowed down rather than accelerated.

Similar considerations apply to educational and health reforms. Thus, has ObamaCare worked? Or has the common core improved achievement scores?

Likewise, did Head Start enable minority student to catch up with the majority? You know the answers.

So why do we keep expecting miracles? Is it because our current situation is so intolerable that we cannot stand it for another minute? Or have we become spoiled children who want what we want when we want it?

Sometimes life is hard. Sometimes we must work for what we get—even if we wish things were different.

Chapter IV

Liberal Failures

A Dream Deferred

Liberals have taken to calling themselves progressive. The implication is that they are leading us into an inevitably glorious future. Their enlightened reforms are thus guaranteed to be superior to our tainted present. These allegations are nevertheless untrue. Liberalism specializes in exorbitant promises. It cannot provide the principled change we desire because its head is in the clouds, while its feet are mired in deceit. Despite myriads of true believers, it has failed in its ambitious designs. If we are to achieve actual improvements, we must recognize the realty of our contemporary experience. If we are to get beyond inflated hopes, we must begin by noticing that what is said does not always conform with what has been done.

I have therefore compared liberals with sugar addicts. They are so desirous of disseminating sweet news that they see it where it is absent. As a result, they inhabit a land of myths and false optimism. So many things have gone wrong that they are no longer prepared to recognize their extent. Instead they build a barricade of deception around the smoldering ruins of their expectations. In many ways, they are like a flying saucer cult. When proven wrong, they merely step up their claims. Nonetheless, reality is what it is. It intrudes upon our consciousness because it is solid and unmovable. Most liberal programs have failed and hence attempts to disguise this via political correctness are doomed to crumple. Burnished words alone cannot cancel out significant disappointments. Eventually people tire of being told what they can say or believe. They become aware that the emperor has no clothes and decide they will no longer play along. This seems to be happening today.

We have, regardless of opinions to the contrary, endured a century of liberal bankruptcy. Wherever we look, be it in education, the economy, criminal justice, the family, race relations, or poverty, the setbacks multiply. Arrogance and self-deception cannot obscure these facts. Despite the grandiose rhetoric and overblown insults hurled at doubters, the veil is being pierced. It has become increasingly clear that liberals are anti-democratic, intellectually broke, the opposite of nice, lacking in compassion, devoid of tolerance, and beret of integrity. Despite a never-ending series of glowing self-encomiums, they are world-class haters. When among themselves, they are endlessly self-congratulatory, but when it comes to those with whom they disagree, they can be savage. Irrespective of their talk about cooperation, unless bargains are made on their terms, they are not prepared to accept accommodations.

Liberals like to talk about love. They believe this pleasing emotion represents their essence. In reality, they are more about envy and hypocrisy. They despise those who disagree with them, although they pretend to be disinterested. Nonetheless, were their love genuine, it would still be insufficient. In a world filled with hundreds of millions of strangers, meaningful differences of opinions cannot be canceled out by way of universal amity. We require other means to distribute scarce resources—especially power. To this end, we must use our common sense. Politicians, of course, regularly extol this quality, but then they substitute vacuous platitudes for genuine insights. We, as a society, and as individuals, must do better. We cannot allow ideological blinders to keep us from dealing with harsh realities—especially when these frames of reference are misguided.

Why Liberalism Does Not Work

Sugar Addicts

Why are so many Americans devout liberals? Why do so many good people—and make no mistake, lots of liberals are very good people—cling to failed social policies with a death-grip? There are numerous reasons, but one of them may be surprising.

Liberals are like sugar addicts. They must get their fix of sweetness and light or they go into a painful withdrawal. Never mind that an excess of niceness is injuring them and those they hold dear.

Once upon a time, sugar was hard to come by. When we were hunter-gatherers, our intake generally came from fruits and berries. Occasionally we got lucky and happened upon a beehive filled with honey. Nevertheless, extracting this treasure took guts and luck.

Eventually, however, we learned to refine sugar from sugar cane. And once we did, the immediate impact was a surge in tooth decay. In time, we also fell victim to an epidemic of diabetes. Our collective pancreases were overwhelmed by a glut they could not handle.

Yet this did not stop people from craving sugar. Nowadays it is even added to pre-packaged foods, crammed into ice cream, and disguised as candy. We simply must have it or we go into paroxysms of distress.

It's the same way with social niceness. Once life was hard. Most people literally earned a living by the sweat of their brows. Nonetheless, the majority just scraped by. They did not have the luxury of endlessly agonizing over the troubles of others.

Still, we are rich and so we worry about poverty, justice, and peace. Happily, those of us who are comfortable also want others to be comfortable. Liberals, unfortunately, over do. They are so concerned with being nice that they cause irreparable damage.

Consider poverty. By the 1950's the United States had grown so wealthy John Kenneth Galbraith argued that an affluent society should share its bounty with the less well off. Within a decade, the war on poverty was launched. This was intended to eliminate destitution once and for all.

Yet what was the upshot? It was in increase in social dependency. People who received more than enough to meet their basic needs without having to work decided it was better to procure a government check than seek employment. On one level this made sense, but on another it deprived them of self-respect.

Or reflect on crime. Once, in the old West, horse thieves were hanged on the spot. Settlers who depended on this mode of transport-ation for survival were in no mood to be understanding when deprived of it.

We, in contrast, and so well-off that when we are robbed, we do not feel existentially threatened. And so we are merciful. We allow thugs to rampage through Baltimore on the theory they need to vent. That this would drive up the homicide rate was recognized only in retrospect.

Or contemplate our desire for peace. Just as in the old Coke commercial, we want the people of the world to hold hands and sing in perfect harmony. Except that they don't. For one thing, most of them are not as well heeled as we are. They still have aspirations to fill.

And so when we go to war we impose rules of engagement designed to abolish collateral damage. No one is supposed to get hurt—not even the bad guys. After all, why should they die when we are living in such comfort? This would be unfair.

And so we behave like spoiled children who want to consume all the candy on the table. We—most often liberals—do not worry about getting a bellyache or, for that matter, contracting diabetes. So what if more people are trapped in poverty, victimized by crime, or ruined by war. At least we tried.

Sadly, a smug inability to recognize our limitations precipitates more harm than good. Virtuous intentions are not enough when an excess of sweetness can be just as lethal as premeditated villainy.

A Century of Liberal Failure

Have you noticed how bitter liberals are at their electoral defeat? They not only expected to win; they felt entitled to do so. They have, as a result, been the sorest of sore losers. As this is being written, they are plotting ways to make sure Donald Trump does not enjoy the traditional presidential honeymoon.

Across the nation, Trump is being attacked as a fascist and terrorist. His victory is described as illegitimate; hence rioters felt free to vent their spleens. Meanwhile, calls for his assassination have been heard, members of the Electoral College urged to break their faith, and voter recounts pursued.

Can you recall any post-election this vituperative? When have Republicans acted this spitefully? Both of the Bushes left office gracefully. Their supporters were disappointed, but they resigned themselves to defeat. Gerald Ford and his allies were also good losers. They had doubts about Jimmy Carter, but were not about to destroy the nation on this account.

Nor can I remember a precedent for Barack Obama's behav-ior. He has gone on what amounts to an "I was really a great President" tour. Both at home and abroad, he elucidated, in mendacious detail, why he was not responsible for his party's loss and urged the new chief executive to continue his policies.

Obama has been known for taking undeserved victory laps. Now he assures us that his personal popularity is proof his two terms in office were triumphs. According to him, he saved us from a depression and single-handedly rescued America's international reputation.

But contemplate how much worse off we actually are. ObamaCare is in a death spiral. ISIS terrorism remains with us. The Iran deal gave an implacable foe cover for terrorism and the right to acquire nuclear weapons. As for the economy, it has never grown at more than 2 percent.

Nonetheless, this is par for the course for liberal administrations. On their watch educational achievement has plummeted, crime rates have risen, and the welfare roles have swollen. Despite their big promises about equality and justice, these were never kept.

Nor is this a recent development. Liberalism can lay claim to a century of failure. Virtually everything progressives have touched has turned to dross. Lest we forget, it was Woodrow Wilson who brought segregation to our nation's capital, Franklin Roosevelt who lengthened the Great Depression, Lyndon Johnson who lost the War on Poverty, and Jimmy Carter who gave us the Great Inflation.

If asked about their achievements, liberals generally cite Social Security, Medicare and Medicaid. But even these are in actuarial trouble. What is more, Democratic attainments in civil rights owe as much to Republicans as themselves. After all, it was the Dixiecrats who opposed voting legislation and Nixon who introduced affirmative action.

Why then are liberals so sour? Why have they gone ballistic over their current defeat? They have had setbacks before and recovered. Nor is it because Trump has egregiously misbehaved. If anything, his cabinet choices demonstrate a sincere intention to reinstate conservative principles.

Nonetheless, this is the problem. If Trump is successful, it might finally dawn on voters that neo-socialist promises are a fraud. Blacks and Hispanics might realize that conservative policies, if given a chance, would leave them better off. So might the blue collar workers at the historic heart of the Democratic coalition.

With Obama in office and the mainstream media guarding his flanks, liberals were able to disguise the depth of their failures. They were able to claim that no one could have done better in protecting our economy and national security.

What will they do if these hyperbolic pretensions are exposed? Already people have grown tired of identity politics and political correctness. Ordinary Americans are fatigued by the lies and angered by the perpetual unfairness. Many long for a return to the old verities.

If Trump delivers on these, liberalism might conclusively be discredited. Implementation of an American Dream that actually provides opportunity, liberty, and integrity may, in fact, reduce the prevailing cynicism. If so, neo-Marxism could go into a fatal decline. No wonder progressives are worried.

Is Liberalism a Flying Saucer Cult?

It was an intriguing question. What would happen to a religious cult that predicted the end of the world when the world was not destroyed on the predicted date? Would the believers go into shock? Would they suddenly realize that they were in error and abandon their faith? Or would they react otherwise?

The answer was the latter. In a classic study conducted over half a century ago, the social psychologists Leon Festinger and Stanley Schachter were in for a surprise. As they reported in *When Prophesy Fails*, members of these groups find a way to rationalize their mistakes. They decide perhaps that they miscalculated the date, or that the space aliens took pity on the human race, or that their own faith forestalled the catastrophe.

True believers have a way of believing no matter what the facts. When these contradict their predictions, they merely alter the predictions. Paradoxically, rather than be embarrassed, they become more committed. Instead of hiding away in shame, they intensify their proselytizing efforts.

But isn't this what we have seen with liberals? Haven't they found a way to rationalize their failures? When they do not deliver on their promises, they merely offer bigger and better ones. Rather than back off, they become more vocal and more certain in what they predict.

Consider the Great Depression. When Franklin Roosevelt's spending programs did not restore prosperity, his acolytes explained that he had done "too little, too late." They insisted that bigger government programs would surely do the trick. Indeed, they are still making such claims. Today, of course, they predict that unprecedentedly large "stimulus" packages will bring renewed growth.

Or what about poverty? Didn't liberals institute a War on Poverty? According to them, providing the underprivileged with larger welfare checks and greater training opportunities would to lift them into the middle class. Only it didn't. Liberal programs actually increased the number of people on the dole.

And how about Progressive Education? Wasn't that supposed to improve student's performances by allowing them to initiate their own projects? Except that this is not what happened. In the real world, math and reading scores went down. Rather than leading the world in educational achievement, the United States fell to the bottom of the pack.

Even in crime, liberal prophesies failed to come true. Liberals told us that poverty was the root cause of crime. They also said that punishing lawbreakers labeled them as criminal and therefore encouraged further crime. They answer was to defend the rights of the accused. In this way, we would stop "blaming the victims." And yet this approach also failed. In fact, under liberal tutelage crime rates skyrocketed.

Still liberals do not give up. Now they want to throw more money at schools and at welfare. They especially want to chuck tons of money at health care. Medicare and Medicaid are going broke (as is Social Security), but they are not alarmed. President Obama, with a straight face, promises that he will find the required funds by reducing waste and inefficiency.

The trouble is that no liberal administration has ever made good on any such promise. They have always managed to spend more than forecast and to spend much of this on political allies—such as labor unions. Why should this time be different?

One of the most amusing spectacles of the Bush administration was when liberal reporters badgered Bush to admit that he had been mistaken about Iraq. The irony was that these same journalists never admit their own errors. Nor do liberal politicians. Obama could not even bring himself to acknowledge that the Iraqi "surge" succeeded.

As true believers, we can expect nothing less from liberals. They are essentially waiting for the flying saucers to land and bring lots of goodies. But fear not, when the date of their predicted arrival comes and goes, they will have a ready explanation. They will tell us that they have not done enough, but next year—or maybe the year after—the millennium will finally arrive.

A Fortress of Myths

Although Liberals have been compelled to protect their outdated beliefs with a bodyguard of lies, this has proved insufficient. Their ideology is so worm-eaten that they have had to erect a fortress of myths to defend it. Fantasies based on wishful thinking are required to do the job.

Not long ago I spent some time with my siblings. Given the present controversy over Israel and Iran, the question of president Obama's motives arose. Why, it was asked, do so many Jews continue to support our president when he is apparently so hostile to Israel?

My brother—who, before I go further, is one of the most decent people I know—rushed to Barack's defense. Our Middle East problems, he informed me, are of our own making. If Muslims are antagonistic toward us, or Israel, it is because they were provoked.

The story goes this way. The United States is rapaciously selfish. Americans are so convinced that they deserve to live in luxury that decades ago they squandered their oil resources. This forced them to appropriate stocks of other countries—most notably in the Persian Gulf.

"We stole their oil!" Naturally they are displeased. As thieves and bullies, we should not be surprised when our victims get angry at us and our allies. Clearly, we deserve their animosity!

When I responded that we did not *steal* Arab oil—that we paid for it, this justification fell on deaf ears. Instead the response was "We stole their oil!"—only issued more emphatically.

No further progress was made in resolving our differences because the notion that we are villainous thugs was deemed self-evident. I had, in fact, run into a stonewall of liberal myths. These sorts of narrative are impervious to facts. They, therefore, serve as formidable redoubts against unwelcome views.

Indeed, liberal myths abound. One of the more recent is "Hands up, don't shoot." That Officer Wilson shot an unarmed black teenager because he was a racist has become an article of faith. Even a report to the contrary by Eric Holder's Department of Justice, changed few minds.

Yet contemplate the many other liberal myths—and they go way back. To begin with, Franklin Delano Roosevelt did not save us from the Great Depression. If anything, he prolonged it. Nor did Calvin Coolidge provoke this downturn. In reality, his policies produced a period of enormous economic growth.

As for the War on Poverty, it was not responsible for lifting the downtrodden out of misery. The truth is that minorities were making faster progress before it was enacted than after.

Meanwhile it was not Republicans who denied African Americans civil rights. For over a century, it was Democrats who did so. As recently as the 1950's, a large proportion of them stood in the schoolhouse door blocking the entrance of blacks. Amazingly, it was Richard Nixon who gave us affirmative action.

Or how about Global Warming? Had enough snow yet this winter? If we have much more due to carbon emissions creating a greenhouse effect, we are liable to freeze to death. No doubt this is why Obama assured us the Keystone pipeline is more dangerous than ISIS.

During my family's discussions I also heard the old chestnut about how Bush lied and people died. But funny how many liberals also believed the CIA's warnings about weapons of mass destruction and hence voted for the Iraq War.

The thing about myths is that they are extremely enduring and can be shaped to rationalize any policy. I find it particularly amusing that progressives style themselves intellectuals. This too, of course, is a myth—as is the fiction of their exceptional compassion.

When I responded to my brother by elaborating upon the history of Islamic aggression, he waved my explanations aside. As far as he was concerned, anyone can cherry pick the facts to prove anything. But isn't this what liberals do when they engage in mythmaking?

Osage Oranges

Most fruits are edible. Their appearance is pleasant and their taste is appealing—at least to some animals. This seems not to be the case with the Osage orange. Native to Texas, when ripe the Osage is spherical and yellow. It looks like a prickly orange, but the compar-ison stops there.

The Osage most certainly does not taste like an orange. Its juice is milky and acrid and its texture stringy. Once thought poisonous, it is merely distasteful to humans and most other creatures. As a result, virtually all avoid it despite its superficial attractiveness.

But why am I writing about Osage oranges? This column has never before been dedicated to the culinary arts. The answer lies in the Bible. While I am not a religious man, even I know that the Bible contains a great deal of wisdom. One piece of it crossed my mind not long ago.

The saying is familiar: You will know them by their fruit (Matthew 7:16). This struck me as an apt warning with regard to Barack Obama and his crowd. Superficially they are an attractive bunch. Well spoken and given to lofty aspirations, they can sound like the heralds of a brave new world.

But we have been living with them for nigh on six years and the fruit of their labors is bitter and noxious. We have not yet perished from their works, but we are in more danger than we once were.

Liberals specialize in promises. They are always telling us about the wonderful protections they intend to deliver. Convinced that they are super-compassionate and super-smart, they evidently know best.

The trouble is that good intensions are like seeds. Too often we cannot tell what they will grow into until long after they germinate. Unfortunately, the Obama promises have turned out rather like Osage oranges. They have not yet killed us, but a steady diet of them might.

The litany of failures has grown too long to be cited every time there is a need to document the incompetence of the current administration. Nonetheless, it includes ObamaCare, the VA scandal, the IRS debacle, the Benghazi affair, a foreign policy from hell and a toxic superciliousness that does not travel well.

What then is the point of stating the obvious? By now even Democrats are acknowledging that Obama is a poor administrator. Detached and surrounded by yes-men and women, he doesn't even learn of problems in his own government until he reads about them in the paper.

So my question is: Why has it take us so long to reach these conclusions? After all, it was less than two years ago that we rejected the stability of a Mitt Romney for the razzle-dazzle of Barack Obama. What were we thinking?

Didn't we have enough evidence that the economy had not recovered? Weren't there enough straws in the wind to suggest that our international stature was declining? Couldn't voters see through Democratic assurances that things were getting better to realize they weren't?

As to the future, are we going to be in exactly the same position when Hillary Clinton runs for president? When she tells us that she will fix the ObamaCare mess or that under her tutelage our foreign relations will improve, will we believe her?

Judging from what she has already achieved, there is little reason to give her promises credence. Wasn't she the one who hatched that reset button with Russia? And didn't she, in another lifetime, attempt to force HillaryCare down our throats?

As for Benghazi, she tells us she had nothing to do with that debacle. Other people messed that one up. But if so, why wasn't she involved? She was in charge, so does that mean she was as much of a hands-off administrator as Obama?

I am beginning to detect the whiff of Osage oranges in the air. Hillary may look good from afar, but do we really want another four years of hyperbole and good intensions?

PC Fatigue

The next Republican debate will shortly be upon us and people are wondering how well Donald Trump will perform. In the previous debates, only his mother and devoted enthusiasts were impressed. He was neither cogent nor forceful in his presentation.

Nonetheless The Donald's aficionados are convinced that he is honest, brilliant, and strong. No matter what he says, they take it as gospel. In fact, Trump is none of what is alleged. To the contrary, he is a pathetic imitation of what a tough-minded leader should be.

So why do so many people think otherwise? Why is he hailed as a national savior in some quarters? This has become an enduring mystery. Indeed, commentators of every political stripe have struggled to explain the phenomenon. About all they can agree on, however, is that the "establishment" got it wrong.

In fact, the answer is not difficult to discern. The Trump boomlet is a reflection of PC fatigue. As the anti-political correctness candidate, he has benefited from a backlash that has been slow in coming.

First, Donald is not an honest man. He routinely denies that he has said what he can be documented as saying. Second, he is decidedly not brilliant. His insights into foreign affairs and domestic politics really are on the junior high school level. Third, he is not especially strong. Anyone who brags about his accomplishments as much as he does is fundamentally insecure.

Still, there is an area in which Trump might be described as strong. Trump has stood up against political correctness. He regularly says things that no sane politician is supposed to say—and then he stands up to the criticism that inevitably results.

Why this has gained him a dedicated following can be understood by examining from whence his support derives. As the polls demonstrate, his most ardent backers are blue-collar whites. They are the ones who cheer when he lowers the boom on his detractors.

But consider the primary targets of PC. These too are straight, white males. They are the folks who are routinely accused of being racist, sexist, and homophobic. They are the ones depicted as mean-spirited boobs who ought to be run out of town on a rail.

Consider too the methodology of the folks who enforce political correctness. These card-carrying liberals, and their naïve young henchmen, are specialists in intimidation. Their primary technique for quashing the opposition is to silence it into submission.

How do the achieve this? Why they march through the streets chanting about how they will roast pigs like bacon. They camp out on Wall Street in order to disrupt capitalist activities. They flood suburban malls to prevent shoppers from patronizing the stores.

The PC folks lie. They insist that "hand up don't shoot" was a reality. They firebomb senior centers. Stand in their way and they rough you up. And, of course, if they can, they will get you fired from your job. Failing this, they will use the law to have you fined for not baking a cake for homosexuals.

It, therefore, takes courage to oppose to these bullies. Yet this bravery is sorely lacking on campus, in the media, and among politicians. As a consequence, millions of Americans are fed up with being treated like second-class citizens in their own land. They have been looking for a champion and believe they have found one in Trump.

Unfortunately, The Donald is a bogus hero. He is coarse, vulgar, and in-your-face, but this is not the same as genuine courage. Truly courageous people do more than hurl insults. They do not call women ugly, Mexicans inveterate criminals, or soft-spoken rivals weak.

Trump is not smart because he says he is. And he is not strong because he promises to bomb the daylights out of our enemies. PC does need to be challenged—but not in the way he does it. A devotee of infantile rudeness cannot halt a plague of self-righteous meanness.

Liberal Arrogance

Just when I think that the egotism of liberals can grow no greater, it does. Who thought that Barack Obama would cross the line in the sand that he himself drew and unilaterally bypass Congress to mandate temporary amnesty for some illegals?

Likewise, who would have imagined that having berated George W. Bush for asserting executive privilege, he would do the same for the Fast and Furious scandal? Attorney General Eric Holder has been stonewalling congress for over a year, but why would the president have joined him in this intransigence?

And as for the mainstream media, I was appalled to learn how little attention they have paid to Fast and Furious. Two Americans die because of an ill-conceived effort to track arms into Mexico and the network television news only devotes seconds to covering the story? Is this *Alice Through the Looking Glass*?

Not long ago I discovered a clue to this mentality. I was reading a book called *Red Families versus Blue Families* by Nancy Cahn and June Carbone. As lawyers, the authors were analyzing the legal differences regarding sex and the marriage statues between liberal and conservative states.

For the most part, they did a credible job. But then I encountered their thumbnail descriptions of conservatives and liberals. Mind you, they labeled them as traditionalists and modernists respectively, but the intent was unmistakable.

According to the authors, conservatives adhere to traditions, respect authority, and desire order, whereas liberals are flexible thinkers, tolerate diversity and place a greater emphasis on equality. Guess which group they favor?

But think about how tendentious and arrogant this is. Clearly the conservatives are the rigid bad guys, whereas the liberals are the progressive good guys. One group is obviously mired in the past, while the other optimistically looks forward to a better future. (By the way, hasn't Obama been touting his moving "forward.")

Anyway, let's start with this business of conservatives respecting authority, while liberals presumably do not. Has anybody read *The New York Times* lately? "Kneejerk liberal" is a hackneyed appellation, but it surely applies to the Times. So what of those readers for whom its authority is Biblical? Are they not slaves to authority?

And as to tolerance of diversity, how come the liberals have difficulty tolerating religious fundamentalists? They insist that they are non-judgmental and give everyone "unconditional positive regard;" that is, unless you are perceived as a political enemy. Then you are obviously stupid and unworthy of respect.

With regard to this business of liberals emphasizing equality (of results, not opportunity), why didn't the authors note that conservatives emphasize freedom? Isn't the pursuit of liberty a commendable quest? Indeed, I personally feel freedom is far more important than equality.

What liberals in their arrogance fail to realize is that a respect for tradition and a desire for progress are not incompatible. If anything, a commitment to the Constitution—an admittedly old document—may facilitate the preservation of the very freedoms that make democratic progress possible.

Being forward looking is not equivalent being in favor of a bigger and more centralized federal government, as liberals desire. Nor does it mean that you must put on blinders and fail to comprehend that very large budget deficits are a prescription for economic ruin.

In truth, it is the conservatives who are looking forward to warn of the dangers of concentrating power in fewer hands. Those old-fashioned traditions of theirs—you know the ones about a separation of political power—tell them that what Obama and company are attempting might just undermine our personal rights.

I may be simple-minded, but the way I see it: those who do not do not grasp this unadorned fact are not flexible thinkers. They are so sure they are "the best and brightest" that it never occurs to them that those who disagree might have a valid point or two.

Now that's arrogance!

A Culture of Self-Deception

Some of the best people I know are liberals. I really mean that! They are kind, dependable, and genuinely compassionate. Nonetheless, when it comes to the political arena, their benevolence fails them. Time and again, they support programs that while intended to do good, achieve the opposite.

Why is this so? How can they not realize that the positive outcomes they promote actually cause harm? It is not from a want of intelligence, because many liberals are highly intelligent. Nor is it from a lack of knowledge, because many are very knowledgeable.

What then is the answer? I suggest that their mistakes flow from a deeply ingrained pattern of self-deception. What is more, I believe their errors are reinforced by the pervasive culture of self-deception in which they are embedded.

The war of poverty did not work. Trillions were spent, but poverty remains with us. Affirmative action did not work. Countless thousands of minority students were admitted to schools for which they did not have the appropriate preparation, and then were forced to drop out.

Progressive education did not work. Social promotions and the new math left American students falling behind the international competition with little hope of catching up. Head Start did not work. Despite temporary improvements, the long-term results were extremely disappointing.

The list of fiascoes goes on and on, now to include ObamaCare and a foreign policy crafted by a kindergarten mentality. Liberals did not ameliorate crime, nor save the family, nor end the cold war, nor bring about economic equality—yet they like to pretend they did.

To hear them tell it, our nation would be in a deep crisis without their generous interventions. If they have not been completely successful, it is solely because mean-spirited conservatives forced them to do too little, too late.

Or is there another reason? Could it be that their proposals are misguided? Would an empirical investigation reveal that they have over-promised and under-delivered because whatever their intensions, their policies are grounded in fantasy.

The only way for good people to remain ignorant of these facts is to engage in willful self-deception and to support an agenda of public mendacity. In short, it requires them to lie to themselves and to everyone else.

They must believe that Barack Obama "misspoke" when he told Americans they could keep their health plans and doctors. They must somehow miss the deceit at the center of the assertion that women earn seventy-seven cents on the dollar compared with men—for the same work. Even the census bureau disowned that last one.

And what about Obama's policy of bringing peace by apologizing for American grandiosity? We are not exceptional, so who are we to tell the Iranians they cannot have an atomic bomb or the Russians that they must not annex a nation whose borders they pledged to respect?

Nor should we pay down a national debt that was once decried as unpatriotic or investigate an IRS scandal that had been denounced as shameful. It is time to move on because there is nothing to see; that is, nothing the liberals wish us (or themselves) to see.

Liberals are good people; hence they can do no bad—ever. Liberals are extraordinarily smart; hence they can make no mistakes—ever. If others claim they do, it is because they are racist, sexist, and homophobic idiots.

For some liberals, the endless cycle of self-congratulation will never stop. They are on a merry-go-round energized by ethereal ideals that they will not allow to founder on the shores of a harsh reality. Trapped as they are in a community high on pipe dreams, the best they can manage is to legalize their drug of choice.

Self-deception can be comforting. It can wish away bad economic news or conjure up a political rainbow at the end of a social storm. Meanwhile, the rest of us are tossed and turned by the consequences of their self-inflicted follies.

Liberals Are Anti-Democratic

Every now and then I read a book that alters my perspective. Fred Siegel's *The Revolt Against the Masses: How Liberalism Undermined the Middle Class* is such a work. It makes it clear that liberals have *always* been vociferously hostile to democracy.

While I have long realized that the "Democratic" party is misnamed, how far its roots lie from the egalitarian traditions of the United States came into much sharper focus. Liberalism is—and was—a program designed by elitists for elitists. It never was for, or appreciative of, the little guy.

Although I have a fairly large vocabulary, Siegel uses a word with which I was not familiar. It is "clerisy." According to the dictionary, this is a synonym for the literati. This is also the clique that Siegel identifies as having launched and kept liberalism afloat.

From its beginnings a century ago, modern American liberalism has been dedicated to promoting literary causes. Its chief proponents were self-styled intellectuals who deemed themselves superior to the common ruck. Convinced they were smarter, kinder, and more sophisticated than ordinary persons, they could afford to look down on them.

But more than this, they had to persuade themselves that they were not really snobs. As a result, they styled themselves as knights errant on the mission to save humanity from its own defects. They, albeit highbrows, would lead the lowbrows into a brave new world of gentility and equality.

Of course, they did not really mean this. Utterly convinced of their own superiority, they were certain ordinary people could not govern themselves. These boobs could not tell the difference between a Kandinsky and a toad and therefore they could not be trusted to make important decisions.

No, the clerisy would have to make the decisions—even for the personal lives of those they were destined to govern. Persons of lesser ability would have to defer to their betters so that they could be saved from themselves. Indeed, if these fools had to be manipulated into complying, it was for their own good.

Isn't this what Barack Obama and his merry band of pseudo-democrats are attempting to do? Don't they habitually assure us that ObamaCare will rescue us from the mean-spirited insurance companies? Aren't they confident our nation's hegemonic ambitions must be thwarted lest we corrupt the rest of the world?

And if we are not in favor of these things, they must persuade us to go along. Should this require lies, lies will be told. Should it entail misdirection, red herrings will be trotted out. Should the truth lead people to come to the wrong conclusions, it will be withheld from them.

Why not? Ordinary Americans are regarded as so dim that these forms of manipulation will slide by them. Obviously, young women can be persuaded that conservatives hate them by repetitively making unsubstantiated charges of a "war against women." Clearly, the poor can be rallied to legislation that will make them poorer if offered a few small bribes.

Hence we witness the New York Times, the bastion of elite Liberalism, a newspaper that prides itself on providing "all the news that's fit to print," deciding not to cover the IRS scandal. Ordinary people surely cannot be trusted with knowledge of how Lois Lerner plotted to deny tax relief to conservative organizations; ergo memos that reveal this are omitted.

Then there is Harry Reid who tells the masses that accusations ObamaCare is hurting people are all lies. Or Nancy Pelosi who opined that if we were to find out what ObamaCare contained, congress would first have to pass it—naturally assuming that average Americans would never read the bill.

As for the president himself, he believes that his rhetoric can always get him out of a bad scrape. Given the right honeyed words, and the appropriate cadences, voters can even be persuaded that ObamaCare is working. Failing that, he can divert attention with lurid tales about why the climate-change sky is falling.

Intellectually Bankrupt

Robert Putnam is an important thinker. Not only is he a Harvard political scientist, but he is an extremely influential liberal intellectual. His current book

"Our Kids: The American Dream in Crisis" is therefore an alarming indicator of where progressive thought is headed.

Putnam understands that American families are in trouble. He attempts to dramatize the unfolding calamity by contrasting the small town America in which he came of age to the urban and suburban landscape of today. Thus, on virtually every measure from family viability, though schooling and community integrity, he establishes that we are worse off.

This is not news. Nor is the fact that the middle and lower classes are dissimilarly affected. Charles Murray has already plowed this ground from a conservative perspective. In "Coming Apart" he too documented the tragic decline of the American poor.

Both Putnam and Murray agree that unwed parenthood is tearing American families apart. They also agree that the damage done to children raised by single parents is substantial and is concentrated at the lower end of the social spectrum.

The difference between them lies in their policy recommendations. That children raised by single parents receive less emotional support, do less well in school, are more prone to crime and unemployment, and are apt to replicate their parent's mistakes, is beyond question. The issue is how to remedy these facts.

Putnam and Murray also agree that the problem has a moral dimension. The difference is in how they assign the blame. Where Murray argues for increased responsibility among the poor, Putnam places this duty on the upper classes.

Like Obama, Putnam wants us to be our brother's keepers. He therefore begins his chapter on "what is to be done" by assuming that widespread illegitimacy is here to stay. He does not even ask the poor to abstain from bearing children they can neither afford nor know how to prepare for personal success.

Instead, like a good liberal, he asks us to spend more money. Although he is acutely aware that transfer payments have hitherto made little difference, this is his principal solution.

For one thing, he insists that public schools institute more extracurricular activities. Somehow this is supposed to provide poor kids the structure they do not receive at home. Why, he does not say—except that these programs benefit the better off kids.

Putnam also knows that teachers have limited impact and that we presently spend as much on schooling the poor as the rich. Nonetheless, he wants to double what we devote on the latter. Despite his awareness that there is no correlation between funding and academic success, he can conceive of no other recourse.

Putman likewise wants the poor to have more job options. He believes that if they do, their families will be under less stress. But then he asks that the rich be further taxed. It does not occur to him that by diverting resources to the government, there will be less available to invest in jobs.

This is intellectual bankruptcy. It is tax and spend liberalism dressed up as insightful social analysis. The lesson to be derived from Putnam's examination of family breakdown is therefore that liberals have learned nothing from the failure of their ideology.

Hence it is no surprise that we see this vacuousness is the current presidential campaign. Retread left-wing ideas proliferate like weeds. Once more there are the reputed wars against women and blacks. Once again we are asked to raise the minimum wage and to demand that the rich pay their fair share.

But where is the call for responsible parenthood? Where is the demand for morality when it comes to bringing children into the world? If we really want to help the poor, we must start by insisting on personal discipline. Liberals, on the other hand, are enablers. Their emphasis on spending is permissiveness disguised as altruism.

Our children deserve better. Let's give them a chance by actually strengthening their families!

The Myth of Liberal Niceness

Should I be fired from my job at Kennesaw State University? Some readers of the Marietta Daily Journal seem to think so. They complain that my columns are too conservative and therefore provide evidence that I am too stupid to be a college professor.

Indeed, some of my colleagues and students at KSU have felt the same way. They too have been offended by my political convictions and recommended my termination. Mind you, my job is safe because I am a tenured full professor; nevertheless their sentiment is telling.

Liberals think of themselves as especially nice people. They believe that they are uniquely tolerant and kind. This attitude, however, does not extend to those with whom they disagree. Just ask the tea party activists. Far from being commended for their political activism, they are castigated as stupid, violent, and racist.

Liberal activists, in contrast, are uniformly applauded for their patriotism. However violent or obscene their conduct, they are praised as fighting for justice. The result is that they are allowed to break windows, spit on police officers or steal conservative newspapers with impunity.

Nor, from the liberal perspective, should their lack of niceness necessarily be ruled out of bounds. If I, or my conservative peers, are as threatening to the public well being as alleged, there is no reason they should be extremely polite to us. We should, in fact, be called out and asked to reform our errant ways.

It is just that liberals are hypocritical in their public posture. They proclaim that they are more tolerant than others, whereas the truth is that they are merely selective in their benevolence. Thus, there are very few traditionalists, entrepreneurs, or Republicans they like, while there are even fewer criminals, Arab terrorists, or Black Panther hooligans they seem to dislike.

This imbalance might be dismissed as an innocent matter of style, except that a pretense of universal amiability can have devastating consequences. One of the best examples of this was provided by the Amadou Diallo scandal.

It has been more than a decade since then mayor Rudy Giuliani was castigated by the *New York Times* for allowing the city's police department to run wild. For month after month, the paper accused Giuliani of condoning police brutality by tolerating the shooting of an innocent citizen.

The fact that Diallo was killed by officers who mistakenly fired over forty shots at him was taken as irrefutable evidence of recklessness. Although the officers responsible were subsequently acquitted of wrongdoing, they remained guilty in the eye's of one of the nations' most liberal journals.

Why does this matter? Why is this ancient history relevant today? It is because the Times stance was not without consequences. The papers editors were convinced that the police were not sufficiently nice to minorities and therefore demanded repentance. They insisted that the authorities back off so that similar mistakes never recur.

But what was the actual outcome? When the police did back off, the crime rate shot up in the affected neighborhoods. More innocent people were killed, robbed, and raped thanks to their increased caution.

To be blunt, niceness that results in increased violence is not necessarily nice. Truly nice people worry about the implications of their compassion. They do not abstain from harsh actions for fear of being perceived as mean-spirited, but neither are they gratuitously nasty.

This outlook not only applies to petty criminals, but to large-scale malefactors such as Iran. Being too nice to Mahmoud Achmedinejad today may result in his being incredibly nasty to many millions of others a few years hence.

The same applies to Republicans being too nice to the Democratic legislators who passed ObamaCare. Civility yes, but allowing them to win uncontested re-election—no. Niceness is not absolute, but relative. Sometimes it is essential, whereas reflexive, misplaced, or sham niceness can have dire consequences.

Niceness, Liberal-Style

Liberals are nice. Don't they keep telling us as much? They have compassion, whereas those mean-spirited conservatives do not. Liberals are tolerant of differences, while their adversaries are singularly intolerant.

Just how nice liberals can be was plainly on display when a crowd of demonstrators roughed up folks coming from a Trump rally in California. Accordingly, when they threw eggs at a young woman they had trapped outside a hotel, they were merely instructing her on the error of her ways.

As a college professor, I am routinely exposed to liberal arrogance. As a sociologist, I am doubly and triply subjected to it. Not long ago, I was interviewed for a book entitled *Passing on the Right*. It chillingly documents the tribulations of conservative academics in our universities.

Of the more than one hundred and fifty scholars who were interviewed for the book, a grand total of nine were sociologists. This is not surprising in light of the fact that no more than three percent of sociologists identify as conservative. Fully one third actually profess Marxism.

I get to see this bias at sociological conventions where I have literally been told to shut up when I say something out of the radical left mainstream. I have similarly witnessed it in sociological organizations that have refused to publish my articles in their newsletters because the editors disagreed with my opinions.

But the problem is not confined to sociology. When I started teaching at Kennesaw State University, a colleague from a different discipline advised me that I was in for a bumpy ride in Georgia. The state was then voting Democratic and she assured me that it always would.

Well, the world turns and the solid south has become the conservative south. Nonetheless, southern colleges have remained dependably liberal. At least in the humanities and social sciences, their faculties are overwhelmingly left-wing. These folks consider anything that is not "progressive" to be hard-hearted.

A few weeks ago, the liberal columnist Nicholas Kristof wrote about this attitude in the New York Times. In his piece, he bemoaned liberal intolerance. Describing it as a blind spot, he cited a quote attributed to Voltaire to wit: "I disapprove of what you say, but I will defend to the death your right to say it."

Yet liberals not only refuse to defend opposition to their orthodoxies, they will not hire colleagues who do not heave to the party line. The reason, they say, is that conservatives are just not smart enough. They are not academically-minded and hence are unfit to teach the young.

This was why my wife, not long ago, compared liberals to raccoons. As an Ohio farm girl, she had, in fact, raised some of these creatures from infancy. The experience taught her to be careful about feeding them. "Give them an inch and they will take a mile," she warned.

Liberals too are insatiable. They are never satisfied no matter how much they get. Differ with their positions too vociferously and they attempt to silence you. Fail to agree with their social prescriptions and they will seek to penalize you.

Regardless of how they slice it, this propensity is not nice. Nowadays, many Georgians insist on an independence of spirit and personal responsibility. Unfortunately, this perspective has gone out of fashion in other sections of our country. Genuine niceness, however, requires nothing less.

If we are to rescue our nation from the current doldrums, we must thus understand that niceness is not only about tolerance. It is also concerned with the consequences of its policies. If, in advocating for the underdog, it imposes a totalitarian grip on society, this ought to be shunned.

Colleges, for instance, should be marketplaces of ideas, not one-size-fits-all indoctrination centers. Political rallies should likewise be violence free zones. Yes, Trump goes over the line with his boastful tirades. But so do those who object to his jingoism. Genuine niceness demands tolerance and good sense from all sides. Even Liberals!

Counterfeit Compassion

Liberals are convinced that they are particularly nice. They are certain that they are more compassionate than others. Nice to women, blacks, gays, foreigners, and the poor, they sympathize with everyone—save perhaps conservatives.

The problem is that this compassion is largely counterfeit. It sounds like the real thing when liberals pontificate about how dedicated they are to improving the lot of the downtrodden, but it vanishes when they are put to the test.

Nancy Pelosi provides a wonderful example. When the news channels were full of pictures of young children languishing in holding facilities on our southern border, she gushed about how concerned she was for their welfare. With her arms spread apart, she declared that she wished she could take them all home with her.

Of course, she knew she could not. She was aware that many thousands of Central Americans were streaming into the country, and she bemoaned their plight. Yet she was not prepared to do anything about it except prattle on about how worried she was.

Nancy might tell us that at least her heart was in the right place, whereas conservatives are heartless. Nonetheless, if your head is not also in the right place, neither is your heart. If you are not ready to do something that genuinely helps, you are all talk and no real kindness.

I am reminded of the years I spent working in a psychiatric hospital. It was grueling, discouraging work because so many of the patients were terribly ill. They suffered from schizophrenia, affective disorders, and manic-depression. Of these, the schizophrenics were worst off, trapped in their agony and delusions.

More painful still, the vast majority of the psychotics were not going to get better. They might be medicated to control their symptoms, but they were never going to approach normality.

For those of us who genuinely cared, this broke our hearts. We were fond of our charges and wished them the best. Nonetheless, we knew that the big dreams of their childhoods would never be realized. Even so, we worked with them to make their lives as comfortable as possible.

There were others, however, who were transient workers. Almost always sweet young things, they arrived at the hospital full of hope. Because they possessed boundless compassion, their love was sure to rescue those with whom they came into contact.

Then, thanks to their magical kindness, the patients they saved would be eternally grateful. Except this never happened. The fairy-tale cures never materialized and even when patients improved, few were appreciative. They took this help as their due.

So how did the sweet young things react? Well, they disappeared. Crushed by an empathetic overload, they saved themselves by changing jobs. Only the tough souls, the ones prepared to handle agonizing frustrations, remained behind to continue ministering to the patients. They were the ones who actually cared.

Liberals are like those sweet young things. They are all aflutter about how they are going to remake the world, but when the going gets tough, they hide behind a screen of words. Better yet, they blame others for exacerbating the problems they were not equipped to solve.

We see this in Texas, where the liberals declare the breakdown of border security a humanitarian crisis. Their hearts go out to the huddled masses yearning to breath free. But do they acknowledge their role in creating this emergency? Do they rush to change the laws that set it in motion? No, they just kvetch!

We see this in Gaza, where the liberals rush to send millions in relief to Hamas, but then sidetrack moneys intended to replenish Israel's Iron Dome. They also propose a ceasefire that will allow the Islamists to regroup and start again. No thought is given to those who may perish in the renewed fighting two years from now.

Is this compassion? Is this genuine help—or a pretense of concern? I, for one, am no longer fooled by the crocodile tears.

Liberal Tolerance

Some weeks ago I was invited to give a talk at the *Aeropagus*, a devout Christian organization. The organizer, Dr. Jefrey Breshears, and the discussant, Dr. Richard Howe, could not have been more gracious. Intelligent, open-minded, and decent, they treated me with unfailing respect.

The same could be said of the audience. All present knew that I am an agnostic and hence disagreed with my convictions, yet no one was discourteous. Indeed, people were warm and supportive even when attempting to explain why I was wrong.

I bring this up because it contrasts so markedly with the reception I received at a Regional Sociological Association's recent annual meeting. This liberal organization could scarcely have less gracious or more intolerant.

Many readers have inquired about how I, a conservative, can survive in so liberal a discipline as sociology. Part of the reason is that my colleagues at Kennesaw State University are fair and congenial, even when our perspectives diverge.

With unfamiliar sociologists, however, it is often a different matter. Once they learn where I stand, I get treated like the skunk at the garden party. I am either told to shut up or coldly ignored. This is what occurred at the afore mentioned conference.

A hint at what I was to experience could have been gleaned from the title of the event. Called "The Stalled Revolution: Gender Inequality in the 21st Century," the goal was to promote "social justice"—especially for women.

The opening plenary speaker set the tone by explaining how cutting edge couples were creating the intimate relationships of the future. While her research demonstrated how unhappy these people often were, and how frequently they divorced or remained single, they were presented as positive models of what is to come.

Many years ago, I began my career as a philosophy major. At the time, one of my goals was to learn about life. Nonetheless, I left the discipline when I ascertained that there was no objective way to settle differences of opinion. I balked when persuasiveness and power reigned as the arbiters of acceptability.

Sociology was supposed to be different. As a social science, its disputes would presumably be decided by appealing to empirical data. Not moral commitments, but first-hand observations would determine the facts.

Not any more. Too many sociologists have become inflexible moralists. They are not trying to learn about the world, but to promote their causes. Because they are convinced they know the truth, they are confident there is nothing to learn from dissenters.

Just how left wing sociology has become was evident at the conference's book display. Virtually all the featured works high-lighted what is wrong with contemporary America. To judge from their content, we are residing what amounts to one huge concentration camp.

Why is this so? Why are sociological liberals so intolerant? Once, a mere few hundred years ago, Christians were as fanatical. Back then dissenters were not only disparaged, they were killed. So what changed?

After many bruising wars, during which no side definitively prevailed, the participants realized that tolerance made more sense. Their doctrinal differences remained, yet people discovered they could accept these without insisting on rote compliance.

Liberals, including most sociologists, have yet to learn this lesson. They are so dedicated to their ideology that they cannot stomach opposition, especially from those presumed to be on their side. This makes outliers, like me, particularly objectionable.

Something similar prevails in the political arena. Liberals are so firm in their moral convictions that community members who differ are considered either stupid or evil. Why then would a virtuous person put up with such villains?

Liberals still believe they can win the culture wars. Even when the facts go against them, they are not discouraged. One day, equality and androgyny will surely prevail. All that is needed is for the good guys to stick together and beat the bad ones (e.g., me) into submission.

Liberal Integrity?

Once, liberals stood proud and tall. They were confident in their abilities and convinced they knew how to reform the world. Under their guidance, ordinary people would move forward into the sunny uplands of which Winston Churchill spoke.

For one thing, liberals were certain that they were more intelligent than others. They were also positive they were nicer. As such, they believed it imperative that they lead the way toward a brighter future.

But oh my, how the mighty have fallen! These would-be philosopher kings have been discovered to have feet of clay. The recent debacles of the Obama administration have put their self-assured assertions in doubt. Worse still, it has left their integrity in tatters.

Barack Obama lied. He lied many, many times. He lied when he told people could keep their health plans. He lied when he said they could retain their doctors. He lied when he said our ambassador in Bengasi had been killed by a flash mob incited by an offensive video.

Now Obama has compounded this mendacity by violating his previous declaration that the senate's filibuster rule was sacred. It has not been many years since he vehemently maintained that this practice was essential to protecting minority rights. Suddenly, however, this analysis is non-operative.

What is worse is that many partisan liberals have gone along with his malfeasance. They have defended their president and voted to eliminate a legislative procedure they too once endorsed. Abruptly, power has become more important to them than honest dealing.

Anyone, but the most zealous liberals, must acknowledge that Obamacare is a cancer metastasizing into on the body politic. Anyone, not blinded by ambition, must realize that manipulating the American people with false promises and ignoring constitutional safeguards puts our democracy in danger.

Unhappily, too many liberals have sacrificed their integrity for a mess of stinking pottage. They have excused their president's lies by claiming that he merely misspoke and/or was not sufficiently clear in his language. They have likewise joined in trashing centuries of Senate precedent for a temporary political advantage.

Even as recently as Franklin Delano Roosevelt's administration, senate Democrats bridled at packing the Supreme Court. They understood that the court was obstructing their presi-dent's policies, but they valued the nation's traditions even more. Evidently such patriotism is no longer part of the liberal creed.

So why is this so? Why have so many liberals become blatant shills for deceit and demagoguery? Part of the answer can be found in a psychological insight enunciated a half-century ago. It was then that Leon Festinger alerted us to the potency of cognitive dissonance.

Festinger noted that when people are confronted with information that contradicts strongly held beliefs, they are apt to deny the obvious. In an effort to defend their self-images, they repudiate reality. They simply cannot bring themselves to acknowledge their personal limitations.

But isn't this what is happing to liberals? Aren't they being confronted with shortcomings they are loath to admit? ObamaCare has clearly been a case of over-reaching. It and its rollout have been both inept and injurious. The website has plainly been a technical humiliation; while the program's irrational demands have placed millions of people in jeopardy of losing their health insurance.

How then is this smart? And how is it compassionate? Could people who fancy themselves to be among the best and brightest have perpetrated this abomination upon the fellow citizens who trusted their words? This could not possibly be true—and so it must not be.

Accordingly, with this bit of mental gymnastics, liberal integrity is tossed out the window. Facts no longer matter. Human decency no longer matters. Promises cease to count. And as for tradition, it is a millstone to be hastily discarded.

The only thing that does seem to matter is self-preservation. Liberals have thus become parodies of the virtuous saviors they long portrayed themselves to be. Having descended into the gutter, they wallow there before our eyes.

World Class Haters

Republicans are congenitally mean. Conservatives are downright hateful. Liberals, on the other hand, are filled with love and compassion. This was the central the theme of the Democratic National Convention. Nearly every other speech was dedicated to telling us that love is all we really need.

Sure, the Beatles told us the same thing—but is it actually true? If we can convince the ISIS gunmen that we genuinely care about them, will they lay down their arms? If Franklin Roosevelt and Winston Churchill had given Adolf Hitler a few more hugs, would he have refrained from invading Poland?

If these examples seem silly, make no mistake about it, many liberals would free criminals from prison on the grounds that this would make them better citizens. They would also disarm the police in the belief that inner city thugs are merely reacting to official violence.

After all, didn't the mayor of Baltimore tell the police to stand down as rioters ravaged her city? And didn't the Department of Justice condemn the Ferguson police for bringing riot gear to a riot? And wasn't that a former Miss Alabama who said she felt compassion for a man who killed five officers in cold blood?

Faux niceness is evidently the stock and trade of liberals. Thus, they insist that they are tolerant to the core, whereas their opponents are discriminatory wretches. Only progressives really care about others. Only they want to make the world a better place.

And yet all of this is belied by their behavior. No sooner do progressives tell us that we should love everyone than they turn around and call conservatives awful names. Is this love? Is it tolerance? As importantly, is it non-judgmental?

But you say that they do with a smile on their faces and the milk of human kindness flowing from their bosoms. What then was that business about radicals burning the American flag outside the convention? And why was a good liberal like Geraldo Rivera spit upon by a demonstrator?

The truth is that liberals are world-class haters. At one point or another, they have vented their spleens at men, Christians, the rich, whites, and straights. Although they routinely disguise this venom under protestations of magnanimity, it is ever-present. Theirs, they assume, is righteous indignation. Nonetheless it is deep and unforgiving. Whatever it is, it is anything but loving toward its targets.

When Hillary Clinton was delivering her diatribe during the convention, there was fury in her eyes. If you doubt me, go back and look at recordings of her speech. While she claims to be full of sweetness and light, she also says she is a fighter and those eyes confirmed it.

Hillary and her allies may be justified in their hostility toward some of their opponents, but to call this love is a stretch. Nor is their anger antiseptic because it is moral. Rage has a way of getting out of hand. It does not just ask cops to be nice; it threatens to kill them.

Neither is hate moderate. When it is at full bore, it prevents people from thinking clearly. Haters are so determined to destroy their foes that they do not consider whether their own policies have the intended effect. Clearly, they want to win more than do good.

The progressive agenda has been implemented many times in many places. Nowhere, however, has it lived up to expectations. Why don't liberals realize this? In part, it is because they are too busy blaming their adversaries. They assume that if they could annihilate these folks, truth and justice would automatically prevail.

As for love, if they genuinely loved children, wouldn't they promote stronger marriages and families? Likewise, if they genuinely loved the poor, wouldn't they help these folks become more responsible?

It is easy to say that one is loving. It is quite another to demonstrate it. Liberals consequently make a habit of self-congratulatory nonsense. Although they routinely maintain we should love everyone, they might consider being a little nicer themselves.

Love Is Not Enough

Decades ago, when describing his approach to dealing with autistic youngsters, the psychologist Bruno Bettelheim wrote that, "love is not enough." Without providing these children understanding and discipline, they would never overcome their disabilities.

A few weeks ago I said something similar at a panel sponsored by the Cherokee County Republican Assembly. I argued that love alone would never enable us to triumph over the social challenges we face. Indeed, I claimed that we can never love millions of other Americans.

This may sound harsh—but I meant every word. The term "love" is thrown around with abandon. People use it when they want to sound kind or generous. Nevertheless, anyone who has been in love knows this is a unique emotion reserved for a very few.

The experience of falling in love is totally different from being nice to a panhandler. Giving a homeless person a spare dollar is not accompanied by paroxysms of joy. Nor does it entail the intense commitment that sustains long term relationships.

I love my wife and willingly make sacrifices for her. Most parents are similarly prepared to endure hardships to protect their children. Nonetheless, while I like many of my KSU students, my devotion to them is far less robust. I will not even lend them money.

Anyone who has been in love knows this takes a lot of energy. They are aware of how it fills the mind. They have dealt with their inability to focus on other matters and felt that special thrill which comes from being around the object of their affection.

As it happens, love is generally reserved for those with whom we are related. It is earmarked for family members—including our spouses. Evolutionary psychologists tell us it results from selfish genes that aim to reproduce themselves in the next generation. Love thus generates an altruism that defends our biological legacy.

How different it is with strangers. When I go to the supermarket checkout counter, I often joke with the clerk. She frequently does the same with me. But I don't love her and she does not love me. We are polite; we are even friendly. Yet there is no passion in our transaction.

In our modern mass society, we deal with most others in terms of their social roles. We know their jobs and they know ours and this shapes the way we treat each other. At the supermarket I am a customer and the woman across the counter is a cashier. As a result, she rings up my purchases and I pay for them.

In a world filled with interdependent strangers, how else could we get along? Because it is impossible to know so many others personally, we make do with identifying their social niches. Actually we often judge them by the symbols of their positions. What a person wears, or where he is standing, alerts us as to how we are to approach him.

This may seem callous, but it is a practical solution to living in a mass society. Back in the days of hunter-gatherers, strangers killed one another. Because they could not be sure of an outsider's intentions, they were wary. We are less so because we judge other's objectives by the jobs we impute to them.

In other words, when we talk about loving everybody, this is no more than an analogy. We are being asked to pretend others are members of our family and act accordingly. In fact, we are to conduct ourselves as if we belonged to a "loving" family. Everyone knows authentic kin can be disagreeable.

So where does this leave us when dealing with strangers? We need to be nice if we are to survive unexpected encounters. We need to be responsible if we are to be economically inter-reliant. One way or another, we have to trust unknown others. Consequently, if we cannot rely upon love; we must commit to shared ground rules. Morality has to substitute for genuine affection.

Morality may be cold. It may be impersonal. But if we are to respect others, we must honor the boundaries it sets. This may not be love, but it furnishes some of the same safeguards.

Common Sense

They say that common sense is uncommon. This is certainly true with respect to politics. As a result, whenever a politician touts a proposal as "common sense," we must brace ourselves for something that is probably wrong-headed. To date, the Obama administration has not disappointed.

But let me start with something different. This summer, when I was teaching about social class differences, I explained that research demonstrates that spending more money on education does not improve the outcomes. There is, in fact, no correlation between school funding and student performance.

I went on to explain that almost no one wants to believe this. Ordinary folks regard the opposite conclusion as common sense. Obviously if we pay teachers more, reduce the number of students per class, and introduce additional computers, students will learn more.

Except that they don't. We have spent trillions of dollars more on schools than when I was a child with negligible impact. If anything, achievement scores have gone down. Certainly minority students have not caught up with majority students.

What the research shows is that parental attitudes count for more. Hence, when parents value education, their children usually do. Schools have less impact than we desire because the reverse is also true. The only exception, and it is a small one, is that peers can influence one another.

As a consequence, magnet schools don't work, bussing didn't work, and Head Start hasn't worked. But who believes this? And why not? Clearly, because we want them to work! When we have a problem, we wish to do something about it. We are not willing to sit around allowing it to fester.

And so when someone says that he has an answer, we listen. We then allow our good intentions to substitute for concrete results. Instead of checking to see whether a program has previously succeeded, we are persuaded by rosy pictures of what is supposed to happen.

Nowadays we see this when Bernie Sanders promises socialistic extravagance. Nowhere on this planet has socialism ever worked. It has always delivered less than expected. The young do not know this, however, because they have not been paying attention.

The same tendency exists among conservatives. When Richard Nixon told the nation he would end inflation by introducing price controls, his partisans wanted to believe. This strategy has never succeeded—including in ancient Rome—but who among them knew history?

We see this predisposition today when the poor agitate for a higher minimum wage. Many of them would lose their jobs, but they are convinced it won't be them. Nor will inflation nibble away at whatever benefits they receive. After all, it is common sense that higher wages can buy more things.

And then, there is gun control. Of course, it is common sense that if we take guns out of the hands of terrorists, fewer people will be massacred. Conservatives protest that it is people who kill people. Still, they do so more effectively with assault weapons. So let us identify these individuals and deny them the opportunity.

Doesn't President Obama tell us over and over again that he merely wants "common sense" gun legislation? Doesn't he imply that anyone who disagrees has no sense? Those mean spirited members of the National Rifle Association are so enamored of their guns and Bibles that they cannot see straight.

But what about the fact that gun control has not worked in Chicago, or France, or, for that matter, anywhere? And what about the data showing that an earlier assault rifle ban in the U.S. did not reduce crime? This evidence apparently means nothing. Since it goes against common sense, it has to be wrong.

Will this inclination to go with our gut feelings change any time soon? I doubt it. The politicians also doubt it. Bernie Sanders went a long way with his version of common sense. So have Hillary and Donald. Millions of people will therefore continue to believe what they want, while the rest of us pay the penalty.

Chapter V

The Neo-Marxist Connection

The Socialist Essence of Liberalism

Liberals have long protested against being called socialists. They did not want to be associated with communist Russia or anything that smacked of Marxism. To this end, they invented a slew of misleading labels. Among their descriptors of choice have been *progressives, social democrats,* and *conflict theorists*. They have also favored *social justice, political correctness,* and *identity politics*. The goal in this has always been to sound moral and traditional. Whether they pursued a *New Deal*, a *Fair Deal* or a *New New Deal,* the objective was to pave the way for greater government control, while simultaneously making it seem that they were seeking to implement the American Dream.

With the advent of Bernie Sanders, however, it is now acceptable for liberals to be overtly socialist. The leftward tilt of the Democratic Party has become so pronounced that its underlying neo-Marxist ideals bubbled to the surface. This development decidedly includes Barack Obama. As the most left leaning of recent presidents, he encouraged Americans to be one another's keepers. He hoped by this means to employ the government to create equality and justice. Marx advocated a system in which the means of production was controlled by the state. This hegemony would purportedly reduce selfishness, while concurrently increasing fairness. Obama, in contrast, was going to achieve this outcome by a mixture of federal regulations and taxing the rich into compliance. Although this would not produce overt government ownership, it would extend government control.

Like most socialists, Obama assumed that he and his henchmen were smarter than ordinary citizens. They knew what was best and therefore ought to be entrusted with the protection of others. The trouble is that their self-regard was grossly inflated. A look at the record of neo-Marxist fiascoes is illuminating. Despite constant claims of success, whether at home or abroad, peace and prosperity were never entirely forthcoming. Thus the Great Depression lasted for a full decade and the Obama economy remained flat, while North Korea and Iran blossomed into genuine threats. Although liberals followed the roadmap of the Italian communist Antonio Gramsci and seized control of the media, our educational system, and the entertainment industry, these cultural triumphs did not translate into constructive political accomplishments. In an effort to mobilize public support, they consequently attacked capitalism. The middle classes were relentlessly propagandized to regard the *one per centers* as the enemy. Depicting the wealthy as stealing from the poor, then hoarding the proceeds for themselves, would achieve this. Even more importantly, minority groups were urged to believe they were oppressed. This sense of victimization was to provide the motivation to demand social justice and vote for socialist candidates.

Nonetheless, social justice is a scam. It is not what has customarily been regarded as fair. Instead of enforcing the same rules for all, it endorses identity politics in which favored groups receive special allowances. Blacks, women, and gays thus obtain preferential treatment. This is not democracy. It is government-enforced parity. Moreover, in order to make it happen, the state had to dominate the market economy. It needed to radically reorganize the way our society is run. ObamaCare was part of this scheme. It would allow Washington bureaucrats to dictate what took place in one sixth of our economy. In fact, the burning question is whether such a shift is in our collective interest. Can an ever-bigger government deliver enhanced medical benefits?

Ronald Reagan did not think so. He bemoaned our bloated federal bureaucracy. The Gipper intuitively realized that socialism could not exist without overweening central direction. Three centuries ago, Louis XIV of France hoped to be an absolute monarch. He intended to dominate everything that happened in his domain. He did not succeed because he could not. As it happens, the invention of the modern bureaucracy was necessary to make socialism feasible. It provided the machinery to consolidate unlimited governance. By utilizing metastasizing rules and reams of paperwork, the smallest activities of ordinary Americans could be regulated. Their freedoms would thereby be sacrificed on the altar of collectivist rationality. Except, of course, that rampant regulation became sclerotic. Far from being reasonable, it took on a life of its own that profited the bureaucrats at the expense of those they bullied.

Like it or not, the Democratic Party has become the bureaucratic party. It could not be anything less in the pursuit of its socialist ideals. The only way to expand the reach of federal officials was to codify the system under which they operated. The problem is that this had unintended side effects. While it justified penetrating every aspect of our national life, it also became a self-perpetuating behemoth. Thus was born the *deep state* in which civil servants could veto the intensions of elected representatives. Bureaucrats who were dedicated to enhancing their own powers genuinely came to believe that they always knew best. After all, they were the experts. They were the legitimate decision makers. In what might nowadays be characterized as a *shadow government*, socialist-minded administrators threaten our traditional understanding of democracy. Their liberalism has morphed into an updated and overweening version of Marxism.

Marxism and Bureaucracy

Is Barack Obama a Socialist?

Is Barack Obama a socialist? And does it matter? Certainly the president's most ardent supporters publicly bridle at the suggestion. They consider it an insult hurled at them for partisan purposes. So far as they are concerned, he, and they, are merely compassionate progressives seeking to move the nation into the 21st century.

Sometimes the president and his allies characterize themselves as Social Democrats. They compare their policies with the left-of-center parties that regularly preside over European welfare states. As they see it, it is long past due that we catch up with the government-based programs pioneered by their heroes.

While it is true that some European countries have national-ized economic interests in the name of fairness, their American admirers do not propose emulating Britain's Labor party by taking over our steel or coal industries. These, they say, are free to remain in the hands of their current owners.

Generally speaking, American leftists seem to believe that as long as the government does not literally confiscate private property and as long as its machinery remains officially democratic, the term socialist does not apply.

So let us take a look at history. Surely Karl Marx qualifies as a socialist. He obviously thought of himself that way. Indeed, he described himself as a "scientific socialist." According to him, it was inevitable that a proletarian revolution would one day confiscate capitalist holdings, then operate these for the benefit of all.

Still, we must dig deeper into Marx's thinking to evaluate how he understood socialism. Central to his theory was the belief that at nearly every stage of history two social classes contended for control over the means of economic production. Then the victors used their superior power to exploit the losers.

Thus, during the Middle Ages the nobility, who owned the land, suppressed the peasants and bourgeoisie for their own benefit. Next, after the Industrial Revolution, it was the capitalists, who owned the factories, who did the same vis-à-vis the proletarians.

Obama and his allies are quick to point out that they, unlike previous ruling classes, have appropriated no private property. They may tax the rich so as to assist the poor, but this is not the same as seizing the means of production.

What we must remember, however, is that Marx spoke of "controlling" the means of production—which does not require ownership. He who determines what is done with property, irrespective of its legal possession, has it within his power. He is in *control* despite what a certificate of ownership might say.

And isn't this what Obama and his co-conspirators have done with respect to health care? They make no pretense to owning this one-sixth of our economy, yet they insist on calling nearly all of the shots. Ergo, they get to say what insurance policies must cover. And they get to impose what they call the "best practices."

Or how about what the Obama administration is doing by way of the Environmental Protection Agency. Thanks to idiosyncratic interpretations of the clean air and water statues, this outfit is in the process of running coalmines out of business and will soon be dictating what private citizens can do in their backyards.

Nor is that all. These acts of economic aggression have often been perpetrated in the dead of night. Contrary to promises of total transparency, bribery, intimidation and subterfuge have been the tactics of choice in implementing what are frequently unpopular policies.

In other words, just like many socialist regimes, Obama's is sliding toward totalitarianism. He and his fellow travelers intend to have things their way no matter what Congress or the American people may think.

This is not democracy, as we have known it. Nor is it the free market, as we have known it. The Obama administration and its friends in the media may use every propaganda trick at their disposal to convince us they are not heavy-handed socialists, but if it walks like a duck, and quacks like duck....

The New Leftist Intelligentsia

Karl Marx got it started. Indeed, it was one of his most successful ploys. He not only advocated for a communist revolution, but argued that its proponents were special. Not only were the nicer than their capitalist foes, they were smarter. They understood the arc of history in a way the establishment did not.

Marx described himself and his allies as the "intelligentsia." They were well-educated intellectuals. Rather than motivated by greed, they employed their insights for the betterment of all humankind. Thus, they, and they alone, would mobilize the downtrodden to take their rightful place in a new world order.

As Marx saw it, the working classes were held back by a "false consciousness." They had been fooled by the propaganda of their bosses. Hence, if shrewd people, such as himself, could make then see they were being exploited, they would rise up in sure-fire rebellion.

Marx insisted that he was scientific. He had studied history and deciphered its logic. Thanks to his brilliance—and realism—he discovered the material dialectic. It revealed that social classes invariably compete for control of the means of production. Now it was the turn of the proletarians to wrest power from the capitalists.

Progressives of every sort take this as gospel. Their tactics have varied, but the goal of obtaining social justice by putting ordinary workers in charge has not. These erstwhile reformers have no doubt that their prescription is correct and that victory is preordained.

Never mind that Marx's predictions did not come to pass. The workers in industrial nations did not become impoverished. The proletarian revolution never occurred. Socialist societies, in fact, never developed into bastions of democracy. To the contrary, they were uniformly totalitarian.

Worst of all, Marx never anticipated the emergence of the middle class. He did not understand that post-industrial societies would need to become professionalized. A man of his times, he could not see over the horizon to realize that the free market would generate unprecedented wealth and freedom.

Marx can be forgiven his limitations. But that does not mean we should accept his flawed reasoning. In science, investigators make predictions that they subsequently test empirically. If these do not turn out as forecast, they are set aside in favor of alternate hypotheses.

This, however, is not what happened with regard to Marxism. Its adherents refused to admit their errors. They instead became apologists for what amounted to a secular religion. Having bought the canard that they are smarter than others, they expressed no regrets for their mistakes.

As an academic, I am constantly amazed by the lack of historical perspective demonstrated by so-called progressives. So convinced are they by the Marxist orthodoxy that they do not take the time to verify it against what occurred in the past. Were they to do so, they would find the dialectic fatally defective.

I am also amazed by the ease with which neo-Marxists insult the intelligence of their opponents. They do not listen to those who disagree with them. Nor do they read their books. Instead, they dismiss them as boobs whose opinions are not worth consideration.

The global warming controversy is a prime example. Those who question the extent of increased world temperatures, or their cause, are scorned as "deniers." They are said to be so tiny a minority as to merit no notice. That, in science, minuscule minorities, have often proved right, leaves them cold.

Yet is this attitude smart? Is it open minded? Liberal policies have been wrong about crime, education, and welfare. Nor have they been fruitful in international politics. Why then would intelligent people now assume they are automatically correct?

The truth is that liberals are no cleverer than their rivals. Franklin Roosevelt's brain trust was a bust. John Kennedy's best and brightest made a host of miscalculations. Meanwhile Barack Obama's dulcet cadences could not disguise his simplistic understanding of the economy and foreign relations.

Pretending to be smarter than others can prevent one's opponents from questioning half-baked ideas, but only if these others are intimidated into believing they are inferior. They need not do so. The neo-Marxist intelligentsia is a fraud. Their brilliance exists solely in their imaginations.

The Neo-Marxist Record

A couple of weeks ago I wrote about what a repulsive tyrant Mao Tse-Tung was. In that piece, I remarked at how the world has turned upside down, with Marxists currently commended for their compassion and capitalists portrayed as vicious oppressors. This was not the nation in which I grew up.

A few days later, I received an email from a reader of my own generation. He too lamented at how many people nowadays have forgotten the legacy of Marxism. Not having personally experienced it, they romanticize the horrors perpetrated by butchers such as Che Guevara.

As a sociologist, I am surrounded by Neo-Marxists. Many of my colleagues, especially at other universities, advocate socialism. They sincerely believe that a collectivist economy presided over by experts, such as themselves, promotes social justice. Only this, they are convinced, can create egalitarian prosperity.

And yet, over the last century, socialist experiments have wrought little but destruction. Their partisans proclaim a multitude of successes, whereas failure has been the norm. Whether in Russia, Eastern Europe, China, North Korea, Cuba, and now Venezuela, a succession of dictators delivered poverty and repression.

It is the same in the United States. The damage done has not been as extensive because neo-Marxist control has been less far-reaching. Nonetheless, although liberals regularly boast about their accomplishments, their path here is also strewn with the bones of rotting social programs.

Do you remember how Jimmy Carter was going to be a man we could trust? He would bring down inflation and apply his engineering expertise to foreign policy. But what did he give us? Well, it was a roaring inflation and dozens of hostages held by the Iranians.

Do you also remember how Bill Clinton would extract us from a recession and preside over a peace dividend? But he tried to give us HillaryCare and higher taxes. Only a conservative congress saved him from himself. Without this, there have been no balanced budget or growing economy.

Lastly, do you remember when Barack Obama assured us he would oversee a rebirth of transparency and peace? Yet his was the most secretive administration the nation has ever had, while "strategic patience" allowed Syria to splinter and Russia, China and Iran to assert their hegemony.

Look too at how progressive policies have dumbed down education, expanded welfare dependency, brought violence to inner city streets, exacerbated race relations, over-regulated the economy, and turned health care into a battleground. Was this supposed to be progress?

Words are not deeds. Promises are not performance. Neo-Marxism, whatever it is called, has never worked. Its sorry record of repression and over-sold salvation springs from the contradictions at its core. Collectivist regimes depend upon humans being what they are not. As a consequence, these governments dole out the opposite of what they undertake.

First, ordinary people never love others with equal intensity. Love, of necessity, has a narrow focus. Genuine love is only of a few. Second, ordinary people are not egalitarian. They want to be special. They want to be winners, not mediocrities.

Third, this means that neo-Marxists must use force when imposing their solutions. Why? Because people resist what goes against their nature. Fortunately for the collectivists, they enjoy employing force. They are, as a result, determined to assemble so much personal power that no one can resist them.

Ironically, we are seeing the fruits of these propensities in the Trump presidency. To begin with, Trump would not have been elected had not millions of Americans rebelled at being treated like sheep. They were no longer prepared to delegate their fate in an insensitive federal government.

Next, liberals would not be so upset with Trump had they not provided him the tools to undo their legacy. By concentrating additional power in Washington, he was enabled to use executive orders to nullify what was created by executive order. Now Democrats have difficulty stopping what they designed to be unstoppable.

Here then is the supreme irony of Neo-Marxism. The dictatorial government machinery it bequeathed us can be turned against itself. When people recognize how feckless the progressive record has been, they are able to reverse it with the same imperious techniques used to create it.

Exposing Cultural Marxism

Not long ago I had an opportunity to hear Dr. Jefrey Breshears talk to the Georgia Tea Party about "The Origins of Cultural Marxism and Political Correctness." Although, as a student of social change, I have some knowledge about these matters, his presentation was so masterful that I too saw many things from a new perspective.

Before I continue, I must disclose that Jefrey is a friend of mine. He has been a history professor at Georgia State University and Kennesaw State University. He is also the founder and guiding light behind the Areopagus, a Christian study organization.

Although Jefrey and I disagree about some things, most notably religious issues, I have learned to respect his intellectual honesty and devotion to moral causes. He not only wants to promote Christianity, but to make the world a better place for us all.

To this end, he has sought to uncover the Marxist roots of contemporary progressive beliefs. Most Americans are not aware that what they have been told is "compassion" is a disguised effort to usher in a communist utopia. The idea is to discredit the present to make room for a fictional future.

Dr. Breshears covered far too many aspects of cultural Marxism to be discussed within this short column, but let me mention two. Each concerns intellectuals who are largely unknown to the public, but who laid the groundwork for what many people think.

The first is the Italian communist journalist Antonio Gramsci. Writing back in the 1920's, he became aware that Marx's predictions about the proletarian revolution were not coming true. Ordinary workers were not rising up to support a socialist insurgency. Most were happy to be left alone, as long as they had good-paying jobs.

Gramsci did not believe that this would change and so he sought another avenue to social transformation. He decided that the change agents would have to come from the middle class. If these folks could be converted to the communist cause, they would use their skills to promote it.

How could this be achieved? Why, by educating them in socialist orthodoxies. And how could this be accomplished? Why, by taking over the schools and mainstream media. In case you haven't noticed, this is exactly what has happened in the United States and Europe.

As a college professor, I can attest to the fact that most of my colleagues are dedicated to advancing "progressive" ideals. This is what they teach; it is the criterion they use when deciding who to hire. Because they also indoctrinate future teachers, it is what is largely taught in K-12.

As you may also realize, most journalists are imbued with neo-Marxism. They too, despite the many failures of communist regimes, are convinced that only extreme egalitarian ideals can rescue us from the alleged oppression and discrimination inherent in capitalism.

Nowadays neo-Marxism is often labeled "social justice," but it is just old wine in new bottles. The same goes for "sexual liberation." This was the brainchild of Herbert Marcuse. He argued that unless people are freed from bourgeois sexual repression, they can never be happy.

The real goal, however, was to disorganize society so completely that it would be vulnerable to a communist takeover. Once people could no longer depend upon secure family attachments, they would be ripe for control from centralized authorities.

Today we see this attitude represented by the radical feminists. Although they say their goal is to allow women to live up to their potential, their means of doing so is by destroying the commitments between husbands and wives and parents and their children.

The consequences of this cultural upheaval can be seen in the proliferation of divorce, cohabitation, and unwed parenthood. Yet despite propaganda to the contrary, anyone who believes this development has increased the store of personal happiness is badly mistaken.

Cultural Marxism has been a disaster. Dr. Breshears reminder of its roots is therefore a necessary corrective. Unless we understand how our values have been perverted, we are unlikely to defend them. If so, our path to ruin will be paved with the broken bottles of neo-socialist snake oil.

False Consciousness—American Style
Karl Marx sought a revolution. He wanted workers, whom he called proletarians, to rise up and overthrow their capitalistic bosses. Instead of passively allowing themselves to be exploited, they needed to take control of the government and institute a dictatorship of the proletariat in which fairness would prevail.

The trouble was that the workers were not aware of their plight. Rather than recognizing how badly they were being exploited, they tended to identify with their employers. Many actually accepted pay to serve in militaries and police forces dedicated to defending the very people who were misusing them.

This had to stop. The workers had to become conscious of their own interests. They needed to realize that they constituted a social class to which they owed allegiance. Accordingly, someone was required to help them pierce their false consciousness. Someone, such as Marx, with an objective perspective, had to educate the masses.

Fast-forward to today and liberals continue to regard themselves as a social vanguard dedicated to waking the working classes from their political slumber. In their view, workers must understand that the "one percenters" are not their friends and hence that wealth must be transferred from the top to the bottom of society.

Contemporary liberals are not as militant as Marx, but they too intend to remake society. Obama called this "hope and change," and its cat's paw is ObamaCare.

The difficulty with this strategy is that today's exploitation is primarily lodged in the public, rather than the private, domain. It is now the government that is controlling workers and limiting their options. It is a bloated governmental bureaucracy that is standing in the way of prosperity and freedom.

Who now sets society's rules? Washington. Who collects the confiscatory taxes? Washington. And who calls the tune in Washington? The liberals. Consequently if there is today a false consciousness, it is a lack of awareness of who is exploiting whom.

Once capitalists sought to convince their employees that they were on their side. Among other things, these bosses used religion to pacify the proletarians and convince them they would get their just deserts after they died and went to heaven.

Nowadays, it is the liberals who are trying to convince voters they are on their side. Just you wait, they tell them, and ObamaCare will provide everyone with quality medical care at lower costs. Just be patient and raising the minimum wage will pull everyone out of poverty.

But don't look behind the curtain to see how much money we are wasting. And don't notice that we are funneling your tax dollars into the pockets of our political cronies. And for goodness sake, don't realize that the rules we are instituting to protect you from yourselves are actually intended to enhance our power.

The radical feminists, who were gender Marxists, sought to arouse women to overthrow their male oppressors by making women aware of how badly they were abused. One vehicle for doing so was "consciousness raising" sessions in which the sins of men were enumerated in gory detail.

Political liberals, however, favor use of the media and educational systems. These routinely publicize the alleged transgressions of business leaders, while whitewashing the deceits and power grabs of Democratic politicians.

The object is to divert attention away from the real oppressors. We are thus to believe liberals when they tell us they care about our welfare. We are instead to aim our indignation at the Koch brothers for funding conservative causes. Who is actually helped and hurt does not matter.

And so the poor continue to be hurt. They are driven into a hopeless dependency from which they may never emerge. And the middle classes are hurt. They are tied down with bureaucratic shackles that limit their entrepreneurial aspirations.

As for the rich: they are doing just fine—especially if they donate to liberal causes and are allowed to feed at the federal trough.

Marx and Identity Politics

Karl Marx wanted workers to identify as workers. He believed than only when they began looking after their own interests would they be able to throw off the yoke of capitalist oppression.

Today, liberals purvey a similar attitude with respect to women and minorities. Women are thus told they must identify themselves, first and foremost, as women, while African-Americans are asked to consider themselves primarily as African-American. Being American—or human—come in a distant second.

Marx advocated this tactic because he didn't want workers to side with their bosses. Liberals likewise do not want women or blacks to support their reputed oppressors. In the case of women, these are men; whereas for blacks, it is whites in general.

In both instances, the goal is to prepare the way for a rebellion. For Marxists, this was intended to destroy capitalism; for liberals, it is to totally remake America along neo-socialist lines.

And so women and African-Americans are encouraged to think of themselves as oppressed workers. If they do, they will surely align with the proletarian cause and help defeat their common tormentors.

This makes false consciousness, that is, identifying with men or whites, a serious transgression. Men, particularly Republican men, they are repeatedly told, are waging a war on women, while whites, particularly conservative whites, are obviously trying to reinstate slavery.

These arguments would be risible—except that many young women and most blacks seem to buy them. They do not appear to understand that identifying with liberal causes today constitutes the true false consciousness.

Consider the situation of women. If men are the enemy, does marriage make sense? And if marriage does not make sense, does having children make sense? "Sleeping with the Enemy" made a wonderful movie title, but it is a terrible way to create a family.

Married women know this. They are therefore more likely to vote conservative. A majority of single women do not. They fail to realize that they are being encouraged to become old maids and/or unwed mothers. As a result, they are prepared to sell out their own interests for the sake of free birth control.

No! Women and men are not enemies! To the contrary, they ought to be allies. Yes, some men are abusive, but this is not the norm. If it were, we would all be doomed.

Consequently, young women must learn that this business of men earning more for the same work is a liberal canard. They instead need to discover that success and intimacy are not necessarily inconsistent. They must likewise realize that when men win, they also win. This is not false consciousness, but reality.

With respect to African-Americans, don't they remember that Abraham Lincoln freed the slaves, that Republican votes helped pass the civil rights laws, and that Richard Nixon started affirmative action? Since when have conservatives been pro-slavery—except in liberal propaganda?

Conservatives insist that blacks learn to help themselves, but how is this anti-black? Has helpless dependency somehow morphed into the contemporary version of freedom? Successful parents demand that their children perform so that they too can be successful. Shouldn't we, as a society, make similar demands of blacks so that they can be successful?

So what has the liberal parody of false consciousness delivered in the way of benefits? Not much! The sad fact is that women are discovering a bad economy is bad for everyone—not just men. After all, women too are losing jobs, and women too are suffering under ObamaCare.

As for African-Americans, they may cheer at rhetoric that castigates conservatives as their nemesis, but they are doing even less well on the job market. A black president is a wonderful symbol, yet symbolism alone does not put food on the table.

No, women and blacks are Americans and should be proud of it. They must also realize that because we are all in the same boat, hurting the whole hurts them too.

The Social Justice Scam

The self-congratulatory strain in contemporary liberalism is boundless. Many of its adherents actually believe themselves exempt from criticism because their moral rectitude is beyond question. This is so because they think of themselves as "social justice" warriors.

Nonetheless, there is a problem with this outlook. In part, this is because these folks are not as pure as they imagine and, in part, because of the flaws inherent in social justice. The objective they are promoting is not nearly as honorable as they imagine.

Social justice, you see, is often at odds with individual justice. In attempting to do right by groups, individuals are regularly injured. Rather than personal merits being acknowledged and advanced, these are submerged in a sea of impersonal posturing.

The Declaration of Independence told us that all men (and women) are created equal; that they are endowed with an array of inalienable rights. It did not say that groups are created equal or that they have immutable rights. In other words, the nation's founders were concerned with personal liberty, not group entitlements.

Yet liberals think in terms of groups. They are obsessed with the injustices done to collections of individuals. Central to their concerns are the biases visited on blacks, women, and gays. It is these evils they wish to undo.

Who can doubt the historic wrongs done to slaves or their descendants? Who can question whether women or gays have often been treated unfairly. But are group remedies the way to correct group wounds? Might it not be better to switch to an individualist mindset.

Once many Jews were denied entrance to Harvard because they were Jews. The college set a quota based on religious affiliation. Now, despite affirmations to the contrary, it has a quota for accepting African-Americans. They are not excluded, but rather recruited, because of their race.

Is this fair? In setting race over merit, doesn't it diminish the value of personal accomplishment? Praising the virtues of diversity does not refute this truth. Nor does it undo the damage done by rewarding a biological condition instead of ability or effort.

If our society is to thrive, if its members are to perform at their best, what people do, as opposed to the status of groups to which they belong, must claim priority. If not, then inherited standing takes precedence over personal deeds.

This, however, would be as socially sclerotic as favoring elites just because they have always been favored.

My mother used to tell me that two wrongs do not make a right. Creating new injustices does not rectify past injustices. If we are ever to be color blind, we must treat minorities by the same standards as everyone else. The same goes for women and gays.

Genuine fairness does not ask people about their group connections. It assesses them according to who they are and what they have done. Their personal opportunities are neither restricted, nor elevated, by a relationship outside their control. They, not their parents or grandparents, must be the measure of their virtue.

Imagine, if you will, that I graded my students at Kennesaw State University on the basis of group inclusion. Suppose that before I assigned a score, I put their tests onto separate piles based on race and gender. Suppose further that I employed different criteria for each stack. Would this be justice?

Why then is it justice when we expand this procedure to society at large? Using the phase "social justice" as a mantra should not obscure the immorality of treating people differently because of accidents of birth. Yes, blacks, women, and gays deserve a fair shot at success. But this ought not imply socially enforced equalities.

If people differ—as they always do—shouldn't these differences be recognized and evaluated for what they are? While people must be afforded an opportunity to improve themselves, these advances ought to be acknowledged. If not, this contradicts the notion of opportunity.

"Social justice" is a scam intended to elicit votes based on group membership. It is not a moral "get out of jail" card. Liberals who believe this makes them exceedingly ethical are fooling themselves. To the contrary, it feeds a phony self-righteousness that ought not be honored.

Major Surgery

Barack Obama is fond of telling us he intends to take a scalpel to fixing social problems. Not for him an indiscriminate meat cleaver that will cut away the healthy flesh along with the diseased tissue. Unlike his critics, he can tell the difference and therefore, like a good doctor, refuses to do harm.

Then again Barack Obama has never met a bureaucracy he didn't like. Whatever the difficulty, he plans either to throw money at an existing government agency or to create a new one expressly to supplement the old one.

No wonder our president has dithered in his approach to resolving the Veteran's Administration dilemma. He does not understand that some bureaucracies can only be repaired by grabbing an axe and cutting them down to the roots.

Bureaucracies gone wrong are analogous to cancers. They grow uncontrollably and metastasize wildly. Rogue organizations always employ more people than they need—especially administrators. And they always spew out toxic regulations that destroy whatever they touch.

This is why sclerotic bureaucracies must be drastically slashed. Whether they are governmental, educational, medical, or commercial, tiptoeing around their edges only allows their occupants to devise defensive strategies. They become experts in obscuring their malfeasance from outsiders who do not know better.

Among commercial organizations, market discipline takes care of the more egregious bad actors. Because they must compete with other enterprises, they need to be efficient or go out of business. The result is that during economic downturns, executives fearful of becoming unemployed downsize.

Government workers have no such fears. Often in cahoots with the politicians who hire them, they know their financial contributions and votes will keep their "friends" in line. All they need to do is rattle their checkbooks and plans to curb abuses are set aside.

This is why public bureaucracies must be reformed from the outside. Those who lead and sponsor them are usually motivated to maintain the status quo. Since both benefit from organizational gigantism, whatever they tell aggrieved outsiders, they persist in feeding the beast.

Nor can genuine correctives be modest. Small wounds are readily papered over. Organizational functionaries isolate them so that they do not weaken the basic structure, or culture, of the enterprise.

Bureaucracies, it must be understood, are networks of interlocking offices and lengthy ladders of authority that are linked together by a communal culture. Upset one element and the others are upset. As a result, those not yet touched by a change rush into the breach because they know their own positions will be in jeopardy if they do not.

We have seen this at the VA. It is also true of the IRS, the Pentagon, the EPA, the Department of Justice, the State Department, the CIA, Social Security, Head Start, the Department of Education, and, of course, the Department of Health and Human Services. Rest assured, it will also be true of ObamaCare.

Many commentators have observed that the VA's problems are not new. They also realize that stopgap fixes have not worked. They therefore recommend that the agency be replaced by another program—such as vouchers.

This is a good first step. But it is only a first step. The federal government has become absurdly bloated. Just as Ronald Reagan advised, but was unable to accomplish, it must be reduced in size. –Not eliminated, but reorganized and streamlined.

Standing in the way, however, is the Bureaucratic (aka Democratic) Party. Despite protests to the contrary, the liberal ideal is socialism. The objective is for the government to own—or control—virtually all of the economy. This is regarded as essential for social justice.

Yet real justice is grounded in freedom and freedom cannot flourish when trampled on by government bureaucracies. So let's get out the meat cleavers because government officials will not take the appropriate action on their own unless forced to do so.

Bloated Government Is The Enemy

Years ago, Ronald Reagan warned us that over-sized government was a serious problem. The evidence that he was correct keeps pouring in. The VA scandal is just the latest example of how organizational gigantism can injure people.

Liberal Democrats, with Barack Obama in the lead, keep telling us they must protect us from ourselves. They assure us that their programs are intended to promote social justice and rational planning. Be this in energy or health, they argue that they know best.

Then something like the Veteran's Administration cover-up of incompetent scheduling comes to light and we learn—as we should have known all along—that bloated bureaucracies have a way of getting things wrong. Especially when part of the government, and therefore not subject to marketplace discipline, they often go rogue.

At moments such as this, the president's apologists explain that the executive structure is simply too large for anyone to administer effectively. The president is, after all, just one man and he can't be everywhere. Nor can he know everything; hence he must depend upon his subordinates.

But who are his subordinates? Jack Kennedy depended upon advisors that were regarded as "the best and the brightest." FDR, of course, had his "brain trust." And what does Obama have? A kiddy-corps! And a crony corps!

Let us start with Harry Reid and Nancy Pelosi. They are not part of his administration, but they have been delegated essential tasks such as writing the stimulus legislation and designing ObamaCare. Thus, in many ways they are as responsible as anyone for the recent additions to the Washington mess.

Question: Does anyone trust Harry or Nancy? Does anyone regard them as mental giants? Who believes that they are incorruptible public servants that deserve to be in charge of setting our communal agenda?

Remember Nancy told us that we had to pass the ObamaCare legislation in order to find out what was in it. This was not only an example of abdicating legislative responsibility, but of engaging in a crapshoot with the health of the nation. Some leadership here!

As for Harry, when he is not accusing the Koch brothers of global warming or asserting that Mitt Romney did not pay his taxes, he is seeking a constitutional amendment to overturn the Bill of Rights or staging an attack on senate procedure via the nuclear option. More brilliant leadership!

What about the executive branch itself? Does anyone believe that Jay Carney is an honest and penetrating analyst of administrative policy? Or is he more like Art Carney; that is, a sideman in a comedy routine? Reporters are tolerant of his badinage, but does he really deserve to be the voice of the United States?

And what about those other voices, such as the spokespersons for the State Department? Jen Psaki obviously has the experience and gravitas to represent our country to the rest of the world.

And how about Obama's advisors? Tommy Veitor was a wonderful example of their maturity with his, "Dude, that was two tears ago," explanation of the Benghazi cover-up. He gave us confidence the nation is in good hands.

As for the political advise Obama gets, which frequently seems decisive, David Plouffe and Daniel Pieffer constantly impress with their deep thinking. They may have the president's interests at heart, yet do they have the nation's?

This list could be extended indefinitely, but it gives an idea of what can happen when the management of an already bloated government is delegated to a band of incompetents. When a gang of venal ideologues, supplemented by juvenile ciphers, takes charge, we get the mess we are currently enduring.

This puts the lie to the entire Liberal agenda, which asserts that centralizing decisions in Washington promotes rationality. The truth is the opposite. The larger the government gets, the more un-manageable it becomes—a problem that is exacerbated when those who naively think they know best take the helm.

The Bureaucratic Mentality

When I went to high school during the 1950's, my very liberal teachers encouraged students to go into government service. They were aware of the failures of Franklin Roosevelt's New Deal and blamed this on the absence of talented administrators. If these managers had been smarter and more creative, workable solutions would have been found.

I took these admonitions to heart. As a good student, it was my duty to make socialism succeed. This, of course, had to begin by making the government more responsive. Unless this occurred, it might be unwise to place the entire economy in state hands.

For the next several decades I sought, and obtained, government employment. I was not going to be one of those greedy capitalists who put self-interest before communal interests. Only after many years of trying did I realize that a deeply ingrained bureaucratic mentality prevented accomplishing my dream.

To illustrate, when I went to work for a state vocational agency, the first thing a new colleague told me was CYA. At the time, I was so naïve I did not know what this meant. For the uninitiated, it stands for "cover you're a—." That is, don't make waves and you won't get in trouble.

In other words, a great many government bureaucrats intend to follow the rules—and only the rules. They are not looking to be creative. They are not geared to taking risks. As a bus driver uncle advised me, if you keep your head down, the pay is good and the security can't be beat.

The degree to which this attitude discourages originality also became plain at the vocational bureau. Having obtained a Ph.D. in sociology, I sought to apply it to helping my clients. Over the course of several years, I therefore developed a program I described as "Resocialization."

So far as I could tell, it worked well. Then the boss of my boss came to ask what I was doing. To my surprise, after I explained my innovations, I was ordered to stop. There was no follow up to determine if I was aiding people. I was simply told to desist.

Naturally I asked why and was startled by the response. The answer was that this superior did not understand what I was doing and therefore I must not continue. There was no assertion that I was hurting clients; only that he could not comprehend my methods.

Sadly my Ph.D. was not respected. If anything, it made my colleagues wary. The fear was that I would use it against them. As a result, no one asked how my expertise might assist them. Their goal was to get along by going along.

Earlier in my bureaucratic adventures I discovered how detailed paperwork prevented disruptive novelties. This time I was working for the New York City Department of Welfare. More particularly, national social workers had recently succeeded in getting the federal government to sponsor social interventions for our clients.

The benefits of this change were to be twofold. First the department would be allocated more money and second the caseworkers would be professionalized. As a consequence, clients would we better served, while those assisting them received greater respect.

The surprise was in how these modifications were implemented. All that happened was that caseworkers were required to fill out forms that documented the services they provided. What they did, did not change. Only the way they reported it.

For example, caseworkers had always been required to check that clients paid their rent. This was intended to make sure they did not squander their resources. Now caseworkers were to describe this activity as providing clients with financial advice.

Today I am a professor at Kennesaw State University, but I am still required to pretend to do what I don't. Thus, the state of Georgia recently decided it wants to encourage faculty members to be more involved with the community. So how are we implementing this? I bet you can guess.

We are filling out a form that documents community in-volvement. We are not changing what we are doing. We are merely changing how we report it. No doubt this will look good in legislative hands.

Some things never change. The bureaucratic mentality is always about professing to do more, while doing less.

The Paperwork Blues
I hate paperwork! Even when I was employed as a clinician, I resented the amount of time I was required to devote to recording what I had done. Instead of counseling, I was compelled to fill case folders no one read. This seemed to me a waste of time.

I was therefore both surprised—and pleased—by the reactions of my colleagues at Kennesaw State University to the arctic blast of paperwork we are currently enduring. The growing volume of documentation we are expected to produce also appalled most of those with whom I have recently spoken.

This is the season of our annual reviews. As is true in most organizations, we professors are asked to report on what we have accomplished this past year and to project ahead what we hope to achieve the next. This in no way adds to our productivity, but allows administrators to keep track of what is being done.

The problem is that our reports keep expanding. Just as in bad science fiction, they continue to grow in scope—almost reaching to the heavens. This year has been made even more onerous by the introduction of a new reporting system—Digital Measures. Computer based, it was advertised as making our task easier.

But when has a new computer tracking system ever made life easier? This one not only invites us to elaborate on the details of our accomplishments, but it does so in an open-ended manner. The upshot is likely to be an arms race in which each participant tries to make sure that no one has documented more triumphs than he or she.

We have already visited this storyline with respect to the portfolios we professors must submit in applying for tenure and promotion. When I first arrived at KSU, these were limited to two volumes. Now they are unrestricted. As a consequence, an administrator recently recounted an applicant who tendered ten huge binders.

My eyes rolled when told this story. Whose wouldn't? Can anyone read and digest this much information, especially when there are many dozens of similar offerings to scrutinize? What initially looked like a reasonable a way to ensure that no one's successes are overlooked, guaranteed that most would never be read.

Then there is the problem that in attempting to improve reporting instruments, they are constantly revised. As a result, people spend more time learning a new system than using it. Instead of teaching or researching, they are at their computers attempting to figure out what goes where.

Over thirty years ago, when I got my first computers, I also purchased the fanciest programs I could afford. One of the latter was for desktop publishing. It enabled me to do brochures and pamphlets on my own. This ability was nearly magical—and I loved it.

That is, I loved it until I wanted to use the program a second time. In the interim, I had forgotten how to access its bells and whistles. And so, I had to relearn them. In other words, their complexities, forced me to spend more time on programming than on writing.

It is the same with these new reporting systems. Because we professors do not use them regularly, we forget what is in which pull-down menu. We must then seek out computer specialists to save us from ourselves, for without these helpers we would remain frozen in our ignorance.

All this, incidentally, is another instance of how bureaucracy is strangling our nation. Increased levels of administrators demand so much paperwork that this becomes our primary product. Forget about teaching, learning, researching, or creating. What matters more is the appearance of each.

Were we faculty members trusted, this charade would be unnecessary. As professionals, we would do our jobs because we were committed to them. Instead, we get a paperwork charade. From top to bottom, people pretend to work, rather than actually do so.

Call It the "Bureaucratic" Party

When Thomas Jefferson inaugurated the State Department, it employed under a dozen souls. Today Foggy Bottom employs thousands upon thousands. Like government in general, it has become bloated beyond the imagination of those who founded our nation.

Everywhere we look, bureaucracies are taking over, but no more so than in the federal government. Today its rolls number in the millions, with little hope in sight of bringing them under control—never mind reducing them.

Amazingly, bureaucracy of the sort we know is a relatively recent invention. The Roman Empire possessed a small slave bureaucracy, while the Roman Catholic Church maintained a loose knit one. It wasn't until modern armies began to grow that this mode of organization took off.

But what really made bureaucracy commonplace was the advent of big business. With the rise of industrial conglomerates, it became impossible for owner-mangers to control these entities on their own. They required something more predictable, and more reliable, than their personal efforts.

As Max Weber tells us, this is the forte of bureaucracy. It permits a few people at the top to control a great many at the bottom by creating a defined hierarchy of authority that oversees the implementation of numerous rules and procedures. It also utilizes a myriad of files and records to impose its will.

Weber believed that bureaucracy was the only practical way to bring rationality to bear on large organizations, but he also feared that it locked those at their base in an "iron cage." So effective was it in controlling their behavior that they lost much of their freedom.

Many people, especially liberals, agree that larger and larger bureaucracies are the wave of the future. So efficient do they consider these, that they wish to concentrate more and more power in the hands of fewer and fewer "experts." Confident that they are the "best and the brightest," they aim to grow the federal bureaucracy so large that it can impose their vision of justice on everyone.

I propose, therefore, that the Democratic Party be relabeled the Bureaucratic Party. It has already been accused of being the party of "big government," but this is too clunky a designation. So-called "low information" voters, in particular, require an evocative term to drive home the essence of liberalism and progressivism.

One of Parkinson's Laws informs us that bureaucracies have a tendency to grow. However big they are, those who control them wish to see them get larger. This is because the people who run bureaucracies love power. They are empire builders who perceive their success as lying in the management of more and more people.

Liberals are fond of portraying businesspersons as power hungry and therefore dangerous, but they ought look in the mirror if they wish to view genuinely ravenous wolves. These bureaucracy-lovers have never met a government program they did not like or a government regulation they did not believe necessary to solve problems of their own invention.

Hence it is by these means that the Bureaucratic Party keeps encroaching on the freedoms of Americans. Small business owners have known this for a long time. Ordinary citizens are learning it via ObamaCare. As newly federalized health bureaucracies continue to impose rules on them, they are beginning to feel the pain.

As per usual, adherents of the Bureaucratic party tell us this is for our own good. They assure us that they must protect us from our personal limitations. Nevertheless, the real reason they keep piling rules and procedures on rules and procedures is because they want to be in charge of everything.

Almost no one—except those who run them—likes bureaucracies. It is time for those who value their freedom to take advantage of this antipathy. Call the Democrats what they are, namely bureaucracy-lovers. Paint them in the colors (e.g., red tape) they have so richly earned, and they may be less attractive to potential voters.

The Shadow Government

President Trump's advisor Steve Bannon has been accused of every political sin in the book. He is supposedly an anti-democratic monster who must be stopped before he—like Godzilla—stomps all over our freedoms and way of life. As a staunch critic of the press, he is obviously a vicious brute.

It was therefore with some pleasure that I listened to him when he appeared before the recent CPAC conference. Given that he usually operates behind the scenes, it was nice to hear his voice and governing philosophy.

What impressed me most is how deftly he delineated what is starting to be called Trumpism. Most listeners focused on the economic nationalism he espoused. I, however, was captivated by his discussion of administrative bloat. As a longtime critic of bureaucratic over-reach, it was nice to hear that someone in power is aware of this threat.

We have, in our society, at least two governments. There is the official one and the shadow one. The first we elect; the second gets hired and then pulls the strings out of sight. This second, which consists of career civil servants, always thinks it knows best and is increasingly determined to veto initiatives of which it does not approve.

To make matters worse, operatives in the shadow government can remain in place for decades. They do not get dismissed when a new party is voted into office. To the contrary, it is almost impossible to fire them—even when they commit grave malfeasances in office. They just hunker down and await the next opportunity to assert themselves.

We see this phenomenon at the Internal Revenue Service, the State Department, and the Department of Justice. It is also on display at the Environmental Protection Agency, the Federal Election Commission and the Veteran's Administration.

Americans wonder why things change so slowing in Washington. This is one of the primary reasons. Unelected functionaries, most of whom have a liberal bent, see to it that some policies are never implemented and that meddling politicians are chastised. To do so, they leak information, slow walk programs, or apply laws selectively.

The question is what can be done about this? One thing is certain; bureaucrats will not reform no matter how eloquently their faults are explained. Too many are power-hungry ideologues who will not listen. Others are simply creatures of habit who do not want their perquisites disturbed.

The answer is that we must be draconian. Small fixes around the edges only alert these folks to put up their defenses. Like the husband who does not want to do what his wife asks, they say yes and then they do as they please.

So what must be done? First, agency budgets have to be slashed. Superfluous personnel must be let go. If they will not leave, they should be shunted into positions where they can do the least harm. Some might be sent to North Dakota in the dead of winter.

This, I think, is what Bannon has in mind. If so, it is understandable why he is hated. If he means that the federal government must be reduced in size, those who feed at its trough are bound to be terrified. Since the only way they can be stopped is to eliminate them, they realize their careers are in jeopardy.

And so they will tell us that without them the government would grind to a halt. We will hear horror stories about how aunt Minnie in Missouri died of starvation because her social security check did not arrive on time. But don't you believe it. Uncle Charlie in Arizona has already died waiting for the VA to set up an appointment.

As Parkinson's Law tells us, work expands to fill the time available to it. Give the bureaucrats less time by hiring fewer of them and there will be less gossip around the water cooler. There will also be less time to get into mischief—and that is what really counts.

Chapter VI

The Assault On Our Social Integrity

Moral Collapse

Because massive bureaucratic control proved to be a nightmare, liberals were compelled to assail our collective moral compass. They could not allow traditional values to hold sway as long as these conflicted with their intensions. The result has been widespread corruption. There has been a wholesale assault on our social integrity such that we are in danger of tearing our social fabric apart. Lies have become commonplace, as have rationalizations for irresponsibility and unfairness. As a consequence, it is more difficult for people to trust one another. We have been divided into competing factions that are determined to defeat each other at any cost. Even if they suffer as a result of their depravity, they forge blindly ahead.

Liberal corruption has been a long time in coming. The failures of excessive government power were not immediately apparent. Nonetheless, once the exaggerated promises of leftists hit a roadblock, a tainted version of morality was rolled out to protect their authors. The very tools we use to guard against interpersonal conflict were perverted. Morality, it appears, can be employed to promote immorality. This is possible because we humans are gullible. When our convictions are appropriately revised, we can be led to endorse the opposite of what we have hitherto believed. The result of this ploy has been to turn morality on its head. Liberals have been able to depict lies as truths and truths as lies. Instead of recognizing which way the needle points toward the moral south, we head north into an ethical blizzard.

Even so, morality is what it is. It is not what people say, but what they do that matters most. When we use this truth as our guide, it is clear that Barack Obama was one of the most mendacious of American presidents. Although he regularly bragged about leading an extremely transparent administration, it has become obvious that he and his minions specialized in immense cover-ups. No doubt, he and his followers believed they were telling noble lies. Convinced that they knew best what was good for the nation, they sought to mislead voters in order to help them. Like all politicians, they were compelled to repackage hard truths to make them palatable. Thus, if people wanted to be told that they could keep their doctors and health plans—when they could not—they would later be grateful after they discovered the immense benefits of ObamaCare.

Liberals truly believe they are the designated custodians of social justice. Their idea of justice, however, is taking from the rich in order to give to the poor. They do not have faith in the same rules for all. On these grounds, they have no compunctions about surrounding their collectivist ideals with a bodyguard of lies. Unpleasant realities must be disguised lest Americans reconsider their allegiances. To this end, a perverted pubic relations industry was invented. Talking points, not truths, were manufactured so as to capture the imagination of the naïve. Dishonesty became institutionalized. A host of progressives soon earned a living this way. Like the former Senate majority leader Harry Reid, they did not worry about what was factual as long as it was to their advantage. As he told reporters when confronted with a gross fabrication, "Well, it worked, didn't it."

But this orientation bred other disturbing trends. Irresponsibility and unfairness also became institutionalized. If the federal government was to protect everyone, voters had to be discouraged from helping themselves. Likewise, if identity politics was to succeed, different groups could not be handled the same. In the end, the concept of honor lost its currency. A relative handful of military types were still prepared to sacrifice their lives for the good of the nation, whereas in the nation's capital it was every man and woman for him or herself. Justice could be damned—as long as it sounded fair. Who cared if treating people unequally let to street riots? What did it matter if Baltimore burned or if in Ferguson Missouri, blacks were pitted against whites? Perhaps, to paraphrase Thomas Jefferson, a little blood might have to be spilled so as to refresh the roots of democracy.

All of this depravity should be obvious. The discomfort that millions of Americans are currently experiencing is attributable, in part, to the violence done our traditional values. And yet, liberals are in deep denial. Earlier I compared them to a flying saucer cult. The aliens they worship have not landed to whisk them away to a utopia in the stars; as a result they are breaking the nation's furniture and attributing this to directions from their celestial mentors. Unfortunately we are the victims. We pay the price in disorder, and frustration, for their inability to come to terms with decades of well-intentioned fiascoes.

Liberal Corruption

The Roots of Corruption

With Monica Lewinsky back in the limelight, Fox News aired a snippet of Bill Clinton's deposition concerning his affair with her. There was Bill once again dogging and weaving, doing the best he could to change the subject. Alas, he was eventually cornered and forced to tell a bald-faced lie.

This was not an inspiring performance. It was painful to watch the president of the United States behaving like a trapped schoolboy. Worse, however, was to follow. A stained dress was to prove that Clinton perjured himself when he assured the American public he "did not have sexual relations with that woman...."

Yet what ensued? Especially after Clinton was impeached, Democrats rushed to his defense. Among other things, they argued that he was only lying about sex. According to them, everyone lies about sex and therefore it was no big deal.

Nevertheless, what they refused to acknowledge is that not everyone is obliged to lie about sex. Most are faithful to their spouses and therefore do not need to sweat when subjected to legal grilling. To imply that coving up an indiscretion is perfectly all right is thus to endorse it.

One of the things I learned in social psychology over a half century ago is that when people make a public assertion, their commitment subsequently increases. Thus, if they publicly approve of a sexual transgression, they are apt to double-down on their approval later on. Likewise if they openly excuse a lie, they are apt to continue excusing it.

Sadly, the need to "move on" from Clinton's misconduct opened the floodgates. Ever since, we have been sliding down a slippery slope toward accepting more and more political corruption. Lies have become standard operating procedure and character assassination an honored mode of political discourse.

During Clinton's impeachment converting Lewinsky into a media piñata became a national obsession. She was portrayed as a squalid floozy who seduced this otherwise admirable man into committing an understandable peccadillo. Never mind that he had a history of sexual offenses and needed to be protected from "bimbo eruptions."

Or consider the unhappy case of Kenneth Starr. Before he investigated Clinton, he was a respected attorney. Yet while doing so, he was transformed into a religious fanatic who scandalously abused his power by asking questions of witnesses such as Lewinski's mother.

Bill, and his wife Hillary, had a field day vilifying anyone who delved into his reckless behavior. Still, for this, journalists lionized them. They were evidently skillful politicians because they won the battle for public opinion. That they did so viciously and dishonestly did not matter.

In this manner are political cultures born. Thus do corruption and mendacity become accepted ways of transacting business. One of the subsequent manifestations of this development was the barbecuing George W. Bush received for allegedly lying about WMD's in Iraq. In fact, it was his Democratic accusers who lied.

Bush was mistaken about the WMD's; nevertheless he told the truth, as he understood it. Assured by the intelligence agencies that these weapons were there, he too was a surprised when they were not found. Hence, calling him a liar was not based on facts, but a need to balance the books. For Democrats, moral equality could only be reestablished if a Republican president was dragged down to the level of his predecessor.

Nowadays this same pattern of deception and vilification persists. Indeed, Barack Obama has transformed it into the normal way of operating. Like Clinton, yet more so, he regularly charges his political opponents with being dastardly scoundrels. Thus Romney was depicted as depriving a dying woman of medical care and aching to start a cold war with Russia.

So here comes the next act. With a special committee having been appointed to investigate Benghazi, we can be sure its Republican members will be portrayed as vengeful partisans. As for the evidence they uncover, it will be dismissed as dishonest and/or irrelevant.

The Immorality of Morality

Ray Rice shouldn't have done it! Even I was taught that a gentleman never hits a lady. To this day, I remember the thrashing I got from my father after I struck my sister in the back with a roundhouse punch.

It did not matter to Dad that she had provoked me by digging her nails into my arm so hard that she drew blood. He hadn't even asked if she had done anything wrong. The rule against hitting a girl was absolute.

This same sort of attitude arose in the Rice affair. When pictures emerged of him knocking out his then girlfriend, a hue and cry went up. He was a fiend who had to be punished.

That his girlfriend might have goaded him by taking the first swing was scarcely mentioned. That the two could have been intoxicated at the time drew no notice. These were not considered mitigating circumstances. What mattered was that a much stronger man had knocked a woman out.

This event, which undoubtedly mirrors numerous others, was deemed national news because of who was involved and because it had been captured on videotape. Both male and female commentators were incensed that the perpetrator got of so lightly. A two game suspension, without jail time, was obviously not enough.

The conventional wisdom alleged that Rice received favorable treatment because he is a celebrity. Clearly the district attorney and the NFL commissioner gave him a better deal than Joe Blow would have received.

But is this true? In fact, it is not! It does not even come close to the truth. A non-celebrity, who did not have a criminal record (as Rice did not), would have received a slap on the wrist. Rice, in contrast, lost his job and forfeited millions of dollars.

But even this was not sufficient. The critics demanded that he be banned for life and that the commissioner who let him off be fired. This was a sin of such a magnitude that only the equivalent of a blood sacrifice would do.

Yet consider the implications. Do we really want to insist that everyone who commits any sort of crime must lose his job? In addition to jail time and/or a fine, are malefactors routinely to be deprived of their livelihoods. In an era, when we have been reducing the penalties for murder, this seems excessive.

Plainly, when people are in high dudgeon, morality becomes a lethal weapon. What amount to lynch mobs engage in behavior that they might otherwise consider immoral.

Examples of morality gone haywire are legion. Lest we forget, Adolf Hitler massacred millions in the name of morality. As he saw it, he was protecting the rights of the German people from human vermin. The Jews and Slavs deserved to die because they were taking bread out of the mouths of the master race.

ISIS too perceives itself as defending moral principles. The organization has a right—if not a duty—to severe the heads of infidels. Only in this way can the end of times arrive and the faithful receive their just rewards.

About forty years ago, sociological research revealed that domestic violence was initiated about 50/50 by men and women. The men, however, finished the job because they had greater upper body strength.

Then, because a crackdown on intimate violence led to more men being arrested, the ratio changed. Now women were twice as likely to be the initial aggressor. Regarded as helpless innocents, they were given a free pass.

How does this help strengthen marriages? If one side is always right and the other wrong, how does a couple arrive at an amicable settlement when they disagree. Yes, men should not hit women, but neither should society deal with them as if they were monsters.

We must be moral, but we must also be wary of excessive moralism. When it seeks vengeance rather than equity, it too can be a danger.

The Gullibility Factor

I almost laughed out loud! Here was the president of the United States postulating a way to bring down the budget deficit that had been ridiculed several months before. When Harry Reid had proposed it during the battle over increasing the nation's debt limit, it gained no traction whatever and even prompted Representative Paul Ryan to mock it on the floor of the House.

So what was this howler? What was this plan to save money that was so obviously not a plan to save money? It was asserting that the cost of a new stimulus could be off-set by not spending a trillion dollars on the wars in Iraq and Afghanistan that no one had proposed spending.

Ryan said that this was like first passing a bill to cover the moon in green cheese and the next day rescinding it amidst of flourish of trumpets heralding Congress's frugality. This was nothing other than a transparent verbal gimmick. It did not even pass the smell test.

Hence my question is: Why are so many people accepting Obama's scheme at face value? Why aren't many more millions of Americans doubled over in laughter at the temerity of such nonsense?

It isn't as if no one has noticed that our president is a habitual purveyor of falsehoods. Nor is it that he has never been called out for inciting class warfare.

It cannot even be said that the late night TV comedians haven't been finding humor in his pious incantations about being non-political. They certainly have.

It is also true that the president's ratings in the polls have been slipping. Nevertheless, they have not plummeted. Many people are still more prepared to blame the Republicans for Washington's gridlock than they are him. So once again I ask: Why is this so?

One reason is simple human gullibility. Lincoln told us that you cannot fool all of the people all of the time, but you can apparently fool a great many of them almost indefinitely. They are so determined to believe that they put their rational faculties on hold and cruise along oblivious to the most ridiculous twaddle.

So who are these gullible people, and what is the source of their gullibility? One group is the rabid partisans. These are the left-wing Democrats who are upset that Obama has not squandered more trillions of dollars on failed policies. They will continue to blame conservatives for our troubles no matter what Barack does. Although no longer enthralled with him, they hate their traditional enemies even more.

Another group consists of the politically detached. They don't read newspapers, watch cable television, or check the Internet for current events. For them, what happens in Washington does not exist. They, therefore, continue to support the president because they have no idea that many of his policies might injure them.

Then there are the authority sycophants. They are prepared to defer to people in charge regardless of what they do. These folks do not question what the most powerful man in the world says because they always accede to power—especially if it is articulated in an authoritative manner. And Obama, of course, is good as sounding confident.

Next there are the people who believe in giving the next guy a chance. These tend to be good people who do not want to jump to conclusions too quickly. They are inclined to allow others a great deal of latitude before they conclude that they have failed. For them, three years of ineptitude is still not enough.

Finally, there are those who always believe. They are therefore liable to credit the last voice that they hear. Because they do not analyze what was said so much as take it at face value, they are frequently swayed by a rousing speech.

Obama, as we know can give a wonderful speech—and gives lots of them. Consequently, for these folks he is often the last persuasive voice they hear.

If we put these all of factors together, although the president is down, he is not out. Indeed, he is counting on his ability to convince the gullible to join his cause. He is apparently hoping that there are enough of them to provide him with the margin for another term in office.

I, for on one, am hoping that he is wrong. I have my fingers crossed that more people will listen to what he says, rather than the way he says it.

Our Faulty Moral Compass

One of the subjects I teach at Kennesaw State University is the sociology of morality. This often includes a small demonstration intended to help my students understand the nature of moral rules. It goes as follows.

Apropos of nothing, using my finger as a weapon, I pretend to shoot someone in the first row. "Bang, bang, you're dead!" Then I immediately switch to an entirely different topic. The students are a little confused, but otherwise unruffled.

But then I again switch gears. "How would you have reacted," I ask, "had I really shot someone?" It is obvious to all that there would have been pandemonium. Besides being terrified, the class would have been outraged by a cold-blooded act of murder.

And that is my point. Had I committed a nakedly immoral act, they would have been incensed. Most would have been furious and demanded that I be punished—if not immediately, then shortly thereafter. Business as usual would have abruptly ceased.

At this juncture, I observe that when a moral rule is broken, we generally get angry. We do not simply carry on as if nothing had happened. In fact, if we do not get angry, then we do not really believe that a rule was violated.

Moral rules are important rules. Hence they are resolutely enforced. At the minimum, we use anger to inform the offender that this conduct is unacceptable. We do not remain neutral.

If this is true, then how are we to understand the state of contemporary American politics? On the one hand, we have a candidate who was derelict in her duty to protect national secrets. On the other, we have one who brags about having bribed public officials.

So where is the outrage? Do ordinary Americans truly perceive this sort of behavior to be wrong? Evidently not! They plainly take it in stride. So accustomed are they to moral corruption that they are no longer offended when it is rubbed in their faces.

Surely one of the strangest phenomena of this very strange political season was Dr. Ben Carson endorsing Donald Trump. A man who grounded his campaign in asking the nation to return to its moral roots, suddenly found Trump's vulgarity and dishonesty "business as usual." We were actually told that we shouldn't get upset because this is the way politics is played.

And what about those Democrats who know that Hillary is a confirmed liar? They keep voting for her anyway. Why? Because she has experience—and is a woman. Apparently being female and a practiced dissembler are now sufficient qualifications to be an American president.

What too of those Christian evangelicals who voted for Trump? They knew that he was morally sleazy, but didn't seem to care because they perceived him to be strong. Does this mean that his alleged strength canceled out his lack of personal integrity?

Americans time and again complain about lies. They likewise grumble about the dreadful condition of political affairs. But then they vote for the liars and demagogues. Clearly they do not consider this sort of behavior reprehensible. As a result, we keep getting more of it.

There were good candidates this cycle, yet we brushed them aside as unworthy of support. And so we will get what we deserve. If we have become an amoral society, then we ought not be surprised by the mischief created by the devious leaders we choose.

As I see it, too many Americans have lost their moral compass. To judge by their actions, they can no longer tell right from wrong. Although they protest the current situation, it is what they have wrought.

My conclusion: we need a moral reformation! We need one desperately! Our democracy, prosperity, and national survival all depend on an ethical revival, yet there is none in sight. As long as we attempt to counter the immorality of Barack Obama with that of a Donald Trump or Hillary Clinton, there is little hope.

Moral Is As Moral Does

Liberals like to present themselves as conspicuously moral. The recent election, however, as exposed them as shallow poseurs. For all their talk about compassion and truth, they have demonstrated a penchant for rank dishonesty.

Although liberals regard themselves as upright, they revealed a callous disregard for morality. Moral people behave morally. They do more than congratulate themselves for their superior values. They live by them. If they don't, they don't have them.

One of the things I teach at Kennesaw State University is the sociology of morality. I explain to my classes how morality operates. The goal is not to tell students what is right, but to analyze how moral rules work. This includes how they are enforced.

Moral rules tell us what to do and what not to do. Don't lie! Don't steal! Don't murder! Proscriptions of this sort are at the heart of the enterprise. We learn them when we are young and insist that they be honored when we grow older.

Without this, society would be anarchic. Because human beings have incompatible interests, we compete to see who will prevail. Thomas Hobbes long ago warned that this could precipitate a war of all against all. Thanks to our selfishness, we might be so aggressive that few escaped without serious injury.

The first line of defense of moral rules turns out to be anger. When someone violates a regulation to which we subscribe, we get upset. We let the malefactor know, in no uncertain terms, that this was unacceptable. Often enough, because an angry rebuke is distressing, people conform. Thus, if they told a lie, they cease telling it.

In class, I illustrate this with a demonstration. I pretend to shoot someone and then act as if nothing had happened. After this, I ask the students what would have occurred if there had been an actual murder? Over and above their fear, wouldn't they have been out-raged?

But what if they weren't? What if we all proceeded as if there wasn't a corpse in our midst? Wouldn't this indicate that we didn't consider murder a serious offence? Wouldn't it demonstrate that we did not believe a rule against it had to be upheld?

But isn't this the situation we find ourselves with respect to Hillary's lies? She told us untruth after untruth. She lied about her server. She lied about pay-for-play. She lied about Benghazi. Many of these were big lies. Others were small. Nonetheless, there were no apologies. There was no contrition.

Did Hillary's supporters call her to task for these fabrications? Did they ask her to clean up her act? Were they angry at her for her many deceits? If they were not, did they believe she committed any infractions?

The answer is obvious. Hillary's backers applauded her misrepresentations. Because they wanted her to win, they hoped these would work. Far from getting angry at her, they reserved their wrath for her opponent. He, and only he, was the dissembler.

The point is that Hillary and her crew did not consider their own duplicity immoral. They never worried about crossing an ethical line. So far as they were concerned, they were always moral. Because theirs was a good cause, they had done nothing of which they should be ashamed.

This is consequently a case of justifying immorality with morality. On the other hand, moral is as moral does. Whatever rationalizations allowed Hillary people to excuse their transgressions, they were rationalizations. Corruption is corruption. Lies are lies.

Liberalism, unfortunately, is plagued with self-righteous vices. People convinced that they are saving the world often permit themselves latitude. They do not apply to themselves standards they employ with others. As they see it, the good they do outweighs any shortcuts they may take.

This is why liberals are seldom dismayed when their policies backfire. So what if the poor are getting poorer. Given progressives good intentions, any missteps they might make are canceled out. As a result, they simply move on from one aborted policy to the next.

Harming people in the name of helping them is not, however, a virtue. Even if disguising one's failures is done unconsciously, this predilection is not praiseworthy. It is an anteroom to folly; a gateway to perpetual transgressions.

Yes, Obama is Transparent; Transparently Dishonest

Scarcely a week goes by when the president of the United States does not tell several whoppers. He stands before the television cameras and blithely states a series of blatant untruths. He lies and lies, and then he lies some more. The mystery is why the public is not completely scandalized by this performance.

The latest of his falsehoods, of course, concern the cap-and-trade legislation recently passed by Nancy Pelosi and her Democratic poodles. Obama tells us these will create work when they will actually cost us millions of jobs. He further says that the price of this unnecessary social engineering will be modest, whereas it will be excessive. Then he has the audacity to declare that the debate over global warming is over, when it continues to heat up.

Earlier the president assured the nation that he believed in pay-as-you-go policies at the very moment he was proposing trillions in additional unfunded spending. Likewise he insists that he believes in transparency at the same time he urges congress to pass legislation no one has read. No doubt, these latest bills will include the equivalent of his previously "shovel ready" projects.

Conservatives, to be sure, are outraged by this hypocrisy. Having endured a "bipartisanship" that repeatedly excludes them from policy discussions, they realize that this president is not a man of his word. They understand full well that extremist measures are being rushed into law in the hopes that this will avoid close scrutiny.

Liberals, certainly left-leaning liberals, are, in contrast, delighted by what they see. As true believers who agree that only collectivist solutions can save the nation from inequality, they detect no dishonesty. No matter how manifest Obama's rationalizations, they give them credence. Indeed, they add justifications of their own. No doubt, if the president's policies exploded in his face, they would hasten to praise the psychedelic colors of the blast.

No, the mystery of why more people are not offended by this festival of deceit is to be found in the middle of the political spectrum. The question is, Why are moderates inclined to allow this cynical demagogy to go unquestioned? Don't they realize that it violates the premises upon which our democratic institutions are founded?

The answer has several parts. First, moderates won't allow themselves to recognize the president's mendacity because they don't want to see it. Having voted for the man, they are on record as believing his many promises. To suspect him now would be to admit their earlier error; something most people are reluctant to do.

Second, they do not want to give up hope. As *The Shawshank Redemption* proclaimed "hope is a good thing." Maybe "the best thing." Why would they want to renounce it? Much better to give Obama the benefit of the doubt and allow him time to fulfill his many pledges.

Third, there is the emotional message the president communicates. Just as Bill Clinton convinced many people that he had nothing to be ashamed of in the Lewinsky affair by being publicly shameless, Obama does the equivalent by being relentlessly earnest. In gracefully, and sincerely, espousing his various falsehoods, he conveys the message that they are true. The ease, and indeed the elegance, of his delivery implies that he has nothing to be embarrassed about; hence that he does not fear being caught in a lie.

Lastly, there is the issue of race. Sadly many people agree with Janeane Garafolo that challenging the president's words is tantamount to racism. They fear that if they are affronted by his mendacity, they will be accused of prejudice. Yet in capitulating to this sort of intimidation, they make it impossible to engage in an honest debate. The logic of honoring the race card is that the president can never be wrong and hence must never be contradicted.

This said; lies are lies. It may seem mean-spirited to point this out, but the truth is the truth. Moreover, only if we as a nation have the courage to stand up for the facts, can we preserve ourselves—and our democracy—from descending into a morass of deceit and failure. It is the truth that will save us, not a polite ac-quiescence in dishonesty.

Noble Lies

Themistocles had a problem. The Athenians had beaten the Persians at Marathon and were feeling pretty good about themselves. So far as they were concerned, if their archenemies reappeared, they would lick them just as handily.

But Themistocles feared the worst. He suspected that when—not if—the Persians returned, it would be with a more massive army and navy. Thus, for Athens to survive, it too would need a much larger navy. The city would have to build many more triremes if it were to match its foe's fleet.

Yet the Athenians were in no mood to spend money. So Themistocles resorted to subterfuge. He lied. He told his fellow citizens that a small nearby island posed an immediate threat. For this, they were willing to open their purses—and the ships were built.

The result was that when the Persians returned, Themistocles was able to defeat them at the battle of Salamis. By most accounts, this, and the courageous Spartan stand at Thermopylae, saved Greece, and Western civilization, from falling under an Asian yoke.

Why am I telling you this story? It is because many people—including myself—have been mystified by Barack Obama's ability to get away with an unending series of lies. How could the American people have reelected him, or continue to hold him in high regard, when he is so challenged by the truth?

The answer, I believe, is that Obama's lies are also regarded as justified by many people. These too are thought of as noble, and therefore as are needed to save us from a dreadful fate. Most liberals, in particular, assume they have a duty to protect us from ourselves. Because like the Athenians, we do not know what is good for us, they must lead the way.

Sometimes lies can help, but Barack Obama is not Themistocles. Contemporary liberals do not know what is best for us. They think they do, but their misplaced faith in large government is creating far more problems than it solves. The fact is that they, and specifically Obama, are making things worse, and in many cases, much worse.

Let us take an example. In attempting to pass ObamaCare, our president assured us that costs would go down and that people could keep their own doctors. Now, of course, as this program is being implemented, we are learning that these pledges were false.

But anyone who was paying attention back then was aware of this. So why did so many liberals suspend disbelief? The reason is simple. It was because they were committed to government provided health care. For them, this was an article of faith and therefore any tactic employed to bring it about was acceptable—including lies.

The same scenario is again unfolding with regard to the budget deficit. Where months ago Obama agreed that spending would have to come under control lest an ever-expanding deficit sabotage our economy, now he tells us that spending is not a problem.

He also tells us that he has met the Republicans halfway even though he as not proposed any significant spending cuts. Instead, a man, who boasted that he had not raised taxes, continues to seek new ways to increase government revenues. This, he says, will reduce the deficit, even though the numbers tell us it will not.

Why then the drama and the deceit? And why are the president's supporters so ready to believe? The answer again is that they too have faith in a much larger government. They thus forgive what they could easily detect as lies because they regard these as noble lies.

I say "forgive," but I actually mean "embrace." These lies are believed necessary and therefore are not considered "lies," but good strategy. As a consequence, the opinions of these true believers will only change when a disaster forces them to do so. –As, unfortunately, it soon may.

All Politicians Lie?

"All politicians lie!"

By now I have heard this mantra thousands of times. Almost always it is issued for the mouths of liberal students trying to defend the latest deceit offered up by a liberal politician. Often nowadays, the person in question is the president of the United States—but his minions are also on the line.

The next thing I usually hear is that Bush lied too! Or that Republicans and/or conservatives are liars. If I suggest that not all politicians lie to the same degree, this may be acknowledged, but is treated as an incidental fact.

In contemplating how common this scenario is, several things strike me. The first is that these students, and the politicians whose example they are following, have become addicted to a strategy that most mothers warn against. They are essentially saying that: if everyone does it, it is okay.

Instead of defending a particular lie, they decide to accuse their opponents of the vice of which they stand accused. This shifts the focus of attention and when it works takes them off the hot seat. It may even succeed in establishing an equivalency between different instances of deception.

The way this often goes is: Well, Bush lied too! It doesn't matter whether he actually lied or that he may have done so years ago, the current canard suddenly becomes unimportant. Now the fight is over whose lies are worse.

But that was not the original issue. The question was about this present lie and its implications. If the "everyone does it" ploy succeeds, then everyone is equally guilty and there is no current mendacity that should disqualify what liberals are arguing.

This seems to me a remarkably cynical gambit. Committed liberals appear to have become so jaded by the habitual deceits of their heroes that they no longer consider a lie wrong. Their criterion is now: Does it work? And if it does, then it is political wizardry.

We saw this recently when Democrats were accused of voter fraud in the Wisconsin recall election. Fraud is a kind of lying that, in this case, is utilized to change election results. Yet Wisconsin Democrats went on television, not to deny the fraud, but to assert that it was no big deal. After all everyone engages in fraud and it does not really alter the course of events.

Then there is the Department of Justice refusing to allow states like South Carolina to use picture ID's for voters. This is said to protect equality, but what about protecting against dishonest manipulations. Evidently the fact that votes by felons, though illegal, probably allowed Al Franken to become a Minnesota senator does not matter.

There is also the spectacle of the President telling the nation that he has spent less than his predecessors. Given the fact that Obama increased the national debt by nearly six trillion dollars, this would seem to be a joke. But no, it was said with a straight face.

Barack's defenders quickly rushed forward with a bogus accounting to demonstrate that black was white and white was black; an exercise that would have been unnecessary had the president been honest. Even so, many of his partisans swallowed this invention as if it were true.

Yes, everyone lies, especially if they are liberals. They have to because what they stand for is so egregiously fraudulent. Moreover, they are forced to defend their lies with another cordon of lies. They know that to do less would place their credibility in jeopardy.

But I submit that the credibility of people who have grown so comfortable with lying should be in jeopardy. The deceits emanating from Washington, be they about national security leaks or attacks on political opponents, have come so fast and furious, that they ought to be alarming to people who value honesty.

I have my fingers crossed that most Americans fall into the latter category.

Two Theories of Social Justice

Rest assured, disputes over what comprises social justice are going to arise during the upcoming presidential campaign. The Democrats, in particular, are going to assert that they are the paladins of social justice; that only they can protect the little guy from exploitation.

The validity of this claim, however, rests on how we understand "social justice." To this end, let us examine two rival views. These may be summarized as the "Robin Hood" and the "Three Little Pigs" theories.

In the Robin Hood version, it is necessary to steal from the rich to give to the poor. According to it, because wealth is unequally distributed, a champion must level the playing field. Only this person can correct unfairness by forcing the affluent to disgorge their ill-gotten gains.

This theory is obviously favored by the Democrats. They insist that everyone must pay their "fair share" and therefore increased taxes must be levied on the upper one percent. Only this can provide a modicum of decency.

In contrast, the Little Pigs version of justice allows the players to keep what they earn. It notes that of the three pigs, only the industrious one invested the effort into building a house of bricks and therefore only his dwelling resisted the efforts of the Big, Bad Wolf to turn him into a pork dinner.

The Republicans favor this parable in that they too believe individuals deserve to benefit from their own efforts. For them, justice is not about achieving full equality, but about guarding human rights—including property rights.

If we translate these theories into contemporary politics, then Barack Obama hopes to play the Robin Hood role. There is, however, a small problem with this. Barack is the president. In this sense, he is the sheriff. He is not a humble outlaw seeking to redress governmental wrongs, but can draw upon the coercive power of the state to enforce his mandates.

Yet, what if we do regard Obama as an outlaw. He has, after all, flouted the constitution at many turns. Then does he, like Robin Hood, get to pick those whom he plunders, as well as those upon whom he showers his favor? Might he, for instance, choose to force one company into bankruptcy while forgiving the debts of another—that is, as long its owners contributed to his campaign?

And what of those Republican pigs? They are presumed to be irredeemably selfish, yet the original little pigs presented a different picture. The industrious pig, it will be remembered, offered his siblings the shelter of his abode. They came to his sturdier house for protection against the wolf.

In the real world, it turns out that conservatives give far more to charity than liberals. They may believe in private property, but that does not mean they are without compassion. The difference is in how people are helped. On the one side, individuals provide succor, while on the other, virtually all assistance is channeled through the federal government?

But what if the latter took over? What if we decided that only the government should provide fairness? With respect to the three little pigs, would this translate into Obama decreeing that each pig be provided with exactly the same number of bricks?

Let's, however, take this supposition a step further. In taking bricks from the industrious pig, wouldn't this leave him with too few to build a substantial structure? And, as to the other pigs, what guarantees that they will use their bricks to improve their dwellings?

In the end, the probable outcome of this arbitrarily enforced equality is three ramshackle edifices and one very well fed wolf.

If this sounds absurd, we have, in fact, witnessed the outcome of government enforced social justice elsewhere. It occurred in the old Soviet Union. There the government controlled all of the strings and distributed goods according to formulae of its own devising.

So what did people wind up with? As history records, they were rewarded with both poverty and tyranny. Or, as the libertarian John Hospers used to say, they were well on their way to "splendidly equalized destitution." —Some justice!

Pinocchio's On Parade

Winston Churchill famously said, "In wartime, truth is so precious that she should always be attended by a bodyguard of lies." To judge by this standard, liberals, such as Barack Obama, must be guarding extraordinarily valuable truths.

The opposite, however, is the case. The center they are protecting is hollow. Liberalism has long since rotted out at the core. As an ideology in crisis, it no longer provides valid answers to the problems we face—if it ever did.

Think about it! What, if anything, are Obama and his entourage reluctant to lie about? Is there any policy, foreign or domestic, that has escaped the stultifying hand of deceit? So common has dishonesty become that it is no longer worthy of outraged notice.

Why is this so? When public policies have miscarried, those promoting them have two choices. They can either admit their failures or lie about them. Nevertheless, as ideologues, who believe they are infallible, liberals, in fact, have but one choice. They can only lie. The result: Pinocchio's on parade.

What have liberals been wrong about? Where can we begin? Did they improve the economy as promised? Six years have gone by and trillions of dollars have been spent, but we still have the slowest recovery since the Great Depression.

As importantly, the administration routinely vows to grow the economy from the middle out. In reality, the rich have done well and the poor receive larger transfer payments than ever, whereas it is middle class jobs and salaries that have gone on permanent hiatus.

Or how about education? If we are no longer engaged in a race to the bottom, someone forgot to tell American students. Despite the money expended trying to finance a college education for everyone, our young continue to lag behind the rest of the world.

Or what about race relations? Do blacks and whites trust each other more now that we have an African-American president? Actually, our president cannot even bring himself to admit that "hands up, don't shoot" was based on a lie.

As for foreign policy, are we safer? Claims that we are, are obviously absurd. And why trash Netanyahu? Or cozy up to the Iranians? Or kowtow to Vladimir Putin? Or allow the Chinese to hack into our secrets? Such gross neglect can only be excused by lying.

Barack Obama is surely incompetent. But the problem goes deeper. He is the symbol of liberal ineptitude. He has messed up ObamaCare, immigration, and the IRS not merely because he is a poor administrator, but because liberal prescriptions cannot work. They are grounded in ignorance and wishful thinking.

And so not only does the president lie; so do those who work for him—whether they are in the State Department, the Department of Justice, or the EPA. All must participate in the cover-ups if they are to prevent their doctrinal bankruptcy from being revealed.

Nor is this all. The liberal media are complicit in the lies. As card caring liberals, reporters and editors conspire to keep the public misinformed. They routinely reinterpret failure as success and refuse to report disconcerting news.

Thus, rather than embarrass the president, they will not cover stories such as Jonathan Gruber's admission that the public was intentionally deceived about ObamaCare.

Nor indeed is that all. Ordinary Democrats, what were once called "knee-jerk liberals, do not want to know the truth. Whatever the scandal rocking the capital, they prefer to discount it. Hence they look away. Far from demanding the facts, they cease paying attention to uncomfortable details.

And so lying has become the new norm! It does not shock because the alternative would be to admit that liberalism is a god that has failed. People high and low might have to recognize that their political shield is a moth eaten sieve. As a result, they turn to transparent fabrications to do the job.

Lies Incorporated

During the 1930's, Jewish and Italian gangsters created an alliance to further their illegal activities. Characters such as Bugsy Segal and Lucky Luciano teamed up to wipe out anyone who stood in their way. So effective were they in eliminating the opposition that the New York media dubbed them Murder Incorporated.

Today more dangerous conspirators have supplanted these felons. The mafia-associated villains of yore were small in number and restricted in their area of operation. As a result, their modern successors make them look like amateurs. Nowadays, the reach is international.

What might be called "Lies Incorporated" is a massive operation. Many tens of thousands are involved in a multi-billion dollar enterprise. These players are, to be sure, loosely associated. Nevertheless, they are responsible for far more damage than their predecessors.

I am talking about none other than the crowd answerable for what Donald Trump calls "fake news." Many of these folks are journalists, but PR firms, Super PACs, Non-Profits and Think Tanks employ legions of others. What these scoundrels have in common is a desire to manipulate public perceptions.

What they also have in common is an utter disregard for the truth. Many do not care whom they hurt. If a lie accomplishes their mission, they do not hesitate to embellish and disseminate it. The goal is to win; not to advance our common store of knowledge.

Fortunately, former CBS reporter, Sharyl Attkisson, has done a masterful job of exposing this underworld of creeps and character assassins in her new book The Smear. She makes it plain that they reside in a universe where day can be turned into night in an instant—then change back even more quickly.

You've seen this sleight of hand on television thousands of times. Alleged experts come on screen to debate the latest political sideshow. They then spout talking points fashioned by those Attkisson describes as "shady political operatives." These narratives are not designed to illuminate, but persuade.

Did Hillary Clinton try to hide embarrassing emails? No, she turned everything over to the State Department. Is global warming about to inundate our shorelines? Those who doubt it are unscientific "deniers." They are like the cretins who question the holocaust.

Oh by the way, today we talk about "climate change" rather than "global warming" because these shadowy manipulators determined that the former term worked better. The substitution had nothing to do with an empirical discovery. It was about effective propaganda.

A recent example of verbal slight of hand occurred once it was discovered that the Hillary campaign hired Fusion, GPS to create a Russian dossier intended to discredit Trump. Within hours, conservatives were blamed for starting it. Only later did it come out that the Washington Free Beacon had commissioned entirely different research.

In any event, firms like Fusion GPS are in the business of confusing us. They invent stories out of whole cloth; they plant misleading accounts with congenial reporters; they besmirch the reputations of inoffensive bystanders. The underlying objective is to make money or advance a particular agenda—or both.

The casualty in this? The truth, of course. It becomes ob-scured in a blizzard of lies. So pervasive are these fabrications that it is virtually impossible to keep track.

To make matters worse, most Americans are not even trying. They are satisfied with parroting the fake news distributed by their allies. Many do not care if these are lies. As long as they promote the interests of the erstwhile good guys, they are content.

This is tragic. Not only is the truth put in jeopardy, but so is public trust. When fake news and phony innuendo suck the air out of the public arena, people don't know whom to believe. Everyone becomes suspect.

The smear merchants have thus replaced the search for truth with a quest for the cleverest way to slander the next guy. Flood the Internet with spurious Tweets. Tell whoppers on Facebook. It's all part of the game. As long as ordinary folks cannot tell the difference between reality and fiction, the dissemblers might come out on top.

Isn't this comparable to murder? Aren't we killing our souls—as well as our national integrity—when we allow this miasma of deceit to spread?

Institutionalized Dishonesty

The left has been decrying "institutionalized racism" for some time. These partisans say that even though overt racism is less common, a deep-seated brand of bigotry is built into our nation's traditions and psyche. Although this bias is often unconscious, it is alleged to be vicious.

Once upon a time, it was undoubtedly true that racism was part of our country's fabric. Blacks were not allowed to vote. They were lynched if they were too assertive. A host of jobs were completely closed to them. What is more, the media invariably portrayed them as simple-minded criminals.

That has obviously changed. To engage in this sort of blatant discrimination would cause more problems for the racist than his target. Paradoxically, this is why the institutionalized racism charge has become prevalent. It is a way of decrying bigotry without having to prove its presence.

On the other hand, we are besieged by a torrent of institutionalized dishonesty. Starting with a flood of untrue accusations about race, gender and political bias, we find fraudulence in a variety of venues. Thus, we encounter it in the government, the media, and education.

The ubiquity of liberal deceit is one of the primary reasons that Donald Trump was elected president. Many ordinary voters were fed up with politically correct cant depicting them as low-life boobs. They realized that all they have to do is hint that some black person in the wrong and they will be vilified.

Likewise, anyone who has been paying attention to the propaganda coming out of the State Department, the Department of Justice, or the White House knows that dishonesty has become normal operating procedure. The folks doing this may call it "spin," but it is a way of disguising the truth and implying what is false.

We saw the same thing during the recent political campaign. Both sides habitually made impossible promises. Although we expect exaggeration from political candidates, the cascade of lies was over and above what we are accustomed to hearing.

But then there were the media. They have always been partisan, but seldom as transparently partisan. Time and again, they misrepresented what a candidate said. Actually, this was almost always directed at Trump. Journalists were so dedicated to a Clinton victory that they felt justified in distorting her vile opponent.

The New York Times, which was once considered the newspaper of record, openly violated its boast to publish all the news that's fit to print. It routinely failed to mention WikiLeaks revelations that were damaging to Hillary. Either that or it buried them in the back pages.

Meanwhile CNN richly earned the sobriquet of the Clinton News Network. Like MSNBC, and the mainstream television networks, it editorialized in what amounted to the front page. Commentators and news anchors alike made it obvious where their sympathies lay.

Even after the election was over, the bias remained. As a consequence, the *Times*, when writing about the Trump victory, framed it in terms of how the losers would react. Instead of featuring Trump's efforts to be conciliatory, it was its own constituents hard feelings that mattered.

As for CNN, it highlighted purported instances of where Trump supporters had violated minority rights. Middle schoolers were described as bigots for chanting "Build the Wall." Graffiti at Louisiana State University about "safe places" was denounced as despicable. Similarly. a man who yanked at a Muslim woman's hijab received national attention.

On the other hand, a Trump voter being stomped in Chicago was virtually overlooked. So were Hispanic Americans who encouraged their children to beat a piñata of Trump. Worst of all, violent anti-Trump riots in Portland Oregon were given short shrift.

As an academic, I can also assure readers that our universities have not been even-handed in teaching about politics. There was precious little joy on campus when Trump prevailed. Nor were there many approving lessons taught about his potential policies.

The fact is that government agencies, the media, and academe are riven through and through with partisans. As a result, these folks reflexively transmit untruths, as well as withhold abhorrent information, because they want to win. They may not believe they are doing so, but this practice has become institutionalized. It is just who they have become.

The Feather Bed Factory

A couple of weeks ago, I wrote about Institutionalized Dishonesty. I claimed that liberalism has incorporated reflexive untruthfulness into our national fabric. Whether in the government, the media, or ordinary life, more people are engaging in what are regarded as justifiable lies. These have become business as usual.

Now I am about to assert that irresponsibility has also become institutionalized. It too has been integrated into the social structures upon which we depend. No longer do most people feel accountable for their destinies. Now they believe they have a right to be protected.

Where did they get this idea? Why are millions of us certain that we are entitled to cradle to grave success and security? The source of this conviction should be obvious. It is an article of liberal faith. Progressives, whether in the media, academe or government, constantly proclaim it as a birthright.

But from whence did they derive this notion? How did they get it into their heads that the state must supply everyone with a good job, as well as shelter them from any hazard an uncertain universe might throw their way?

Although left-wingers sometimes maintain that they are in favor of personal responsibility, their actions shout otherwise. After all, they want to jack up the minimum wage, provide all and sundry with free medical care and higher education, and institute reams of regulations so that no one ever injures anyone else.

This has been called the nannie state, but it might also be labeled the feather-bed factory. The theory is that we all should be able to lean back and be served whatever we desire merely because we exist. We ought not have to work hard—or make decisions we could get wrong. Faceless others are to do the heavy lifting.

So I repeat: How did this peculiar worldview arise? Why did so many of us come to believe that we do not have to support ourselves by the sweat of our brows and that a set of rules emanating from Washington D.C. must ensure that we never come to any harm?

The culprit, I am afraid to say, is Marxism coupled with rampant bureaucratization. Karl Marx taught his disciples that virtually all of the world's evil could be laid at the feet of a few selfish capitalists. If these malevolent oppressors could be overthrown, the exploitation they sponsored would disappear.

But freedom from maltreatment was not enough. People still wanted to live comfortably. The Industrial Revolution had provided a cornucopia of goods and services. No one wanted to see these vanish. They were to be redistributed.

This was deemed feasible because industrial production was regarded as automatic. It was a matter of setting the machines in motion so that the affluence they generated would appear of its own accord. All the government had to do was make sure everyone received their fair share.

The state bureaucracy was itself conceived of as an automatic machine. Once the correct rules and procedures were put in place, these, and not fallible human agents, would guarantee prosperity and social justice. No one would be responsible because personal respons-ibility was now to be unnecessary.

And so here we have it. The government can supposedly make us rich merely by forcing employers to pay us more. It can also render us better educated by making universal education gratis. Our health can likewise be enormously improved by its underwriting the costs of medical care. We have to do nothing—except enjoy the bounty.

We won't even have to worry about being moral. This too will be the state's responsibility—which it will discharge with everlasting compassion. Because the philosopher kings overseeing the bureaucratic machinery are to be unswervingly nice, their kindness will theoretically rub off on the rest of us. We won't need to control our selfish impulses because they will evaporate.

In this brave new liberal world, we need not dread mistakes, because we won't make any. Nor will we have to develop complex skills, because these are to be built into our mechanical servants. Rather than act responsibly, we can concentrate our ever-narrower attention spans on Facebook and computer games. Won't that be fun!

Institutionalized Unfairness

The election is over, but the bellyaching continues. The liberals, in particular, remain deeply disgruntled. They keep casting around for villains to blame for their failure. It never occurs to many of them that they might be responsible for their defeat.

In earlier columns, I have suggested that the electorate might finally have rebelled at the institutionalized dishonesty progressives introduced into government, the media, and education. Political correctness has become so pervasive that millions of voters could no longer conceal their distain.

Liberal commentators, of course, have continued their self-deceptive ways. Despite ostentatious "soul-searching," they are still looking outward to understand why they were rejected. Indeed, some of their recriminations are nastier than ever.

I have also suggested that we are victims of institutionalized irresponsibility. Millions of Americans obviously want to be saved from their follies. They require the government to protect them and to do the heavy lifting. In this case, folks on both the left and the right are implicated.

Clearly those on the left want politicians to guarantee them a good job with high wages, but so do those on the right. They too ask the president to intervene to make sure they are protected from life's hazards. The difference is that conservatives also ask for an opportunity to run their own businesses.

But now I want to turn to the proliferation of institutionalized unfairness. In recent years, there has been a greater emphasis on treating people differently depending on their social category. Discrimination and prejudice have become fashionable—that is, as long as these are applied to unshielded groups.

Another way to describe what has occurred is to label it "identity politics." The citizenry has been divided up into groups that are appealed to in terms of their allegedly distinctive characteristics. Blacks, Hispanics, Gays, and Women are regarded as separate and thus deserving of special benefits.

On the other hand, Whites, Straights, Men, and Christians have been flung into the bowels of the earth. They are told that they are a basketful of deplorables and therefore are not entitled to respect or social preference. The fault for this is supposedly their own and hence they have no right to complain.

One of the most glaring examples of unfairness is affirmative action. People are nowadays ushered to the front of the line if they possess the correct group credentials. Thus they get admitted to colleges although their grades are below par. They also get hired and promoted on the job in order to fit predetermined quotas.

What makes matters worse is that this favoritism is defended in the name of social justice. It is said to be an essential means of returning equity to our society. Never mind that some people get hurt. They must be sacrificed on the altar societal progress.

Many Trump voters caught on that as members of the white working class they were expendable. They realized that if, for instance, only Black lives matter, theirs don't. They began to understand that they were scorned and marginalized.

Liberals have assumed that they can bring about fairness by being unfair. They believe that the only way to correct historical injustices is to institute a variety of contemporary injustices. The new victims had accordingly best shut up and take their medicine.

Except that millions in the heartland decided that they were fed up with remaining silent. They too had grievances that were not being addressed. The new rules told them that they were the cause of other's distress, but now they protested against this demonization.

The fact is that the only way for a society to be fair is to apply the same rules to everyone. A democracy that is based on partiality, no matter how well intended, cannot be stable. The losers ultimately discover they have been cheated and demand recompense.

This is apparently where we have arrived. Relentless appeals to political correctness are falling on deaf ears. Innocent people cannot indefinitely be made to feel guilty for the sins of others. In time, they conclude that they too have rights.

No Honor

Honor! What an old-fashioned word. How antiquated an idea. Surely modern sophisticates are aware that this was a ploy perpetrated by the elites in order to defraud the masses. The goal was to get ordinary people to make sacrifices that were not in their interest.

We, in our world-wise ways, are no longer taken in by such manipulations. We are not about to do something dangerous just because it is "honorable." And so honor has been disappearing from our universe, snuffed out in a whirlwind of cynicism.

But wait! Some things happened a week ago that reminded me there are still a few honorable people in this country; people who are prepared to do the right thing even though it does not personally benefit them.

Last weekend Fox News ran a special on the contractors who were guarding the CIA Annex in Benghazi. Their story was inspiring. Their attitude was even more so. Here were men who lived up to their commitment to protect and defend; men who put their lives on the line to do so.

When the bullets began flying around the U.S. embassy, they did not run and hide. Their first impulse was to race toward the shooting. They were determined not to let their colleagues die unaided.

Then, when superior numbers forced them to fall back, they made a stand worthy of the heroes of the Alamo. Despite being out-gunned, and even when injured, they fought with stubborn professionalism. Cool under fire, they kept the enemy at bay for hours.

These men did what they knew to be right. Although they realized they might lose their lives, they honored their commitments. The same can be said about the heroes fighting the Ebola outbreak in West Africa. They too put their moral obligations before their personal comfort.

Dr. Kent Brantly not only volunteered to minister to the ill in Liberia, but when stricken with the deadly disease, he maintained his dignity. Even though blood was seeping from his orifices—usually a sign that death is near—he kept his composure.

Then, after he recovered, Brantly actually contemplated a return to his duties. Undeterred by his near miss, he placed his devotion to helping the downtrodden before his own interests. A man of genuine belief, he would honor his convictions despite the danger.

How different this is from the spectacle we are witnessing in Washington. Barack Obama and his minions are not above telling any lie or distorting any truth in order to gain a political advantage. Being honest and doing the right thing is not part of their playbook.

The president of the United States is pledged to defend the nation and to protect the constitution. But when the guns began to fire in Iraq and the Ukraine, his first impulse was to run for cover. Unsure about what to do, he decided that the best option was to remain on the safety of the golf course.

Likewise when confronted with a choice between honoring the constitution or enduring a political setback, he jettisoned the constitution. It did not matter whether he had a right to alter the immigration laws or ObamaCare, the question was what would get him the most votes.

As for liberal Democrats in general, they have grown so accustomed to obscuring for their president's inadequacies, that they can no longer tell the difference between what is honorable and not. However egregious the misconduct of their leaders, they find a way to excuse them.

Honor has thus been frittered away very cheaply. Rationalizations, misconstruals, and downright lies have become the coin of the realm. Too many decent people, in order to deny their ideological failures, have sold their souls to the devil.

Nevertheless, morality matters! Honor matters! Once these have been abandoned in the service of ambition or cowardice, they are difficult to reclaim. Hence what today looks like a good bargain may tomorrow precipitate a catastrophe.

No Justice

By 1990, the conventional wisdom had it that big cities were ungovernable. Places like New York City were regarded as sinkholes of despair. Festooned in graffiti, and plagued by crime, their mayors and police departments had lost control.

Two decades earlier, while a student at the City University of New York's Graduate Center, I watched my professors struggle with the task of rehabilitating Times Square. Unfortunately, their social engineering did not help.

Then came Rudi Giuliani. He decided to fight crime instead of surrendering to it. The police were told to arrest people even for small infractions—such as turnstile jumping. They were also unleashed to engage in pro-active interventions in violent neighborhoods.

The results were dramatic. Crime plummeted. The murder rate, for instance, fell by almost three quarters. People again felt safe. They even returned to the newly cleaned up Times Square to celebrate their liberation from squalor.

But this did not satisfy the liberal pundits who ran the *New York Times*. They regarded Giuliani as the enemy. He was perceived as a monster who was oppressing the poor. Instead of being nice to the downtrodden, he insisted that they follow the law—or pay a penalty.

And so the Times fought back. It ran hundreds of articles about police brutality. Despite statistical evidence that police abuses had been reduced, aberrant cases, such at that of Amadou Diallo, were highlighted to demonstrate just how vicious the authorities were.

Today the clock has been turned back and Freddie Gray is the new poster boy for police cruelty. Without knowing the facts, cries for revenge rose from Baltimore's mean streets. Worse still, the city's elected officials echoed these calls. They agreed that without justice there would be no peace.

And so the police were scapegoated. Instead of putting down the rioters, they were asked to expose themselves to the brickbats of an unruly mob. Meanwhile the officers suspected of injuring Gray were indicted for second-degree murder on the theory that they intentionally killed their prisoner.

The upshot: back on the streets there were celebrations. Vengeance, disguised as justice, had won the day. Now the Crips and Bloods were hailed as heroes for maintaining the peace. It did not matter that they directed vandals to loot Asian businesses. Hadn't they, after all, protected their own?

This, however, was not justice. It was a return to a State of Nature in which it is every person for him/herself. Millennia have gone into developing the institutions that shield ordinary citizens from chaos. Yet these were brushed aside as if they were the problem.

With the Al Sharpton's of the world now dictating the terms of surrender, the worst is yet to arrive. Baltimore is about to become Detroit East. Legitimate businesses will flee the city, as will its respectable residents. Nor will the cops do their job. Why should they risk being sent to jail for apprehending evildoers?

So who is responsible? It is none other than the liberal champion of justice in the White House. Intent on vindicating his ideological convictions, Obama is determined to do what the New York Times could not. He aims to dismantle law and order in favor of a squishy niceness.

Baltimore's mayor decided to provide the looters space to foul their own nest. This could only be achieved by disarming the police. Yet this policy was well under way. From Cambridge Massachusetts to Ferguson Missouri, our president had already condemned law enforcement agents for having gone wild.

Nevertheless, Obama and his allies do not know what a lack of control portends. With the gangs and incompetent public officials in charge, there will be blood on the streets. Once the law is fully dismantled, no one will be safe.

This is not justice. It is insanity. Ordinary police officers are not perfect. They make mistakes. Moreover, they should be punished when they do. But destroying law and order is a far greater mistake—with more serious consequences.

Deep Denial

We are in the midst of a constitutional crisis far more serious than during the darkest days of Watergate. Nonetheless, to hear the Democrats and their allies tell it, nothing is wrong. We are merely witnessing business as usual. This, however, is evidence of deep, and persistent, denial.

When I wrote *Post-Liberalism: The Death of a Dream*, I opened with a vignette about a flying saucer cult. Back in the 1950s, social psychologists engaged in an observational study of a religious group that predicted the end of the world. How, they wondered, would these folks respond when doomsday arrived and there was no doom?

The answer surprised them. Although flustered, these true-believers reaffirmed their faith. While they too could plainly see that the saucers supposed to save them from destruction had not appeared, they immediately concocted justifications as to why.

Thus, the sect's leader explained that Armageddon had been called off precisely because her followers remained constant. Their loyalty convinced the extraterrestrials to spare the earth as a reward for this devotion.

In other words, when people are deeply committed to a belief, counter-evidence is explained away. Denial and rationalization rush into the breech; with those who remain steadfast assuring each other they were right all along.

Barack Obama provided a classic example of this impulse with respect to "climate change." Hence, during his state of the nation speech, he assured the country that the case for global warming was settled. Then he winged his way to California to put down a billion dollar bet on saving us from droughts and floods.

Mind you, there has been almost no global warming for seventeen years and the country is gripped by one of the coldest spells in decades, but this did not deter him. Warm or cold, wet or dry, everything proved that what the president said was accurate. The data just had to be *interpreted* correctly.

More serious for the political welfare of the nation was Obama's claim that there is not a smidgeon of IRS scandal and that ObamaCare is finally working as intended. Of course, he also told us that the Benghazi affair was now closed; that we knew all we needed to know.

Worse yet, the president bragged about how he would henceforth go around congress. He had a pen and a phone, and therefore his mandates had the effect of law. This was not unconstitutional because—gee, everyone else has done it.

Only, as I recall, this was what Richard Nixon's defenders also said. According to them, everyone played political dirty tricks and they all covered up this unsavory business. So what was the big deal? Time to move on!

Nevertheless, Nixon never used the IRS to suppress opponents on the same scale as Obama. Nor did his fellow Republicans urge him to do so. Neither did he flout the law in the serial manner of our current chief executive. Nor did members of his party suggest he should.

As for cover-ups, in the Watergate days we were told that the cover-up was worse than the deed. If so, what about hiding the facts regarding Benghazi? Or the IRS? Or the true numbers of ObamaCare enrollments? Doesn't any of this count?

During Watergate, Republicans at first rallied around Nixon; then they were appalled. Not surprisingly, Democrats have rallied around Obama, but concerned more with political survival than the nation's welfare; few show signs of abandoning their leader.

As for the mainstream media, they hated Nixon and were only too happy to tear him down. Obama, in contrast, is their creation; ergo they have a stake in propping him up.

The result: a festival of lies, half-truths, and averted gazes. Forget about transparency; even the *New York Times* tells us that when ObamaCare threatens two and a half million jobs, this is good for the people. They apparently get liberated from "job-lock."

Now if that isn't denial and rationalization, I do not know what is.

Chapter VII

Traditional Values—Updated

Morality is Not Obsolete
　　No society can survive when its moral underpinnings have been corrupted. Without an allegiance to principles appropriate to its situation, conflicts cannot be resolved. The liberal elevation of non-judgmentalism and unconditional positive regard has been a disaster. Were these recommendations taken literally, they would prevent us from entertaining any moral opinions. We would have to practice a toleration so broad that it included behavior, such as murder, that is otherwise considered reprehensible. Nor is this abdication of social responsibility rescued by endorsing moral relativism. To convey to individuals and societies that what is moral is what they decide is moral, essentially provides a rationalization for the most abysmal conduct. It would make killing Jews okay for the Nazis and beating slaves acceptable in the antebellum South.
　　Much of what has historically been considered moral still deserves to be regarded as moral. Our traditional values have not been wiped away by advances in science or economics. They must, however, be updated. Modifications need to be made in order to accommodate unanticipated challenges. Concepts such as honesty, personal responsibility, and interpersonal fairness ought not be jettisoned on a whim. We can begin by admitting the truth. It is what accords with reality. Nor ought persons skilled in moral deception be permitted to get away with their depravity. We must be able to identify such shameful behavior even when the perpetrators portray themselves without shame. The same goes for self-righteousness. Just because people, for instance, liberals, believe they are morally superior does not mean they are. When good people meet bad people, they ought not be intimidated. After all, lies are lies and liars are liars.
　　Unfortunately, the Obama era left behind a legacy of moral nihilism. His administration's lawlessness was often justified by perverting time-honored standards. Over and over again, they created new moral imperatives by asserting them forcefully and repeatedly. The invention of a right to gay marriage was one such instance. Attacking its critics as extremists was a fruitful method for advancing this practice and then deflecting attention from its creators. Barry Goldwater once proclaimed that extremism in defense of liberty is no vice. In

fact, most of what conservatives believe is hardly radical. Indeed, much of it is grounded in human nature. Liberals forget this when they recommend a society in which humans cease having human inclinations—such as selfishness. Having been corrupted by their own power, these progressives lost sight of human frailties. Accordingly, they are forced to encourage "unconditional positive regard" lest they be judged on their own merits.

Given how much has gone wrong in contemporary society, it is fair to ask if we require a moral reawakening. We have experienced religious awakenings in the past; do we need a secular one now. If so, we must proceed with care. One prerequisite is foresight. If we are unable to look ahead, we are sure to miss the side effects of our reforms. We must also avoid the perfection trap. Thomas Sowell alerted us to the constraints imposed by a combination of our humanity and social circumstances. These ensure that we will never fulfill all of our fondest dreams. Nonetheless, we can seek improvements.

First, among the most important distinctions we must make is that between equality and universalism. Perhaps the biggest mistake made by liberals is their pursuit of total equality. Although they call this social justice, it will be impossible to realize because people are unequal in a myriad of ways. We are not all uniformly smart, or attractive, or powerful. Even so, we can be held to common moral standards. Universalism implies that the same rules need to be applied to everyone. Regardless of their social status, all must be chastised for their lies or negligence. This requires that we have the courage to be honest about our personal shortcomings and the difficulties thrown up by an intransigent reality. If we are smitten by the blandishments of romantic idealism, we are bound to suffer. The same is true if we are emotionally immature. If we cannot manage our fears, or anger, or sadness, these affects will manage us. But if they do, we will not have the wherewithal to behave in a principled manner.

Liberals implore us to show compassion for the weak. They likewise chide conservatives for being hard-hearted. Conservatism can, in fact, be benevolent, but must do so realistically. People can be helped—but only if they help themselves. This begins with self-discipline. Unless individuals can refrain from acting on momentary impulses, they are destined to create enormous harm. Strangers must obviously exercise restraint when dealing with other strangers. Despite their personal desires to succeed, they must not violate moral strictures while pursuing their aims. Individuals must also work at cultivating their best selves. This often entails engaging in activities that are not immediately gratifying. Schooling, for example, can require years of tedious study. We can also be certain that we will commit mistakes. Especially when we enter unfamiliar territory, we are sure to make a multitude of poor choices. This, however, should not prevent us from taking chances. Without undertaking risks, improvements are impossible. The real mistake is thus not correcting our missteps. As long as we have the ability to recognize these errors, we have the hope of reversing them.

The bottom line is that we must be devoted to principled realism. Our moral traditions provide a vital foundation upon which we can build. Even so, the rules necessary for a mass techno-commercial society differ significantly from those appropriate in an agricultural one. As we will see in the next chapter, the canons that apply to marriage have therefore been modified. What we today expect from husbands and wives is not the same as what our great-grandparents expected. Forward-looking conservatism must perforce look forward. It cannot simply repeat the past as if conditions had not changed. In other words, although morality is not relative, neither is it absolute. Its boundaries are set by our human capacities, social constraints, and inherited traditions. These interact in a way that is fluid, but not unrestricted. Unless we respect who we are—and what we can do—our unfettered imaginations get us in trouble. That is one of the ironies of undisciplined liberalism.

Principles for a Complex Society

Traditional Values

When I asked my grandfather what it felt like to be old, he replied that he still felt like teenager on the inside. Now that I am older than he was then, I know exactly what he was talking about. This includes feeling the same way about right and wrong.

Every now and then, I am told that this makes me old-fashioned. If so, I embrace the label. Some things do not go out of fashion and morality is one of them. We may need to adjust it occasionally, but we should never throw it out wholesale.

One of the things I like about living in the South is that some of the old ways have survived. Politeness is still considered a virtue and the young continue to be taught to respect the old. Mind you, southerners are no more moral than folks from other parts of the country. They are just less likely to celebrate their transgressions.

Decades ago, when I was living in New York, I remember be told that it was silly to reprimand the young for violating the rules. They weren't going to listen anyway. In fact, they might do more wrong simply to annoy their scolding elders.

The idea was that if we tolerated casual sex, pot smoking, and cursing a blue streak, they would eventually tire of being contrary. Sooner or later they would settle down and support the time-tested truisms.

Well the generation that experienced this permissiveness has now reached maturity and it continues its coarse lifestyle. Divorce is rationalized, dishonesty is accepted as the norm, and out-of-wedlock parenthood is regarded as a personal choice.

Individual responsibility is treated as a concept that comes from straight the Dark Ages. Whenever people do something malicious, it is obviously not their fault. They are merely reflecting the corruption of the larger society. It is up to others to be their keepers, not them to control their own conduct.

Yet what happens if nobody is willing to be anyone's keeper? What if we depend upon the government to prevent nastiness, but it is unable to do so? Then again, how could it, when those who administer it are as bereft of traditional values as those they govern?

Just look at Donald Trump and Hillary Clinton. Does anyone regard them as paragons of virtue? Have they lived up to, or are they living up to, the traditional values? If anyone answers yes to this question, I plan to hold onto my wallet when in their presence.

Donald's marital history is scarcely exemplary, while Hillary's husband had a problem with bimbo explosions that his wife blandly covered up. Neither, of course, is admired for honesty and both have a history of shady business dealings. Each may, in fact, be guilty of criminal activity.

Nothing new here folks—right? What is new is that one of them is liable to be elected president. Oh sure, we have had immoral chief executives before. But have we consciously voted for them?

What is radically unprecedented is that so many ordinary people are utterly tolerant of depravity. They have been told to be nonjudgmental and have taken this to heart. Rather than be mean to anyone, they stand around and allow others to be as mean as they want to be.

The moment we heard about Hillary's machinations with a private server, her political aspirations should have been over. The second that Donald used gutter language to insult an opponent; his campaign should have been history. That this did not occur is more our fault than theirs.

Morality is never automatic. The temptation to violate its strictures is universal. But the traditional values became traditional because we once upheld them. That we no longer do is more than an affront to tradition. It is proof positive that our moral benchmarks have eroded.

As for me, I will continue to be old-fashioned. If those who believe in being non-judgmental find this offensive, I advise them to stop judging me!

Admit the Truth

For many years I had a sign over my desk that read, "Admit the Truth." Not "tell the truth," but admit the truth. Although I hate to make mistakes, and find it even more painful to acknowledge them publicly, I wanted to remind myself that it is better to come clean when you are wrong, than to keep fighting for a falsehood.

I came to this conclusion after witnessing a fight between my father and a favorite uncle. They were arguing about whether soldiers were allowed to bring home money from Europe at the conclusion of World War II. My father insisted that they couldn't, while my uncle said they could.

After going back and forth for almost a half hour, my uncle finally capitulated and agreed that they could not. What made this interesting was that my father had not served in the military, whereas my uncle fought under General Patton. In other words, my uncle had first hand knowledge, while my father did not.

After observing how my father bullied his way to success, I decided that this was a Pyrrhic victory. It didn't matter if my uncle yielded. What mattered was who was right. Simply forcing someone to give in would not change the truth. What was more, the truth was likely to determine later events.

And so I concluded that it did not make sense for me to fight for what was wrong either. Once I realized that someone with whom I disagreed was correct, admitting my error and getting on to the next piece of business would save us both grief. Even I would benefit from adding a new bit of knowledge to my stockpile.

All of this is by way of analyzing Barack Obama's recent speech about how he would address our impending deficit disaster. Almost everyone who has done the math recognizes that the current deficit spending cannot be sustained. They soon realize that the required interest payments alone will eventually swallow up everything else.

Obama, of course, had a few months earlier submitted a budget that increased federal spending. Now he decided that the accounts needed to be brought into balance. This was forced upon him by Rep Paul Ryan's budget plan. It drastically reduced deficits, mostly by reducing what the government spent.

But Obama would have none of this. Most of his speech was very vague about expenditure cuts. Somehow getting rid of waste, fraud, and corruption would reduce government outlays. Still, the Obama administration had not been able to make much of a dent in any of these despite two plus years in office. Nevertheless, the future would be different.

Where the president's heart was, however, was in tax increases. He would rescind the Bush tax cuts so that the rich finally paid their fair share. Never mind that under Bush the wealthy were paying a larger share than under Clinton. Never mind that Obama defined the rich as anyone earning over two hundred and fifty thousand dollars.

All this raised eyebrows, but the worst part of this plan was that it totally ignored history. Whether under the auspices of Andrew Mellon, John Kennedy, Ronald Reagan, or George W. Bush, the evidence was unambiguous. Reducing taxes increased tax-receipts—it did not reduce them.

Indeed, when first Herbert Hoover and then Franklin Delano Roosevelt increased the tax rate on the rich in order to pay for expenditures during the Great Depression, their strategy backfired. Instead of more money flowing into federal coffers, the amount was nearly cut in half.

So low did income tax receipts fall that Roosevelt was forced to nearly double the excise taxes on ordinary Americans. In other words, the rich paid less and the poor paid more. On top of this, with less money available to them, the rich reduced their investments. As a consequence, Roosevelt lambasted them for their selfishness, but they had neither the resources nor the incentive to comply with his demands.

And now it is Obama who is lambasting the wealthy and promising to confiscate more of their incomes. Unable to admit that he is wrong, either he has not read history or he has not understood it. In any event, the truth does not seem to matter to him. Intent on winning reelection, he is more concerned with the bill of goods he can sell the public.

But the truth is the truth, and if it does not bite him in the backside, it is sure to bite the rest of us.

Creating a Civil Right

Three decades ago most people would have scoffed at the idea. A century ago, the vast majority would have been perplexed that the proposition was even raised. Almost no one, until fairly recently, accepted the notion that gay marriage was a human right.

How, it would have been asked, could something, which had not even existed until almost the day before yesterday, be considered a right? That would be like calling the ownership of a cell phone a right.

But come to think of it, some folks are indeed calling cell phone ownership a right. Moreover, nowadays, according to some polls, nearly half of all Americans have decided that homosexual marriages are on a par with freedom of speech and freedom of religion.

What has happened here? How can our moral judgments have changed so rapidly? Have people, in fact, discovered a new civil right? Or is it merely that they have been sensitized in ways their ancestors were not?

One of my specialties is the sociology of morality; hence I find it fascinating to observe a moral right being created right before my eyes. Many people think of morality as eternal and never changing, but the evidence that much of it is socially constructed is difficult to deny. The gay rights crusade is a case in point.

Consider how this new moral entitlement has risen from nowhere to dominate many political discussions. The steps in this evolution are classic. They provide a vivid example of moral entrepreneurship at its creative best.

The first step to establishing a moral right is to affirm it. People who want a novel entitlement to be socially accepted must begin by asserting it. They must proclaim loudly, and energetically, that it is an eternal verity. It does not matter whether anyone has previously entertained the idea as long as they insist it is a universal truth.

Next, they must demonize the opposition. Those who disagree with them must be portrayed as the essence of evil. Only their vile, mean-spirited natures could prompt them to deny so valid a claim. If need be, they must be punished to provide an example of what happens to villains.

As part of this process, the pain and suffering endured by the purported victims must be highlighted and driven home. In the case of gay marriage, individual couples whose love has been crushed by the bigotry of the mob need to be offered up as object lessons as to why we need this new right.

In moral negotiations—for that is what these are—the objective is to elicit sympathy for one's own side, while simultaneously arousing loathing for the other. The goal is to convert as many as people as possible to one's own viewpoint.

If all goes well, a bandwagon effect will have been fashioned. The fact that one's allies are increasing in number will then influence the uncommitted to join what seems to be the winning side. As s result, one's own position will become dominant and the new right will have been established.

President Barack Obama's coming out of the closet to support gay marriage was part of this momentum building process. He, and those who agree with him, hope that it will nail down a majority so sizeable that henceforth no one will consider supporting their competitors.

Because rights exist, when, and only when, overwhelming numbers of people subscribe to them, in having swung popular opinion in their favor, the gay marriage advocates will have achieved their objective. What had not been a right will, by virtue of their political efforts, have become one.

That said, the game is still in progress. It is in the interest of the pro-gay marriage faction to portray their victory as inevitable, but it is not. The perception that it is, is itself part of the process of trying to recruit as many people as possible to their side.

Shameless

Bill Clinton taught me an important lesson. This occurred during the Monica Lewinski scandal. Even after the stained dress came to light, our president insisted that he had not had sex with "that woman." What was more impactful, however, was the way that he said it.

Clinton went before the American people without a shred of shame. Whereas most men would have been embarrassed to have been caught with their pants down in the oval office, he acted as if nothing untoward had happened.

Monica might have been an intern and he the president, but what was the problem?

Contrast this with Richard Nixon. Once the tapes began trickling out, he went before the public to declare that he was not a crook. This didn't work, in large part, because Nixon looked as if he had done something unethical. Unlike Clinton, who would laugh things off, Nixon could not hide his discomfort.

What lesson does this impart? It is this. People conclude that someone has done something shameful not just from the act, but from the way that he (or she) responds to exposure. If a person does not appear to be ashamed, that is, is shameless, it is generally assumed that there must have been nothing to be humiliated about.

Most people, when caught in a lie, become red-faced. They begin stumbling over their words and would like nothing better than to disappear from sight. The shameless, in comparison, are bold. They greet ridicule and skepticism with confidence—and even humor.

Barack Obama is a master of this tactic. Hence when he was embroiled in the IRS scandal, he did not run away or become flustered. Instead he brazenly told the public that there was not a smidgeon of corruption—and then he chuckled. Nor, when he lied about ObamaCare, did he feel compelled to apologize for his deceit.

So well does this strategy work that it has become an integral part of contemporary politics. Now that we are in the middle of the political silly season, shamelessness has become as common as cold weather in winter. Candidates on both sides of the aisle are obviously addicted to it.

Consider Hillary Clinton. She learned her trade at the foot of a master. Hence when she is asked about her server or the top secret e-mails that she sent or received, she insists that she is one hundred percent sure that she will not be indicted. And then she gives her patented horse whinny.

The trouble is that although she is shameless, she is not effortlessly so. Altogether too loud and adamant, she does not sound innocent. Nor, with her face thrust forward in a feminine imitation of General Patton, does she look innocent.

Donald Trump is much better at this sort of audacity. For example, he can stand before an audience and boast about having gone into bankruptcy four times. Not once does he allude to the people who lost their jobs or the creditors who were cheated. These fiascoes are all about him and how he came out with his fortune intact.

Nor did having lost in Iowa embarrass him. Despite his initial modesty, he quickly reverted to form and insisted that he had won after all. Clearly, the Donald is never a loser—even when he loses. Indeed, if need be he will cover up a defeat with vulgarity.

Of course, Trump is not alone. Cruz, Christie, and Bush have all been caught in whoppers that they pretend are truths. While some of these are more brazen than others, nowadays political expediency evidently demands a large measure of shamelessness.

So who is at fault? Although the politicians are obviously not choirboys, the real guilt—dear Brutus—lies with us. If we, the American public, cannot see through this lack of integrity, we will continue to get what we deserve. If we allow ourselves to be fooled, wouldn't some of the candidates be fools not to try to deceive us?

Who then should be feeling shame?

Self-Righteousness

A couple of weeks ago, when I attended the annual meeting of the Georgia Sociological Association, I ran into a familiar challenge. It was discouraging, but not overwhelming. Don't get me wrong; I love the organization and most of its members. Nevertheless my colleagues left-leaning attitudes can be discomfiting.

Let me explain. This year I came in a bit late to a workshop on applied sociology. Those in the room were already discussing the best ways to bring social activism into the classroom. For them, this meant figuring out how to promote social justice.

Perhaps I should have kept my mouth shut, but this is not my style. All too often, I am a provocateur. And so I raised my hand and suggested that many liberals tend to be self-righteous. In doing so, it was as if I had thrown a bomb into their midst.

All of a sudden everyone rose to his or her feet to tell me I was wrong. The decibel level rose to unseemly heights for an academic gathering, as I was vigorously instructed about the error of my ways.

My response was that the vociferousness of their reaction proved my point. Had they not felt threatened by the potential truth of my words, they would not have been as emotionally aroused.

Of course, no one heard what I said. They were too busy making certain that I was not allowed to continue my remarks. In other words, self-righteous people do not want to be confronted with their self-righteousness. Just check-out the mainstream press.

In sociology, the left-leaning consensus is so all-encompassing that people regularly expect their opinions to be reinforced. So frequently is this the case that they regard dissent as evidence of a mental shortcoming.

Mind you, most of us think we are right. We do not welcome criticism because we are sure it is undeserved. Whether we are liberal or conservative, we would not believe what we do if we did not assume it was correct.

Nevertheless, there are degrees of certitude. Some people are far more rigid in their viewpoints than others. As it happens, many liberals and progressives are today especially inflexible in their perspectives. They seldom brook principled disagreement.

To hear some leftists tell it, they are never wrong. Whenever one of their programs fails to live up to the advance billing, they blame it on the opposition. Whether this pertains to the economy, foreign affairs, or Obamacare, it is conservatives who obviously prevented success.

As far as these progressives are concerned, every social problem is created by privileged oppression. Some elite group has selfishly harmed the poor, minorities or women. The proper corrective is therefore to counteract these bad guys. Often this entails purging of them from the community.

Those, who are so convinced, are blind to the myriad complications of human endeavors. They do not see the subtleties. Be they proponents of social justice or religious fundamentalism, they cannot accept alternate explanations.

Oliver Crowell, when he was disputing with the Scottish Presbyterians, declared "I beseech thee, in the bowels of Christ, think you may be mistaken." Of course, his opponents came to no such conclusion. The result was a war that left Scotland badly damaged.

Crowell, on the other hand, although he could be stiff-necked, was frequently prepared to modify his course as the circumstances demanded. This made him effective on the battlefield and in Parliament.

Being ready to imagine that others have a valid point is essential to correcting our errors. We don't have to agree with these folks, but there is generally a reason they believe as they do. Being prepared to recognize this often enables us to see where our own position might be strengthened.

Nowadays the extent of our collective confusions is such that our anxieties have stimulated a rash of moralistic posturing. Many of us are not sure of the answers so we conceal our discomfort by pretending that we know everything anyone needs to know. This is a dangerous form of self-delusion.

Strong people can accept their limitations. They can live with their inability to understand or control events. This furnishes them with the flexibility to roll with the punches. Too bad political suppleness is currently in short supply.

When Good Meets Bad

Many years ago, when I was seeking tenure at Kennesaw State University, one of my colleagues promised to help me in this process. She would coach me on what was required and put in a good word on my behalf. I was grateful and looked forward to a long academic career.

But then I hit a stumbling block. On an early level of approval, I was turned down. This came as a shock. My teaching evaluations were good. My level of service was above average. What was more, I was the only member of our department who had written any books. How could this have happened?

Not long after I discovered that the colleague who had pledged to be of assistance had actually written an evaluation that torpedoed my application. This was so surprising that I confronted her to seek an explanation. At this point, she told me that I was "just not fitting in."

When I asked why she had mischaracterized my achievements, she made several demonstrably untrue claims. By now I was in a state of disbelief. Here was someone I had trusted lying to my face. This could not be. No decent human would do any such thing.

At this point I decided to shut up. Suddenly I realized that a purported friend was an enemy. All I could think of at the time was that it would be unwise to give her further ammunition.

Why have I chosen to write about this now? It is because I see a similar scenario working out on a larger scale. The American people have been made numerous promises by liberal politicians. They were told they would be given social justice, and economic prosperity, as well as hope and change.

When this did not unfold as expected, liberals were on the spot. How were they to explain why their assurances fell flat? Honesty would not have worked. Voters wouldn't have been placated by an admission that liberal policies were misconceived and incompetently executed.

And so they lied. And then they lied some more. They accused everyone and sundry of malfeasance. It was those darned Republicans. They were scoundrels to the nth degree. They were intent on sabotaging programs that would save the nation from ruin.

Now that Donald Trump is president and pledges to undo their handiwork, the lefties have gone apoplectic. They have not only doubled their lies, they have quadrupled them and then quadrupled them again. These are no deceptions they are unwilling to propagate.

Trump is said not to have done anything as president when he has done more in a month than his predecessors. He is accused of undermining the constitution, when it is liberal justices who did so. His administration is described as chaotic, when Senate Democrats even denied him his cabinet.

The problem is this. Decent Americans do not know how to handle a blizzard of lies. For the most part honest, like me they are discombobulated by bald-faced fictions. They cannot believe that anyone would do such a thing.

Decent liberals are especially in a quandary. As good people, they cannot imagine that their allies might be bad. Good people expect others to be equally good. When their friends say they are trying to do the right thing, their first impulse is to support them.

And so many liberals believe that the accusations aimed at Trump must be true. He has to be an anti-democratic tyrant, otherwise their fellow liberals would not have said so. He must be a racist, sexist bully or they would not have made the allegation.

But liars are liars. The fact that Trump is condemned even before he does anything is evidence that his detractors care nothing for realities. Their goal is to bring down a hated foe. The rest of us must understand this. We need to see past the over-heated rhetoric to their actual motives.

This is especially the case for good liberals. They need to be honest with themselves and true to the ideals they have hitherto maintained. Our democratic principles ought not to be immolated on the funeral pyre of a lost election.

The Extremism Ploy

Suppose you wanted to radically remake America. Suppose you intended to undermine our democratic institutions and replace them with a centralized autocracy. How would you go about it? What would you do to convince ordinary citizens that this was in their interest?

Further suppose that a major political party opposed to your agenda. Add to this the fact that most Americans are moderate. They do not like radical practices. How would you get a majority of these folks to ignore your own extremism?

Liberals have, in fact, found several ways to achieve this end. Thus, for years they sought to discredit conservatives by labeling them "extremists." The idea was to frighten ordinary citizens into believing those protecting their heritage were actually wild-eyed revolutionaries.

It didn't matter what conservatives supported. Whatever it was, was portrayed as alarming. Did they want to roll back ObamaCare? Why this would leave millions of people dying an agonizing death on our streets. Did they wish to send criminal aliens back home? This would surely break up families and leave children wailing in misery.

The latest iterations of the extremism charge have, of course, been hurled at president Donald Trump. With his shock of yellow tinted hair and podium gesticulations, he is a Hollywood casting director's dream of what a political hooligan might look like.

And so not only do we hear him accused of extremism directly. We also hear it said that he wants to dismantle the First Amendment. He is obviously against free speech and freedom of the press. Given that he is a racist, sexist lout, the only way he can get to torture the weak and helpless is by removing their constitutional protections.

This attack strategy is of ancient vintage. The original progressives used it against the robber barons. Franklin Roosevelt trotted it out against business leaders. Barry Goldwater was accused of wanting to start a nuclear war. Ronald Reagan evidently hoped to do the same.

Now it is Trump's turn to get the wild man treatment. Somehow it is extreme to tell a federal judge that he made a mistake in blocking a presidential order. Obama railed against many Supreme Court decisions, but Trump cannot be allowed to describe a liberal magistrate as a "so-called" judge. That is an intemperate strike on the separation of powers.

Nor can Trump accuse journalists of dishonesty. When he calls them out for months of fake news, this is obviously an assault on the press itself. By now everybody with half a brain knows the mainstream media are deeply biased, but their minions still pose as aggrieved innocents.

As for sending criminal aliens home, what could be more vicious? Closing our borders is anti-democratic. It is an outrageous attempt to deny the third world under class the benefits of American largesse. Nice countries build bridges, not walls.

The extremism poly is therefore one more liberal con-job. It has been repeated so often, from so many mouths, that it has begun to sound like a self-evident truth. In reality, it turns the facts on their head. It is liberals who are the extremists. It is they who want to undo the constitution and substitute a benign despotism for our democratic institutions.

Getting rid of private medicine and placing it under federal control; that was extreme. Enticing millions of Americans onto the dole; that was extreme. Reducing public schools to dumbed down propaganda vehicles; that was extreme. Regulating mud puddles on family farms; that was extreme.

Freedom, as they say, is not free. It has to be defended with our blood and treasure. But is also has to be defended against deception and manipulation. The extremism ploy is just one more way to persuade us to let down our guard. It must thus be seen for what it is and rejected out of hand.

Goldwater said that extremism in defense of freedom is no vice. But neither is it extremism. It is common sense. The American Dream was once decried as a menace to civilized society. We Americans ought not be complicit in propagating this canard.

Unconditional Moral Surrender

I do not like Barack Obama. I was reminded of how much I dislike him when Mitt Romney recently reappeared in public. Here was a decent, and competent, human being who was rejected in favor of a moral pygmy. For reasons I cannot fathom, the American people preferred four more years of lies, manipulation, and bankruptcy to him.

Now I know this is harsh. But the time has come to be harsh. Once more our president has revealed his true nature. In order to gain political advantage, he has knowingly chosen to injure our nation. Even school children are fair game for his destructive impulses.

Everyone in Washington understands that Barack chose to close the White House to visitors in order to demonstrate how damaging budget cuts would be. They likewise know that he instructed his underlings to find other unnecessary cutbacks in other agencies as well.

This has been called the Washington Monument ploy in that it is a very visible way to arouse public ire. Shut down the Washington Monument, or the White House, and ordinary Americans will demand that something be done—such as rescinding the budget sequester.

To engage in this sort of deception, even when knowledgeable observers see it for what it is, is the height of cynicism. It is to treat the American people as if they are mentally defective. But then again, the American people have swallowed so many lies over the last four years that Obama had reason to believe he could get away with this maneuver.

A cardinal doctrine of contemporary liberalism is that we must accord everyone "unconditional positive regard." Whatever they do, we must not be too critical. To do so might harm their self-esteem. And so we must let others know that we love them, even though we do not like what they did.

Well, I am a little bit more old-fashioned than that. When you shoot me in the foot, I do not say thank you, may I have another. When I know that you have intentionally sought to injure me, I do not give you positive, but negative regard. In other words, I am furious with you!

Now some people might characterize this reaction as cruel, whereas I consider it appropriate. Morality exists only when people uphold moral conduct. When they tolerate immoral behavior on the grounds that condemning it might make the perpetrator feel bad, they are actually condoning it.

Taken literally "unconditional positive regard" is tantamount to "unconditional moral surrender." If bad behavior can never be called out for what it is, this is the equivalent of moral abdication. It is to do nothing in the face of wickedness, thereby compounding it.

So I am calling out Barack Obama. I have done so before, and no doubt will do so again. Nor am I alone. This latest piece of presidential mischief may have been a bridge too far. Many other voices have also been raised to object to his transparent manipulation.

The question is, How long will this displeasure last? Will the American people relent when subjected to another charm offensive? Will they agree that the president is basically a nice man and therefore we should be nice to him?

The trouble is that Obama is not nice. He may have a nice smile and a persuasive line of patter, but his actions are not those of a man who is concerned with the well being of the people dependent upon him. He talks a good game, but then he sticks a knife under the rib.

Morality cannot exist when people close their eyes to immorality. It is in particular jeopardy when people consent to corruption in the name of morality. Yes, I have been mean to Barack Obama, but he richly deserves it. And so I will desist only when he changes his ways—although I am not expecting this anytime soon.

Of Liberals, Horse Whisperers, and Human Nature

By now the lesson should have sunk in. The examples set by the horse and dog whisperers should have entered the liberal consciousness, but have not Although the model provided by these animal trainers is much admired in liberal circles, its insights are not applied to human beings.

The horse whisperers, for instance, counsel that horses are prey animals. As such, they are hard-wired to be alert to potential predators. This means that a trainer must avoid looking directly at a horse's eyes lest he be confused with a wolf. Dog whisperers similarly advise that dogs are pack animals and hence dog owners should set themselves up as pack leaders.

Both of these sorts of trainers understand that their subjects are particular sorts of animal. They know that they are genetically programmed to exhibit certain behaviors, but not others. As a result, they operate within these limits.

Liberals, in contrast, seem to imagine that people are completely plastic. Therefore, when they recommend political or economic reforms, they let their imaginations run wild. As long as they can conceive of a particular social program, they assume they can impose it.

Thus, they think they can oblige everyone to love everyone else. They also believe they can impose complete equality. Both of these goals are parts of the Liberal Dream; nonetheless both are contrary to human nature.

And there is a human nature. Violate it and no matter how elevated an ambition, it cannot be realized. As a consequence, promises to implement the impossible eventually fall to the ground unfulfilled. Having aroused unsustainable hopes, they breed cynicism not contentment.

This scenario also applies to another aspect of the Liberal Dream. Liberals believe that once they establish universal love and complete equality, people will be able to flourish as never before. They will become "self-actualizing" individuals who personally achieve their highest aspirations.

This philosophy as infiltrated public education systems to such an extent that they produce ever more ignorant graduates. According to progressive education (i.e., liberal education), learning must always be fun. Students must be allowed to choose what they want to learn, while teachers must encourage them to be their highest selves.

This sounds like it allows students to be themselves, whereas it merely permits them to remain uninformed. We human beings are biologically programmed to learn; including many very difficult lessons. This means that working hard is also part of our nature.

Indeed, one of the things that separates us from other animals is the length of our childhoods. These extend for many years because there is so much to be soaked up. Part of this, it is true, is learned through play, but part must be acquired by conscious effort.

Nowadays, with the emphasis on play, too many students refuse to read books if they are difficult. They would rather engage in computer games or go on Facebook.

Accordingly, the self they actualize is simpleminded and incompetent. They never become the self-motivated experts required by a techno-commercial society because it has falsely been assumed that learning and personal growth are automatic.

A modern middle class society depends on personal responsibility, but a sense of responsibility takes effort to develop. This is dictated by the ways our minds and emotions work. Human nature is such that we can create the complex behavioral repertoires upon which we rely only dedicating many years to doing so.

One more reason the Liberal Dream is dying is thus that it does not acknowledge this simple fact. It takes for granted that people will inevitably become what they must in order to sustain our current prosperity, this is, if the proper social conditions are provided.

This is wrong on two counts. First, liberals cannot furnish the love and equality they promise. And second, even it they could, responsible competence takes years of genuine effort to achieve.

Power Corrupts
A few weeks ago, my wife and I attended the annual meeting of the Georgia Sociological Association. One of the presenters there was a political scientist from Armstrong-Atlantic. He posed an interesting question. Can a Marxist or a neo-Marxist government avoid becoming tyrannical?

This professor did not fully answer the question, yet he, and we in the audience, were aware that Communist Russia, Red China, North Korea, Eastern Europe, Pol Pot's Cambodia and Fidel's Cuba had all fallen into this trap. Each proclaimed its noble aspirations, then proceeded to snuff out any vestiges of democracy.

Was there something about a collectivist ideology that produced this result? While we at the meeting did not come to a final conclusion, there was a rough consensus that concentrating too much power in the hands of a few leaders probably had something to do with the usual outcome.

Marxism, communism, socialism, and even to some degree social democracy all advocate that the state must protect people from social unfairness. The government is supposed to see to it that no one gets a better break than anyone else. Under Marxism there is to be a dictatorship of the proletariat, whereas under socialism the state is to own the means of production.

Social democracy does not go this far. It merely demands that the government regulate virtually all economic transactions, as well as protect individuals from their own foolish choices.

Barack Obama is a social democrat. Not quite a socialist, he wants the government to oversee and regulate virtually all medical interventions, all financial transactions, and every potential environmental incursion. He also wants to increase transfer payments from the rich to the poor, usually by raising taxes and increasing welfare benefits.

These activities are undertaken in the name of the people. The best and the brightest, which is to say the liberals, are to implement the equivalent of Jean-Jacques Rousseau's General Will. They are to provide what the people really want—even if the people themselves do not know it.

The trouble is that all such programs must be put into practice by actual human beings and that we humans are corruptible. As Lord Acton warned, power tends to go to the heads of people who attain too much of it. Liberals understand that this is true for business tycoons; they fail to recognize that it is also true for politicians and bureaucrats.

The Obamacare debacle is a prime example. Politicians infatuated with their compassionate instincts bit off more than they could chew. Utterly incompetent when it came to organizing so immense an enterprise, they jumped into it feet first anyway.

So far the Internet run-out has proved a complete fiasco. Much too expensive, crony-ridden, ill-conceived, and subject to the usual cover-ups, it forecasts what is likely to be the equally inept execution of the program itself.

Mark my words. ObamaCare is sure to be rifled with favorit-ism, multiple hands in the cookie jar, fraud, dishonest evaluations of performance, broken promises, and budget over-runs that would make a convict blush.

While I am sure that some of the people involved in this mess really do have good intentions, imbuing them with so much power is an invitation to arrogance and duplicity. People who imagine themselves to be Gods on Earth somehow find a way to rationalize their mistakes and to overreach their abilities.

Power is a potent narcotic. It distorts the way people under its influence perceive reality and seduces them into over-estimating their capacities. From their perspective they are merely doing good when they send counter-revolutionaries to the Gulag or impose the medical insurance policies citizens must buy.

James Madison understood the temptations inherent in power. He realized that we humans are not angels and that we must be restrained from going overboard. That is why he gave us a constitution in which powers are balanced by competing powers. We would do well to remember why he did.

Do We Need a Secular Great Awakening?

I cannot tell you how many times I have heard it. By now it is so many that I have lost count.

Nonetheless almost every time the subject of politics comes us, some student tells me that all politicians lie. Then someone else generally adds, "Everyone lies and everyone cheats." At this, I am inevitably confronted with a chorus of nodding heads.

Today's young adults are remarkably cynical. Their convention wisdom has it that almost no one can be trusted. Even when they get caught cheating, they brazenly defend themselves by asserting that this is what everyone does. It is merely the sensible way of getting ahead.

Of course, when I was younger dishonesty was also a problem. Indeed, Billy Joel wrote a song bemoaning the fact that honesty is hardly ever found. Nowadays, however, the acceptance of dishonesty has grown to epic proportions. Just how widespread was demonstrated in the recent election.

Even so, no large-scale society can survive if its members cannot trust one another. Strangers must bestow confidence on those upon whose services they depend lest they perish in their separate hovels.

Once trust becomes problematic, we get the turmoil currently on display in the Middle East. People turn on one another so violently that the only persons they can rely on are members of their own families. They certainly cannot trust politicians.

The United States has largely been spared this fate. With the massive exception of the Civil War and its aftermath, Americans have believed in the dependability of their fellow Americans.

Much of this owes to several historic crusades. Although most contemporaries are unaware of them, the first two Great Awakenings shaped the moral landscape of our nation. Taking place in the eighteenth and nineteenth centuries, these religious revivals encouraged personal rectitude. –And they succeeded.

The first Great Awakening introduced Methodism to America and with it came calls for people to live honest lives. The second Great Awakening reaffirmed this commitment, but also sparked the temperance, suffrage, and abolitionist movements. Evangelists literally crisscrossed the country preaching these virtues to huge crowds.

Today, however, the fires of religious enthusiasm have been banked. Like it or not, we have become a secular nation. This too was demonstrated in the recent election. It revealed that the evangelicals were neither as numerous nor as enthusiastic as necessary to elect the person they favored.

This secular trend is also visible in my Kennesaw State University classrooms. Even though the school is in the heart of what used to be called The Bible Belt, when I ask students how many of them are Protestants, no more than two or three claim they are.

Asked, however, if any are Baptists or Methodists, now the hands go up. In other words, these Protestants do not realize they are Protestants. Nor are they cognizant of the particular dogmas of their denominations. While they typically believe in God, their faith is diffuse and not very deep.

If this is correct, then a new religious revival cannot be expected to generate the same results as the earlier exemplars. Yet we may need something similar. Hopefully there are moral principles to which both religious and secular individuals can strive to realize—that is, once reminded of them.

It would also be nice if one of these principles were honesty. Over the last several days I have been speaking to liberals and conservatives alike about our current impasse. While they don't agree on much, one of the things that unites them is a recognition of how dishonest our public discourse has become.

Naturally, fervent partisans view the truth differently. Still, there are truths out there upon which most of us can agree if we have the integrity, and the diligence, to examine things as they are—not merely as we would like them to be. Yes, the truth can hurt, but falsehoods hurt even more.

In Praise of Foresight

Forgive me if I have used the following illustration before, but in the light of our current political situation it seems particularly germane.

As it happens, World War II came to an end just as I turned four. At the time, my family was on vacation in the Catskill Mountains. Coincident with this, my uncle Milton, who had recently returned home after having served with Patton's army, came to spend the day with us.

Having never seen me before, he decided to take me for a walk down a country road. Concerned for my welfare, on several occasions he asked if I had grown tired and wished to return to the guesthouse where we were staying. Each time I replied that I was not and that we could keep going.

Eventually, however, I asked if we could turn around. At this, he once more inquired into whether I was tired and I again responded by telling him that I was not. But then I added that I would be by the time we got back.

My uncle was so impressed with my foresight that he subsequently told this tale many times. He was especially astonished that a child so young could think so clearly into the future. Today I am retelling this story because I am equally astonished by the degree to which adult voters are currently refusing to use foresight regarding the upcoming presidential election.

Let me begin with the Democrats. How is it possible that biologically adult human beings can fail to understand the implications of a national debt that threatens to reduce us to a large-scale version of Greece? With the example of the European financial meltdown before our eyes, how can voters ignore the potential consequences for our children and grandchildren?

Yet instead of reducing government expenditures, the Democrats have decided to engage in class warfare. In the hopes of getting reelected, they have decided that this short-term gain is worth courting long-term disaster. Even worse, they have decided to enrich themselves and their political allies while this catastrophe unfolds.

The Republicans, however, are little better. They may understand that payoffs to the unions, political contributors, and crony capitalists are a recipe for national bankruptcy, but they do not seem serious about replacing the current administration with a more responsible one.

Over the past several months we have witnessed numerous polls revealing an electorate that is operating more like a pack of lemmings than a collection of serious decision-makers. Instead of looking forward to determine who can best solve our shared problems, people have shifted their loyalty from one crowd favorite to another.

Today Newt Gingrich has surged to the head of the pack. People love his feisty debate performances, but why aren't they thinking ahead to the sort of presidential candidate he would make, or, more importantly, the sort of president he would be?

While Newt makes a good showing against fellow Republicans when standing together on a common stage, what will happen if he shares this venue with Obama? Rest assured, Barack will take the gloves off. He won't be reluctant to point out Gingrich's flip-flops, or to condemn his lobbying efforts, or to impugn his character.

There is a reason that the president's campaign managers would rather run against Newt than Mitt Romney. They, at least, have the sense to realize that Gingrich is vulnerable on many counts. A flawed human being and politician, Newt makes a tempting target—however much he declares his eagerness to mix-it-up in debate.

And as to his becoming president, here the past is the best predictor of the future. Don't people remember how hated Newt was when he was Speaker of the House? Back then, just as now, he wrangled with reporters. The difference is that back then he did it virtually every day and that the reporters returned his contempt in kind.

Can you imagine this sort of contention if Gingrich gets elected? Not only would the electorate that put him in office soon come to loath him, but the wheels of government would quickly grind to a halt. With all of the in-fighting, there would be precious little problem solving—to the continued detriment of nation.

Gingrich may have big ideas, but if they are only verbal flourishes that are never translated into effective action, what good will they do us?

The Perfection Trap

About three decades ago when I first attempted to write a book, I ran in to trouble. No matter how hard I tried, I couldn't seem to get past the opening ten pages. These never lived up to my expectations; hence I always wound up putting them aside—never to be completed.

Eventually, however, I got fed up with this self-defeating perfectionism. Thus, instead of stopping at page eleven, I decided to keep going. As a result, I completed a manuscript, albeit not one that satisfied my hopes. That's when I made a profound discovery. I now realized that what I wrote also had to be edited.

Indeed, over the years I have learned that writing is more about rewriting, than instant excellence. One's prose can always be improved and ideas can always be refined. Even after a work is published, improvements are possible.

As it happens, these days people come to me for advice on how to write. But of them, only one has actually written several books. The others generally find that what they put on paper does not match their imagination and they stop. In the end, they join the multitude who believe there is a book in them that never sees the light of day.

Today, a similar penchant for perfectionism has reached its toxic tendrils into politics. To be more specific, Newt Gingrich has accused Mitt Romney of creating a venture capital company that ruined the lives of thousands. Gingrich, and his minions, assure us that Bain Capital was not nearly as successful as Romney claims.

By now, Newt's anti-capitalist rants have been thoroughly discredited (as have those of Rick Perry), but there is more to this mischief than deceitfulness or economic illiteracy. It has also added a fresh layer of juvenile thinking to the acid bath of contemporary politics.

According to Newt, it would be enough to condemn Romney if a handful of the companies in which Bain invested went belly-up. This would presumably demonstrate that Mitt is not compassionate. Never mind, if most of his ventures succeeded; he would still be an economic predator. (Or, as Perry has it, a "vulture" capitalist.)

What this implies is a need for perfectionism. Any mistake, irrespective of how modest, is magnified until it is perceived as a wart that covers the target's entire face. He (or she) is thus distilled down to the essence of a few missteps.

In fact, Bain Capital was wildly successful. It did far better in its investments than most of its rivals. Yet, it too had failures. Many of Newt's examples are bogus, but not everything Romney and his partners touched turned to gold.

The question is—so what? If we were all required to be perfect all of the time, no books would ever be written, no buildings would ever rise from the ground, and no seeds would ever push their way up through the soil to become nourishing ears of corn. Life would come to a standstill, with everyone afraid to put one foot before another.

Actually, the effects of perfectionism run amok are currently on display in Washington. After all, hasn't Barack Obama promised us the world and then assured us he fulfilled his word? Didn't he, for instance, pledge to save or create millions of jobs—and then deliver?

No, wait! There may be some cynics who remain unconvinced of our president's ability to create jobs. These people have obviously not been listening to Obama's recitations regarding his numerous achievements. By his lights, these have made him the fourth most productive president of all time.

For those who remain in doubt, my real the point is that people who promise perfection can only sustain this illusion by making claims of success that are as fraudulent as their initial guarantees. Perfectionism is never in the cards; hence those who deal in it are forced to be disingenuous.

When politics refuses to make allowances for human fallibility, when it instead stoops to adolescent idealism, it bars the door to genuine advances. To make the perfect the enemy of the good, as I did before I learned to write reasonably well, or as Newt has done in ridiculing Bain Capital, is to preclude actual improvements.

This stance embraces fantasies over facts. Sadly, if too many of us adopt it, it will be to our eternal sorrow.

Equality vs. Universalism

A few weeks ago a liberal colleague of mine at Kennesaw State University e-mailed me a short, short story. This was Kurt Vonnegutt's 1961 tale "Harrison Bergeron." I had never seen it before—and it was a revelation.

The story begins "The year was 2081, and everyone was finally equal. They weren't only equal before God and the law. They were equal every which way." Apparently this equality had been mandated by two amendments to the Constitution and was enforced by a "Handicapper General."

Much as horses are handicapped by requiring the most fleet to carry extra pounds on their backs, so people who were smarter than average wore an earpiece that disrupted their thoughts, those who were physically stronger had weights dangling from their muscles, and those who were especially beautiful wore masks to cover their attractiveness.

The reason for this, of course, was that just as some horses are born to be faster than others, some humans are born with superior attributes. The only way to make them equal in every respect was therefore to reduce the advantages of the lucky ones.

Furthermore, because it was impossible to improve the abilities of the less fortunate to such a degree that they matched their betters, all had to be diminished to the lowest common denominator. Even mediocrity would be too exalted if everyone was to be completely equal.

If this sounds absurd, please understand that many liberals desire not an equality of opportunity, or an equality before the law, but an equality of results. This is why they would confiscate the resources of the rich and transfer them to the poor. It is why they institute programs to "empower" the less affluent.

Were this just a left liberal penchant, this proclivity might simply be amusing. Unfortunately, these radicals have been able to convince a sufficient number of voters that this sort of social engineering is essential to create "social justice." They even claim that it is built into the Declaration of Independence.

Needless to say, this is a canard. Jefferson told us that we were endowed with equal rights, not that we were, or ever could become, completely equal. Indeed, in his other writings he advocated an "aristocracy of merit."

So what I propose is that in order to reduce this confusion we start talking about "universality" rather than equality. Universality means that all rules are applied equally to everyone irrespective of social status. No one gets an authorized advantage because of race, ethnicity, gender, social class, or sexual orientation.

Were this standard respected, no individuals would get admitted to college with lesser credentials because of skin color, no woman would be hired for a job because there was a quota for females, and no rich person would have to pay more for the same services as a poor one.

This may sound like a peculiar way to do business, but my students at KSU understand it very well. Were I to award a higher grade to someone just because she was my cousin, they would be outraged. If her work were not up to snuff, they would expect me to grade her accordingly.

Moreover, this seems to me to be the essence of democracy. Democracy is not just "one person, one vote," but a parity in social standards. We do not bow down before aristocrats; we do not kiss the rings of the rich. Even Alexis de Tocqueville, a century and a half ago, noted that Americans did not treat anyone as deserving special advantages because of his/her social position.

This was something to be proud of then; it is something to be proud of now. The United States has assimilated people from around the world—and should continue to do so. But it should do so on the basis of universalism, not an equality of results. Indeed, it is only by being honestly universal that we will induct them into being honestly democratic.

Courage for Modern Times
"I have always thought of myself as a coward." That is the opening line of my new book *Unlocking Your Inner Courage*. I go on to explain what a frightened little boy I was. I talk, for instance, about sitting in the corner of our Brooklyn apartment afraid to go outside. I also describe how my little sister learned to swim before I did.

Not long ago, I ran into a colleague who reviewed the book for the publisher. He began our conversation by asking if it could be true. Had I really been a coward when I was younger? From his experience, he could not imagine that this was the case.

Actually nowadays very few people doubt my courage. They have seen me in action. They know that I am prepared to stand up for what I believe, at any time, against any one. Moreover, as a conservative sociologist and academic, I am always exposed to criticism—some of it vicious. Yet here I stand with my head unbowed.

What happened? How did I go from being the proverbial ninety-pound weakling to a formidable character? Although I am still not a big person and do not relish putting myself in physical danger, on a social level almost nothing today terrifies me.

The changeover came slowly and for many years I did not realize it had occurred. But decades of working as a clinician and even more years of self-analysis taught me important lessons. Still, it was only recently that I decided that I had acquired insights that were worthy enough to share.

What tipped the scale was looking around and realizing that many other folks are more timid than me. Like most people, I was aware of my own limitations. Yet because others did not display their fears, I did not appreciate how profound these could be.

Nor did I recognize how important courage is in our modern era. After all, we are not fighting to open up a wild frontier. Nor have many of us had to cross a dangerous ocean in leaky sailing ships. What then have we to fear with our full bellies, air conditioned homes, and safe suburban neighborhoods?

Nevertheless, we have managed to find bogymen lurking under nearly every sofa. It is not just a few college students who have turned into snowflakes. Many millions of the rest of us melt away when confronted with opinions that differ from our own. As long as like-minded folks surround us we are okay, but let a conservative (or liberal) into the room and we panic.

This is especially unfortunate in that personal courage may be more valuable than ever. Our prosperity has opened up a wide range of possibilities from which we must choose. This has introduced a variety of uncertainties that take daring to confront.

For instance, marriage has become voluntary. We don't marry unless we want to; we don't stay married unless we know how to. Intimacy, as those who have experienced it know, can be scary. People who are emotionally close are able to hurt each other. As a consequence, it takes nerve to get close.

Our more complex occupations also require courage. First, we must choose from an intimidating array of possibilities. Then we must develop the requisite skills. And finally we must make independent decisions in areas of uncertainty. Things can go wrong at any point, which demands a steady hand and clear head.

It even takes courage to recognize what we cannot do. Despite our wealth, we cannot have it all. We cannot fix every problem or make everybody equally happy. Sometimes we must say No, even though we will be castigated for it.

And so a great many of us freak out. We run for the exits—or, more commonly, we look around for a savior. All too often these are politicians who cannot even save themselves. The plain fact is that only we can save ourselves and we can do this only if we have courage.

That is why I wrote my book.

Emotional Maturity

I have recently written columns about *principled realism* and *social individualism*. These were put forward as an antidote to the ideological crisis we are currently experiencing. Yet if liberalism, conservatism, and libertarianism are obsolete, can these alternatives fill the vacuum?

Last week, I spoke about our need for balance. By themselves, none of the old truisms are sufficient for our purposes. None answers all of our questions; nevertheless each supplies wisdom that if supplemented by the others can advance our joint interests.

The trouble is that implementing this balance or my suggested replacements presupposes the existence of a crucial foundation. Ours may have become a mass techno-commercial society in which our affluence offers up a multitude of choices, but we will not be able to take advantage of them without "emotional maturity."

David Goleman authored several books about what he calls "EQ." He compares this *emotional quotient* with IQ, that is, with the intelligence quotient. Both are said to be crucial for social success, but the way he puts it is that IQ will get us a job, whereas EQ is essential for keeping it.

Unless we know how to get along with other humans, we are sure to alienate them. If we can't read people emotionally or control our emotional impulses, we are sure to behave in an off-putting manner. It is, therefore, critical to understand and master our passions.

While Goleman is partial to a comparison between EQ and IQ, I prefer to talk about *emotional maturity*. We are all born with a full complement of affects. Some folks may be more sensitive than others; even so, we all feel fear, anger, guilt, shame, disgust, sadness, and love.

What distinguishes us, however, is how well we learn to use these emotions. They must all be adequately "socialized" if our affects are to be helpful to our adult selves. Were we to experience and deploy them the way that children do, we would be in enormous peril. Our social life would, in fact, come to a grinding halt.

To illustrate, we all get angry. Yet how we get angry differs. An extremely irate infant may literally bite the hand that feeds it. Then again, were an adult to do something comparable, he would probably go to jail. Adults must learn to express their irritation verbally—not physically.

Something similar applies to fear. Adults need to learn the difference between what is dangerous and what is not. Thus, while a ceiling fan might startle a baby, a teenager should be able to take this in stride. The teenager should also have learned to cross a busy street by looking both ways.

Strong emotions must be controlled or they revert to their infantile forms. Without self-discipline, people behave inappropriately. They get angry when they shouldn't. They get frightened when they ought not. Worse still, they lash out when they should keep silent or run away when they should stand and fight.

This is what I mean by emotional maturity. It is not something we are born with, but something we develop. Unlike IQ, it is a competence that we acquire. All of us are able to learn how to be less afraid. All of us can discover how to get angry without throwing a tantrum.

What is more, unless we do, we cannot engage in principled realism. We would instead be so terrified by reality that we hid under a bushel-basket of fantasies. We would also be so enraged by our frustrations that we immorally injured those who got in our way.

Social individualism is correspondingly impractical in the absence of emotional maturity. We would not be able to make wise choices because we did not recognize, or honor, our limitations. We would, in fact, be too busy pretending that we should get everything we desire.

Unfortunately, emotional maturity is currently in short supply. We see this in politics. We see it in the media. We see it in our entertainments. Everywhere we look, childishness is in full bloom. Not only is it ubiquitous; it is celebrated as energetic and optimistic.

Too bad, because in its ignorance and impulsivity, this sort of immaturity is endangering our future. A world that is converted into a puerile sandbox will shortly have all the coherence of a pile of sand.

Genuine Compassion

We hear a lot about compassion nowadays. Liberals are supposed to have it, whereas conservatives are supposedly devoid of it. Theoretically, the former want to help the little guy; whereas the latter are intent on exploiting the vulnerable so that they can line their own pockets.

The problem is that genuine compassion is harder to bestow than it is to express. People may effortlessly brag about how caring they are, but it is an altogether different matter to behave in a caring fashion. Words are cheap; while actions are far more demanding.

Years ago, when I worked in a psychiatric hospital, I watched a succession of earnest young women begin work as helping professionals. They were convinced that they had so much love in their hearts that if they shared this with their patients, these troubled souls were sure to improve.

But then they hit the reality wall. Schizophrenics and other psychotics are, it turns out, difficult to reach. Their mental problems are so severe that they build barriers between themselves and the outside world. This means that love cannot always break through.

This was not only frustrating, but it threatened the self-images of naive helpers. If the love they proffered was not effective, then they were not effective. As a result, most left to pursue more rewarding careers. Only those whose compassion was made of stronger stuff were able to stick it out.

So let's perform a thought experiment. Imagine that you are delegated to help a starving person and you feed him poison. Are you compassionate if you keep feeding him this despite the evidence it is killing him?

If this sounds far-fetched, imagine that you have been delegated to help a poor person. Now further imagine that the assistance you provide makes her poorer and less happy. Although you are furnishing monetary assistance, her living conditions deteriorate and her mental health suffers.

Are you compassionate? You may be attempting to be helpful, but are you constructive? If, in seeking to be compassionate, you do harm and do not desist despite indications of injury, do you care about the person you are purportedly assisting?

Doesn't genuine compassion imply that a person is concerned with the consequences of particular interventions? Doesn't it also mean that a person will continue to provide authentic help, over long periods of time, despite the resistance encountered?

Sympathy, on its own, is not sufficient to be lauded as compassionate. Neither is empathy that is unaccompanied by effective action. Merely feeling another's pain is not benevolent. It may make a person feel morally superior, but does not contribute to concrete improvements.

The reason for this excursion into the nature of compassion is not to make a linguistic point. It is rather to help us understand that political programs intended to help the poor are not compassionate if they do not help the poor. If they keep the disadvantaged destitute and increase their dependency, they are, in fact, unkind.

To repeat, consequences matter. If a healthcare program does not improve the health of the nation, it is not compassionate. If giving people free food does not enhance their nutrition, it is not compassionate. If changes to the criminal justice system do not reduce crime or alternations in the school system do not advance education, they are not compassionate.

Self-congratulatory speeches are no substitute for genuine help. Neither are vituperative recriminations directed at those who champion alternate social strategies. People who care, whatever their ideological preferences, must monitor the impact of their interventions.

Too often people allow their objectives to get ahead of their accomplishments. Just because they believe that a particular form of assistance will have the desired benefit does not ensure that it will. There is, as they say, many a slip betwixt cup and lip.

Genuine compassion is more than a feeling. It is more than an attitude. Genuine compassion implies authentic assistance. It is about what is done for the person helped and not the emotional gratification of the helper.

Self-Discipline

Gesellschaft. It's an unusual word; a word of German origin. It is a word that I did not learn until I took the Graduate Record Exam in Sociology. Nonetheless it is an important word. It is a term that all of us who live in the United States should know.

A Gesellschaft society is a mass society. It is a society that is made up of many thousands, and often millions, of participants. There are so many that most are strangers to one another.

And yet it is also a society in which these strangers are dependent upon one another. Most do not grow their own food, or sew their own clothing, or construct their own homes. They depend upon others to provide these services in exchange for the services they provide.

Members of Gesellschaft communities must therefore be able to count on the reliability of these strangers. They must be confident that these others will furnish what is required. They have to be sure that their food is not tainted and that their automobiles will not fall apart the moment they are driven out of the showroom.

Above all, they must be certain that they can walk down the street without being molested and that unknown drivers will not suddenly swerve out of their lane on the highway.

This requires that such strangers exercise restraint. They must be so reliably self-disciplined that they do what is expected of them. If they cannot control themselves—without external constraints—the world becomes a dangerous place, with interpersonal cooperation almost impossible.

The consequences for a Gesellschaft community when a significant number of its members do not exhibit self-discipline were in display in Baltimore several weeks ago. There, hundreds, if not thousands, of young men lost control and vandalized their city.

Once the police were withdrawn from the streets, chaos broke out. Without someone to stop them, the rioters could not stop themselves from heaving stones, setting fires, or looting stores. They did not possess the personal controls to keep their anger in check.

Most young people learn these controls in their families of origin. Nonetheless many inner-city young people do not come from traditional two parent homes. They are raised by single mothers who do not have the time, or the physical strength, to keep adolescent males within bounds.

Self-discipline, however, is inculcated by reliable external controls. Children are taught to say please and thank you, and to refrain from stealing their friend's toys, by parents who will not let them get away with such transgressions.

But what happens when unassisted mother's are unable to do this? What are we—as a society—to do when thousands, and perhaps millions, of our children never learn self-discipline?

A Gesellschaft society must impose social order if it is to survive. It cannot allow its members to do whatever they want. The results would be disastrous. Over the long haul such a society would disintegrate into anarchy.

And so we enforce order. That's why we have police forces. They are asked to impose external discipline on persons who do not possess the internal resources to do so. A cop's job is to make sure that the rules are followed by individuals who may not be inclined to honor them.

But what happens when the police become the enemy? If the constituents of the thin blue line are punished for imposing restraints, where will the requisite discipline come from? Probably nowhere.

Young people who do not do what they ought to do must sometimes be forced to. If we assume that everyone in our society possesses the same self-discipline as members of the middle class, all is lost. Our fall will be more precipitous than that of the Roman Empire.

We cannot abandon external controls where self-discipline is absent. Doing so would be a form of social suicide. Sacrificing our police on the altar of a liberal fantasy is a prescription for fatal dis-array.

In Praise of Self-Discipline

Life can be hard. We do not always get what we want. Virtually every day we must pull ourselves together to perform onerous chores and/or refrain from attractive vices. Not everything we do is about having fun or satisfying our momentary whims.

I, for one, do not always enjoy getting up in the morning. I would prefer to lounge in bed daydreaming about the glorious deeds yet to be done. Nor do I want to jump in my car to drive down I 575 so as to teach occasionally reluctant students.

Of course, there are days when I am eager to greet the sun and look forward to a stimulating day. It's just that I have duties to complete however I feel. Like it or not, I need to rev up and get on with business.

Something similar applies to expressing myself. I do not always verbalize what I think. Oftentimes when people behave foolishly, but do not point a finger or declare someone a fool. Rather than start a fight, I keep my sentiments to myself.

This goes double for my relationship with my wife. Although I love her dearly, there are moments were her habits try my patience. Never—and I mean never—do I insult her intelligence or impugn her motives. To the contrary, my goal is to understand her point of view so that we can reconcile our differences.

I am no saint, but like a majority of adults in our mass society I have learned the rudiments of self-discipline. Most of the time, I honor my responsibilities and avoid unnecessary conflicts. Civilized society would be impossible were this not the norm.

In previous columns, I have argued for principled realism. Yet this would be unworkable were we entirely impulsive. If we did not stop to think before we acted, we would seldom adapt our endeavors to unpleasant realities. We would instead blunder ahead breaking the furniture.

As importantly, were we wholly spontaneous, morality would be out of the question. We would injure each other without a second thought by violating the simplest of precepts. In brief, we would lie, cheat, and murder as the spirit moved us.

Nonetheless, self-discipline is now in short supply. When we look to the political scene, we see a president who sometimes cannot prevent himself from tweeting inappropriate comments. We also see his opponents engaging in subversive conduct just so that they can injure him.

Perhaps worst of all, we see national journalists throwing tantrums. In an effort to gain personal attention, they play nonstop gotcha games. No longer do they check out the sources of their scurrilous stories.

In fact, narcissistic intemperance has become common. More of us than previously believe we deserve whatever we desire. The mere fact that we want something provides the warrant for being selfish, inconsiderate, and—yes— stupid. Not just political figures, but ordinary folks look for the easy way out.

As a college professor, I tell my students that if they hope to be successful, they must learn to read, write, and organize their activities. If they do not read, they will not increase their knowledge. If they cannot write, they will be unable to communicate effectively. And if they are disorganized, they will squander their talents.

Nonetheless, many of my students do not read. Academic books are often too dry to be stimulating. Nor do they practice writing. Doing so is more tedious than computer games. Lastly, they are unsystematic. No matter how often I urge them to begin class papers before the end of the term, almost none do.

In fact we are cultivating generation of snowflakes. They cannot control themselves enough to listen to contrary opinions. Rather than reflect on distasteful ideas, they scurry off to safe places or shout down opponents.

In a world as diverse as ours, this is a recipe for disaster. It heralds an inability to arrive at shared conclusions or to prevent internecine warfare. Without self-discipline, we are doomed. Chaos is inevitable when people cannot keep their yearnings in check.

Why then aren't we promoting self-control? Why are we encouraging our young to live for the day and indulge in unbridled egoism?

On Making Mistakes

My father was from the old school. He insisted that whatever I did, I had to get it right from the outset. If I made a mistake, however minor, he would land on me like a ton of bricks. This was evidence of my incompetence and therefore unacceptable.

My father also insisted that I learn from his mistakes. Because he had experience whereas I did not, I was to benefit from his example. When he gave me advice based on his years of living, I was to accept it and put it into immediate action.

Naturally, this rankled. Like most young persons I wanted to control my own destiny. I was not my father and hence I wanted to find my own way. Nonetheless, he was my father and there was a price to pay for defying him.

It therefore took me years to put his demands in perspective. Initially, I became risk averse. If mistakes confirmed my ineptitude, the best way to protect my self-image was to avoid anything new. The tried and true path was the one with which I was acquainted; the one where I recognized the pitfalls.

Eventually I realized that this was a prescription for failure. People who do not venture into unfamiliar territory become their own jailors. They never do things worthy of admiration because they keep themselves from accomplishing anything notable.

In time, I came to understand that the problem was not making mistakes, but failing to learn from them. While it was true that mistakes are to be shunned if possible, this is not always feasible. Exercising foresight and caution makes sense; nevertheless previously untried activities almost invariably hold surprises.

I also came to appreciate that although it is difficult to admit failures, I couldn't correct them if I did not. While it was not always necessary to advertise these to strangers, it was not a good idea to fool myself. This only blinded me to what needed to be done.

Today, I offer this advice to my students as they struggle to absorb new materials. I want them to realize that we grow when we allow ourselves to expand our horizons. We likewise become more successful when we incorporate the lessons of our missteps.

So why does Barak Obama not know this? He isn't a child and has had many years of advanced education. He has also been president for nearly six years where he has been privy to information available to few others. Moreover, the best advice from the most accomplished experts is at his beck and call.

So why hasn't he learned. That a neophyte president would make mistakes was predictable. After all, the problems he faces are immense and often one of a kind. But when shovel ready projects did not turn out to be shovel ready, why didn't he make the pivot he proclaimed?

And when relations with Russia soured and the Iranians failed to respond to his blandishments, why didn't he modify his policies? Couldn't he, like George W. Bush and Jimmy Carter, do a course correction? He didn't have to engage in a public mea culpa. All that was necessary was to learn from his experience.

But neither has the Democratic Party learned. ObamaCare is exploding before our eyes, the VA is a basket case, and we recently traded five enemy leaders for a single deserter, but for them it is business as usual. Most Democrats, certainly the leadership, reflexively endorse whatever the president does.

Elected officials, and the party rank and file, may believe that in doing so they are protecting their long-term interests. They are mistaken. So was Charley Wilson. This former president of General Motors once erroneously told us that what was good for the country was good for General Motors—and vice versa.

Democrats should take note. What is good for the nation is good for them, but not necessarily the other way around. They need to learn that their first duty is to help their country—or they too will be in trouble.

The Case for Principled Realism

Several years ago I came to the conclusion that we were in the midst of an ideological crisis. Liberalism was clearly not working, but there did not seem to be a practical substitute. Few Americans were prepared to resurrect laissez-faire capitalism or to embrace a Judeo-Christian theocracy.

So what was the alternative? My sociological analysis convinced me that we were headed toward "social individualism." As our society grew more affluent and complex, there were more personal decisions to make. Yet unless these were based on what was possible, they were apt to backfire.

Liberalism was grounded in a troika of fantasies. Progress-ives told us that social justice depended on universal love, interpersonal equality, and sexual androgyny. Yet I knew these were fairytales. A sustainable social order depended upon being more realistic about the sort of creatures we are and the challenges we confront.

So when I began writing about these issues, I talked about social realism. We were social creatures so we would have to start by understanding our social nature. Love was important, but it was directed toward people we knew well, not strangers. We were also hierarchical creatures. That is, everyone wanted to be special. Lastly there are genuine differences between men and women.

I had also come to believe that in our mass techno-commercial society, more of us would need to be professionalized. We would have to become self-motivated experts in the tasks we performed. Both on the job and at home, we would have to base our decisions on what achieved our aims.

And yet, there was nothing sexy about professionalization, or for the matter social realism. These were not inspirational concepts. Not many people were going to wake up in the morning breathlessly eager to become more professional or socially sophisticated.

Liberalism might be dying, but people crave hope. They need a goal that promises to make life better. Moreover, this goal needs to be easy to grasp. It has to intuitively provide a noble reason for living.

Then it hit me, why not call what I was after "progressive-conservatism." The liberals had appropriated their current label from folks who today would be called libertarians. Turn about was fair play, and progressivism had a ring of inexorable improvement.

Besides, I liked the idea of calling myself a "pro-con." A colleague, however, threw cold water on this by pointing out that conservatism continues to suggest a retrograde orientation. This sent me back to the drawing board.

It was at this point that the notion of "principled realism" dawned on me. Being in tune with reality was not enough. Our shared aspirations had to be in accord with standards that reduced interpersonal conflict. Unless we respected each other's ambitions, we could not cooperate in saving the world.

Then when president Trump gave his speech to Islamic leaders in Saudi Arabia, my hunch was confirmed after he used this very phrase. Trump was referring to political reforms. He wanted to bring contrasting civilizations together to fight a common threat.

But why couldn't a renewed practicality also apply to our personal lives? Why couldn't it relate to strengthening our marriages and reducing social tensions? We have jointly been fed so many myths about gender, race, and social class that might not a dose of truth prove a sovereign corrective?

Reality is a hard taskmaster, but fairytales are more dangerous. Sooner or later, they entice us to place our fate in the hands of monsters. Moral principles too can be demanding. They often require us to sacrifice beguiling dreams for the sake of the common good.

As I write this, I fear that I may be sounding like the college professor that I am. Nonetheless, it seems imperative to me that we as a society wake up from the angry nightmares we have conjointly created. Our unprecedented prosperity will mean nothing if we do not deal with the world as it is.

If we don't recognize our individual and collective limitations, we will not be able to take advantage of our individual and collective opportunities. Life can be difficult, but it is much more difficult with our heads buried in the sand and our hearts dedicated to selfish pursuits.

Chapter VIII

The Mis-education of Our Youth

Perpetuating Corruption

I am an educator. I have been teaching college for over a quarter of a century. As a consequence, I am very sensitive to the damage that education—and in particular higher education—has done to our values and wellbeing. Instead of preparing the next generation to deal with the challenges of a mass techno-commercial society, the young have been indoctrinated in neo-Marxist shibboleths. From kindergarten through graduate school, they learn little else than what is wrong with America. Presumably, this will persuade them that more government control is the answer. My own discipline of sociology is deeply implicated in this undertaking. It has furnished many of the rationalizations for identity politics and collectivist ideals. As a result, it has fallen into disrepute.

Professional educators keep telling us that they have discovered the most effective ways to teach the young. Nonetheless the outcomes keep getting worse. Despite the trillions of dollars invested, the alumna of our K-12 system are often ill-prepared for college. We nowadays promote them based on age rather than achievement. This means that millions of students do not have the qualifications to benefit from advanced schooling. The next question thus becomes, "who is college for?" Many politicians declare it should be for everyone. Liberals regard this as the only way to provide total equality. I suggest that it ought to be for those who have the potential for social leadership. This requires that they have the ability, and motivation, to benefit from what is taught. To do otherwise, so lowers the standards that college degrees become worthless.

That indeed is what is happening. College education, as we have known, it is dying. The bubble is about to burst. The more we spend on useless pedagogy, the more speedily the public catches on. This being the case, in an effort to stave off the inevitable comeuppance, schools are becoming more standardized. Almost entirely liberal in their approach, the last thing they want is promote autonomous thought. Students are apparently on board with this agenda. They now demand to be spoon-fed. Increasingly uncomfortable with ideas that challenge the intellectual status quo, they agitate for safe places. Amazingly, even the brightest among them campaign against academic freedom. Instead of championing liberty, these young people refuse to permit conservative ideas on campus. This is tantamount to book burning. Accordingly, that which is taught is so restricted that counter-information must be acquired afterwards. No only that, but liberal fictions need to be unlearned. Is this, I ask, anyway to run a railroad?

Much of this drift toward know-nothingism might be stemmed if we reinstituted genuine academic freedom. In the near term, however, this seems unlikely. The potential advocates of reform, which is to say the professoriate, have been marginalized. Uniformity-loving administrators have taken over and, in the process, hollowed out the university. Hence, the sort of faculty that might make difference is discriminated against. My own university, for instance, is the victim of salary compression. Senior faculty are denied raises, while junior faculty are paid more in order to attract their services. This destroys the incentive for competent professors to remain. Ultimately, not only are the students dumbed down; so are their instructors.

What we get instead is "defensive education." Rather than sponsor professionalism, bureaucratic palliatives become the norm. Liberal administrators promote what they depict as "best practices." In so doing, they devote themselves to numbers as opposed to actual learning. As long as they can boast of impressive statistics, they do not care if little is behind them. The upshot is that rather than creating havens for cutting–edge scholarship, universities are transformed into Potemkin villages. This decline has been hastened by the proliferation of on-line learning. Because this modality reduces costs, it is lauded as the wave of the future. That students learn less is irrelevant. Besides, the data can be fudged.

Even more distressing is that on-line learning penalizes the students who are most in need of social support. Undergraduates who come from deprived backgrounds often require time, and personal attention, to overcome their cultural handicaps. Merely giving them a credential does not help them catch up with their better-prepared peers. This is driving a wedge between the upper-middle classes and the poor. Although this is the opposite of what liberals preach, it is what their policies have wrought. Rather than instill the self-direction that would allow those from the lower classes to become professionalized, these youngsters are handed a useless sheepskin. Without the accompanying skills, when it comes to performing demanding jobs, they are out of luck.

As a sociologist, I have been especially mortified by the spectacle of my own discipline committing suicide. Because it surrendered to neo-Marxist domination, it is no longer disseminating the knowledge that might reverse current trends. It could, for instance, underline the importance of strong families in preparing children for the rigors of a first rate education. It might also remind us of the social complexities of a post-industrial society. Unfortunately, a commitment to identity politics has shifted the attention of many of my colleagues to insulting Donald Trump. They would rather see him defeated than make genuine scientific advances.

What's Wrong with Our Schools?

Save the Children: Discipline the Teachers

When Georgia was initially hit with our recent financial crisis, it was time for belt-tightening. Everyone knew it, including then Governor Sonny Perdue. And so the word went out that there would be budget cuts. Furthermore these would be across the board so that the pain would be shared.

Only they weren't across the board. Everyone was cut by four, then six, and then eight percent—except the penal institutions and k-12 schools. This presumably made sense. We couldn't very well let prisoners out of their cells or deny small children a good education. After all, we had to "save the children."

Higher education was sacrificed; roads were sacrificed, but these innocents could not be sacrificed. Or was it the children that would have suffered? Somehow, the teachers made out like bandits. They, who, strange to say, had been among Perdue's most vociferous supporters, managed to keep their own nest eggs intact.

Now we witness the spectacle of teachers besieging the Wisconsin State House. They too are claiming to fight on behalf of their students, even as they put in for so much phony sick leave that the schools must close. Nevertheless, they are altruists, whereas their enemy, the governor, is trying to destroy the future of the young.

Before this sideshow, we had heard of teachers unions demanding more pay and benefits than workers in the private sector. We had also heard stories of their defending incompetent teachers. But most people were reluctant to believe these tales. They wanted to help the children and so were willing to assist their helpers.

But now, in Wisconsin, the teachers are prepared to see their state go into default rather than make significant concessions. How is this supposed to help the children? What good will it do the young if there are no jobs waiting for them when they graduate?

Rather than answer this question, let me first share some secrets. To begin with, teachers, despite many significant exceptions, are among the least well educated of our professionals. Anyone who teaches in college (as I do) knows that the worst students congregate in the education department. There they find the least demanding courses, yet obtain the best grades.

Moreover, most of what prospective teachers learn concerns the tenets of progressive education. These essentially dictate that teachers be nice to students. That's it; just be nice. As to the content we might expect teachers to impart, it is a tiny part of the curriculum. Perhaps the fear is that education majors cannot absorb anything too intellectually challenging.

In any event, the time has come to hold teachers to a higher standard. If they are to receive the remuneration to which they feel entitled, they need to work a little harder to accumulate genuine knowledge worthy of being passed along to the younger generation.

The second secret is that the amount of money spent on education is not correlated with educational achievement. More dollars do not necessarily improve learning. In fact, they do not. They barely make a difference. Most people refuse to believe this, but the sociologist James Coleman definitively demonstrated this truth almost a half century ago.

For those who suspect I am mistaken, I offer evidence open to everyone. We have doubled and tripled the amount spent on education over the last several decades, but have the scores on achievement tests gone up commensurately? Of course not. They have barely budged.

Or consider class size. It has been presented as the Holy Grail of education. Smaller classes, we were told, would allow teachers to provide more individualized attention. Well, class sizes have almost been cut in half, but parochial schools with much larger classes are doing better. So did the larger classes I once attended.

As Coleman long ago discovered, the most important factor in generating student success is parental attitudes. Parents who care about education have children who care about it. This is the real secret of the Asian Tiger Mothers. This is why their children are doing so well in school—not because they are more intelligent.

And so the way to get better education is to raise the standards. Raise them for teachers. Raise them for parents. Raise them for children. If we care about education, we must not be fooled into supporting what is essentially in the teachers' interests. We must keep our eyes on the ball. Bankrupting our states to pay for something that does not help us, or our children, makes no sense.

Social Promotion; Then and Now

I think I was in the first grade. Anyway, I remember the commotion. My next-door neighbor's son had been left back. He was only a year older than me, but he was "slow." While he was a nice boy with whom I often played—once even plotting to burn my sister at the stake—he wasn't book-smart.

At the time, I did not understand what the fuss was about. In retrospect I realize his parents were deeply distressed that their only child would be stigmatized by having to repeat a grade. They were equally worried that being surrounded by children younger would stunt his emotional growth.

These parents were not alone in their concerns. Others were equally vociferous in their conviction that demoting a child had dire consequences. What is more, the teachers agreed. They too were lobbying for what was called "social promotion." Children were to be advanced a grade, not because they mastered the materials of the earlier one, but because they were a year older.

The theory was that acquiring social skills was even more important than attaining academic ones. Thus, to leave a child behind was to inflict an indelible scar. It marked him or her as a loser who would be ridiculed by age-mates as "dumb" and shunned by classmates as too "big" to belong.

As a consequence, school policies were changed to keep students with their age peers. In the end, all were moved along ir-respective of what they knew. Ultimately, when they graduated from high school, as many did, they could neither read nor do simple arithmetic. A diploma ostensibly certified that they were educated, but anyone who knew them realized this was not true.

Today many states are about to launch on an updated version of the social promotion, only this time at the college level. (Here it is called *Complete College Georgia*.) Once more the experts and concerned parents are essentially urging us to move students along for their own good.

What is being proposed (and in some cases enacted) is that states fund universities in terms of their number of graduates as opposed to their number of attendees. This is supposed to make schools accountable. They are, in effect, being told to demonstrate their effectiveness before they are bankrolled.

This, at least, is the theory. But put yourself in the place of a college administrator. You need more money to underwrite your programs, but the only way to loosen state purse strings is to raise your graduation rate. So what do you do? Why, you lower the standards required to graduate.

Higher education, indeed, education in general, has witnessed an alarming grade inflation. Individuals who were once "C" students are now pocketing "A's" as if these were jellybeans. A sense of entitlement has taken hold such that many mediocre learners fancy themselves embryonic geniuses.

So now, in the name of improved quality, we are about to see educational criteria take another nosedive. In fact, this is already happening. A colleague of mine who teaches at state university up north tells me when his students cannot read; they have the tests read to them. Not only this, but they have the questions explained to them.

This then is supposed to be progress. No doubt we will shortly be treated to hordes of college graduates who also can neither read nor do simple arithmetic. Our universities are clearly in trouble. Indeed, ordinary citizens are beginning to ask if they are worth the cost. What, they inquire, is the point when their graduates know less than fifth graders.

No wonder that my colleagues and I question the foresight of this brave new world of "rationalized" finance. We, who daily struggle to maintain the value of what we teach, shudder at finding ourselves, and our students, sold out in the shadows of a legislative night. Let us remember that even good intentions can have unintended consequences.

Who is College For?

Rick Santorum does not believe that college is for everyone. Apparently neither does Barack Obama. Both agree that some folks are better off with a technical education. But whom does that leave college for?

Let's agree that it is not exclusively for "snobs." We are nearing twenty-five thousand students at Kennesaw State University and very few of them fit this appellation. Let's also agree that college has become too expensive. Certainly the upwards of fifty thousand dollars that some elite universities charge is too rich for most pocketbooks.

Let's also agree that not everyone has the ability to pursue a higher education. Not only do some people hate academics, but a great many of them do not have the candlepower to deal with the subject matter in which traditional universities specialize.

That still leaves the question as to who can benefit from four or more years of college. Many nowadays think in terms of acquiring marketable skills. They (or their parents) decide that it is worth the effort because they will then qualify for jobs that enable them to earn an additional million dollars over the course of a lifetime.

First of all, let's understand that not everyone benefits from this monetary bonus. The higher the percentage of the population obtaining a degree, the smaller is the financial differential between college and high school. After all, not everyone is going to become a high-power executive just because they take extra years of schooling.

Nor is every major going to have an equal payoff. If you want to be an accountant, college is pretty much the best place to acquire the requisite skills. But if you major in communications—as many nowadays do—the odds of becoming an on-screen television reporter are slim.

So let me switch gears. Let me share a personal experience. Far too many years ago, when I was an undergraduate, I took a course in anthropology. I'm not sure why I did—I was not an anthropology major—but it turned out to be an eye-opening experience.

One of the books we were required to read was about the Tiwi. Who, you may ask, are the Tiwi? They are an obscure aboriginal tribe living on Melville Island just off the north coast of Australia. Although not particularly important; they made a huge impression on me.

Consider that this is many decades later and I still remember them. I recollect how they went to war by symbolically trying to wound the enemy rather than kill him. I also recall how the older men married much younger women, who nonetheless cheated on them with the younger men by having liaisons in the bush.

Why does this matter? Well, on a certain level, it doesn't. Ignorance of the Tiwi's is not going to make or break many careers. Nevertheless, for me, my introduction to them was life changing. It shook me out of a complacency born of an absent-minded ethnocentrism.

Like most people I grew up believing that the world surrounding me was the norm. A majority of Georgians would not agree that the gritty streets of south Brooklyn exemplify the way ordinary people live, but they did for me. It took a college course in anthropology to make me realize that there were alternative ways of living.

Which brings me back to the question of what is college for? My answer is that for many it is preparation to become social leaders. It changes their frame of reference so that they can deal life's complexities better than they would have had they remained parochial in their outlook.

Universities are not merely about honing technical skills. In some cases, that is their forte. But in many more the goal is to shake us out of the lethargy of youth. In these instances, it is much more about growing up to become a multi-faceted human being.

The Death of Higher Education

It sounded so innocuous; so compassionate. Why shouldn't the children of the poor get just as rigorous an education as the children of the rich? Why shouldn't they have just as good an opportunity to be successful as those born with silver spoons in their mouths? Furthermore, why shouldn't the government help out?

These were among the latest recommendations of Barack and Michelle Obama in their ongoing effort to bring social justice to our benighted land. How, they essentially ask, can everyone be made equal if some are allowed to languish without a college degree?

With respect to financial equality, we know that they have sought to tax the rich so as to transfer their wealth to the poor. With respect to medical care, they have also sought to strip the wealthy of their Cadillac insurance plans so as to offer ObamaCare to those without insurance.

But what about higher education? Do they plan to relieve the best educated of their brains and motivation so as to implant these in the have-nots? Do they honestly believe either that everyone starts with the same mental and emotional endowments or that they can transfer these just as they have attempted to do with other resources?

Actually that seems not to be their plan. The real objective appears to be to tear down higher education so that no one can derive an unfair advantage from acquiring more knowledge than others. If they can just make sure that everyone is equally dumb, unfairness will be banished from the earth.

If this sounds like hyperbole, it is not. It is a straightforward extrapolation from what the Obama's have endorsed for educational reform. They tell us that there are not enough poor children attending college; hence they wish to increase their numbers, while providing the appropriate supports.

To hear the Obama's, one would never imagine that scholarships and student loans abound. If they are taken seriously, one might assume that few colleges currently offer remedial programs to unprepared entrants. Nor would one suppose that affirmative action is deeply entrenched at our best schools.

Yet all of these things are in place. What is more, they have not accomplished the mission they were intended to achieve. While virtually any unprepared student can find a school willing to admit him or her, ensuring graduation is another matter. The dropout rates are phenomenal.

But Liberals like the Obama's have a solution. Mandate that colleges must graduate higher percentages of their students. And oh yes, also provide them with more money, more remediation, and greater encouragement.

The fact is that not only don't these policies work; they never can. As long as abilities and effort are unequally distributed (as they are), the only way to guarantee that everyone who enters college obtains a credential is to make college degrees worthless.

If everyone is required to learn as much as everyone else, the only method of ensuring this is to arrange things so that everyone learns as little as possible. Complete intellectual equality can only be attained by insisting on universal mediocrity. After all, the dumb and lazy cannot even rise to be average.

This, to be blunt, is a prescription for destroying our colleges and universities. Whatever they have been, once they are flooded with the students the Obama's want to help, they will no longer be colleges. They may not even be able to teach as much as our high schools once did.

The president and his wife assure us that quality will be maintained. But these are the same people who told us we could keep our doctors and health plans. They are happy talk specialists who live in a world where lollypops grow on trees and chocolate milk gurgles in the streams.

Unfortunately, we do not live in the same universe. For us, if higher education is to be higher, it cannot be for everyone—only those able to benefit from it.

The Coming College Bubble

It's coming! And the causes will be about the same. I'm talking about the college bubble. Just as there was a housing bubble that came close to destroying our economy, we are facing a higher education fiasco of similar proportions.

We got into trouble with mortgages when the politicians decided that everyone should own a house. It didn't matter how sizeable your income was, home ownership was such an unqualified good that the government decided to promote it. Being the lord (or lady) of one's own manor increased individual responsibility; hence it was in everyone's interest to expand its scope.

The way to get there, of course, was to make homes affordable, and that could only be achieved by reducing the cost. If down payments were eliminated and interest rates reduced, even the least privileged could enter the market. All that had to happen was for the government to guarantee loan repayment.

With education the impulse has been the same. Obviously higher education is a good thing. Everyone knows that people who have college degrees earn over a million dollars more during their lifetimes. Moreover, they become healthier, more moral, and better informed citizens. As such, everyone wins.

To this end, altruists from Bill Gates to Barack Obama have advocated universal college enrollment. Indeed, some are now describing a university degree as an entitlement. Every person born in the U.S. (as well as some illegal aliens), not just the rich or intellectually endowed, is said to have a right to a college diploma.

The way to make this happen is, of course, to reform the current system. According to the reformers, it obviously costs too much, takes too long to complete, and teaches irrelevant materials. If instead we get rid of professors dedicated to protecting their outmoded disciplines and replace them with cheaper adjuncts and even cheaper on-line courses, the results will elevate us to the forefront of international learning.

This may sound reasonable, yet it is fatuous! The only way to give everyone a college degree is to reduce the standards drastically. As a college professor I know—first hand—that not every student has the motivation or ability to handle college level subjects. And this, while we still impose standards that deny some folks admission and force others to drop out for lack of performance.

For every potential student to pass, the bar has to be dropped lower than is now the case in secondary education. But if this occurs, what is learned will be so meager that college credentials will be worthless. All they will certify is that a graduate has applied for one.

What is more, the costs will be exorbitant. For the privilege of dumbing down our population, and making it more difficult to distinguish the competent from the incompetent, we will have to furnish trillions in student loans that the recipients will never be able to repay—because they will be unemployed. -- Sounds like a terrific bargain to me.

The fact is that a college education is not a *right*. Not everyone is entitled to a diploma. What people do deserve is the option to pursue a degree. We all, whatever our social origins, warrant an opportunity to prove what we can do. But then we must prove it! If we are admitted to an institution of higher learning, we must demonstrate that we have learned something.

Nowadays with many politicians attacking the integrity of college professors, and some educators apparently intent on watering down what is taught so that it can be inexpensively packaged for the Internet, the soundness of higher education is being compromised. If this comes to pass, an institution that has taken generations to create will be lost.

So let us celebrate those who have learned something in college. We must continue to strive for high standards without opting for the privilege of bankrupting our country both financially and intellectually. Democracy is a privilege. It shouldn't be an excuse for seeking the impossible.

In the Wizard of Oz the scarecrow received a piece of paper that confirmed he was a college graduate. As portrayed in the movie he was wise, yet in the final analysis his head was still filled with straw. Let us not choose only to be empty-headed.

College and The Parable of the Tomatoes

Tomatoes are delicious! Although once spurned as poisonous love apples, Americans have been relishing them for over a century. Indeed, so popular did they become that the demand exceeded the supply. This created a problem because farm grown tomatoes were handpicked. As such, they were expensive.

The only way around this dilemma was to mechanize the harvesting process. This, however, required that as the crop neared ripeness, all of the fruit be plucked at the same time. Because machines could not distinguish between the ripe and the unripe, all had to be simultaneously gathered.

The solution was to genetically engineer the tomatoes so that they matured concurrently. This worked wonderfully, except for one small quibble. These new varieties did not taste as good as the old-fashioned kind. They looked about the same, but were nowhere near as luscious as the juicy ones people grew in their backyards.

Now colleges are under attack. Both from within and without, potent forces are gathering to convert them into what they have not been. Since they are also thought to be too expensive, many critics are proposing solutions akin to that which worked for tomatoes. In the process, universities are being homogenized.

As I have previously written, one reason for this is the move to provide everyone with a higher education. It is forcing universities to lower their standards so as to emulate mediocre high schools. Instead of demanding the best of their students, they lower their requirements so that everyone can pass.

Then there are the effects of the perceived liberalism of college faculties. This left of center attitude is real and gives many parents heartburn. Despite apologetics to the contrary, the latter are correct in believing that many academicians actively promote a left-of-center agenda.

Unfortunately, the response has been to restrain the radicals by controlling the institutions. One tool for doing so has been to demand "accountability." The goal is to make sure that professors impart the information that they should be imparting. If instead of delegating them complete freedom, they have to answer for their efforts, perhaps they will be more careful.

In practice, however, this gets translated into demanding that the faculty abide by standardized rubrics. They are asked to organize their lessons according to pre-digested formats and to test their students by means of equally homogeneous instruments.

But in having their product standardized, it is made second-rate. Professors who are told what to teach and how to teach it become as dumbed down as their students. Asked to leave their intelligence and creativity at the door, it is the least able among them who are motivated to remain on the job.

Yet, we have seen this before. As the number of administrators rose in K-12 schools, the quality of education stagnated—or fell. Although this was done in the name of account-ability—the reverse transpired.

Sadly, in universities the impact is liable to be more severe. Why? you ask. The answer has to do with what is taught in colleges. Higher education deals with arcane and complex materials. Hence, the only persons competent in them are generally the professors. Consequently, unless they are experts, what they teach is inevitably substandard.

Indeed, how are administrators to judge which professors do a good job? Since they cannot do so directly, they impose proxies. One is student evaluations. At the end of each course, students rate what occurred. But which instructors get the best marks? Naturally, it is the popular ones who cater to student desires, not the more demanding ones.

Another administrative strategy is to demand written goals and specifiable learning outcomes. This, however, imposes a need to keep lesson plans within the lines. Getting too innovative is discouraged by a demand to produce exactly what was promised.

The result is a reduction in quality and an assault on academic freedom. What formerly made college distinctive gets excised because it is not easily measured. However, with it goes a professorate worthy of the name and students who learn anything of value. In the end, they all have as much flavor as tomatoes designed for supermarket shelves.

The Study Guide Phenomenon

With the new college term beginning, in many respects it has been deja vue all over again. I can always count on some students to resurrect old chestnuts that I have heard countless times. In so doing, they remind me of the difficulties in teaching materials with which they are unfamiliar.

Every course starts out with a description of what will be covered and how student achievement will be measured. Naturally this includes a discussion of the exams and how they are to be graded. As might be expected, this makes many of my listeners nervous.

As a consequence, one almost always asks if I will provide a "study guide." My answer is invariably no, to which someone, usually a person who has had me before, inquires if I will reconsider. After all, other professors provide these predigested compendiums; why shouldn't I?

First, let me explain what a study guide is. It is usually either an outline of what the course has to date covered, or a series of topics that are apt to appear on the exam. This way students can anticipate what is to come and narrow their focus to what will be be required.

In most cases, I immediately explain why I do not supply this assistance. I tell my students that one of the most important skills they can acquire is how to study. It is up to them to figure out what is important and concentrate on that. They must decide what is mean-ingful, as opposed to what isn't.

I generally underline my point by asking whether they expect to receive study guides from their future employers? Won't their bosses expect them to know their jobs without being furnished with written instructions? If they can't get along without such directives, isn't it obvious that they will not rise to positions of authority?

Nowadays, in our enormously complicated world, where professionalized occupations entail discretion, if people cannot be self-directed, how will they be able to make good choices? If they are unable to deal with uncertainties because they are too frightened to think for themselves, why would they be trusted to lead others?

But where are they to learn to think for themselves? If not in our colleges, then where? Doing so is, of course, difficult in that mistakes are possible. Actually, it is dead certain that beginners will make missteps. We all do—especially when we are in unaccustomed waters.

Yet isn't it also important that we learn to cope with our errors? If we do not allow ourselves to recognize these, how will we discover how to rectify them? And if we don't, won't we perpetuate a myriad of otherwise correctable slip-ups?

Life is filled with landmines and embarrassing miscalculations. Things do not always go as we hope. We therefore require the courage to manage a variety of uncomfortable moments. We must be honest enough to figure out what is going on and brave enough to apply measures we believe might work.

With our colleges having become the land of the snowflakes, this is not their conventional wisdom. Blizzards of politically correct nonsense routinely obscure the vision of the inhabitants. So caught up are faculty and students in the need to bolster everyone's self-esteem that simple facts are ignored.

George Washington and Abraham Lincoln did not have study guides. Neither did Isaac Newton or Thomas Edison. I wonder what Jeff Bezos, the founder of Amazon.com, would say if asked about the study guide he used when creating his company?

These days we have become so desirous of avoiding distress that we want everything laid out for us. But who is going to do this? If everyone becomes a self-absorbed egotist who cannot engage in independent thought, we will have millions of computer game players, but few game designers.

Our colleges—indeed our nation—are sure to be trouble as long as we insist on the easy way out. Success takes effort. Social advances require determination. When these are lacking on either the personal or community level, dreams do not come true. And, lest I be misunderstood, this includes the American Dream!

Snowflakes and the New Conformity

When I was in high school, my teachers regularly warned about the dangers of conformity. They feared that the nation was becoming too materialist and hence that we students might be tempted to join the ranks corporate executives garbed in grey flannel suits.

What could be more enervating than this fate? What could be more drearily boring? We, the upcoming generation, were thus advised never to lose our idealism. We must stand up for truth and justice and not allow our country to slide into self-satisfied vacuity.

The current generation of college students has been steeped in similar guidance all of their lives. They too believe the liberal mantra that it is up to them to save jaded adults from a burned-out conventionality. The young must lead. They must exploit their superior wisdom to join the vanguard of a brave new world.

The paradox at the heart of this recommendation is that the idealistic young are now more conformist than in my day. My peers were asked to avoid the quagmire of excessive acquisitiveness. The current crew is invited to do the same, but also to become combatants in the battle for social justice.

The irony is that this liberal agenda is more conformist than the materialist one. The budding businessmen and women of yore at least had to be innovative, if they were to get ahead. Today's left-wing political agitators have merely to chant time worn slogans and wave vitriolic posters.

Progressivism is not progressive. Its minions have not had an original thought in nearly a century. They always want the same thing, which is to say, more government control. Accordingly, down with the oppressors and up with bureaucratic regulations and programs.

Reality is somewhat different. Ours is a mass techno-commercial society. A market economy and democratic institutions of this sort demand an independence of thought and a willingness to take risks. More people need to become self-motivated experts who are able to make competent decisions in a world filled with uncertainties.

University-bound snowflakes revel in the opposite. They cannot stand uncertainty. When confronted with ideas different from their own, they melt. Instead they demand ideological uniformity. Subversive concepts are offensive and therefore forbidden.

Somehow this regimentation is supposed to promote freedom. With the poor and minorities protected by social justice warriors, these folks will be liberated to carry on without interference. They will thus be spared elite oppression. Well—not entirely. The weak too will have to toe the politically correct line or face remediation.

The truth is that the professionalized jobs of the future require self-direction. Technical and social experts must be able to make independent decisions. They cannot rely on bosses to tell them what to do. Even less can they depend on all-encompassing regulations imposed by benevolent politicians and bureaucrats.

The world is becoming a more complicated place, one that requires personal flexibility. Doctors, engineers, as well as police officers, need the courage to make autonomous choices, as well as to engage in the life-long learning essential to honing their skills.

Snowflakes demand the reverse. They do not believe in courage. Instead they want safe places where they can be protected from micro-aggressions. Nor they do not want to learn from others. As far as they are concerned, the already know what they need to know.

Our overwhelmingly liberal colleges have therefore ceased to do what they ought to do. They do not foster a marketplace of ideas. They do not ask students to deal with differing opinions. No, they specialize in the new conformity.

When colleges disinvite speakers because mobs of student agitators threaten to riot, they are teaching the young how to be model storm troopers. When professors rant about the allegedly fascist tendencies of president Trump and then grade students down if they disagree; they promote a mindless orthodoxy.

The saddest part is that this is not about to change. College campuses are so dominated by political correctness that dissent can find no space to take root. In other words, the snowflakes are safe. The intellectual chill is so pervasive they need not thaw out.

Defending Liberty on Campus

As an educator, I am quite naturally concerned with maintaining the highest academic standards we can. It is, therefore, with some disquiet that I have observed the creeping attacks on liberty on campus. Instead of an honest marketplace of ideas, we have witnessed the rise of political proselytization.

This is why I am so pleased that a ringing defense of intellectual freedom has been published to unambiguously positive reviews. I know that people are reading less nowadays, but Greg Lukianoff's "*UnLearning Liberty: Campus Censorship and the End of American Debate*" (Encounter Books, 2012) is worth the time and trouble.

Almost as wonderful as the book's message is the messenger. Lukianoff, who is FIRE's (the Foundation for Individual Rights in Education) chief lawyer an president is an unrepentant liberal. By his own testimony, he has never voted for a Republican in his life—and never plans to.

As Lukianoff himself admits, much of the demagoguery on campus is coming from the left side of the spectrum. That he too recognizes this as a threat to our democratic institutions is a wonderful sign that Americans may yet come together to defend our legacy of freedom.

If we as a nation are to move forward toward "a more perfect union," it is essential that our colleges and universities create, and disseminate, the innovative ideas that will improve our shared circumstances. This, however, is not possible when only politically correct positions are allowed to flourish.

Almost everyone is aware of how dominant liberals are in the groves of academe. They may be less aware of how this dominance has been translated into censorship and indoctrination. Because he has been fighting these tendencies for many years, Lukianoff provides scores of chilling examples of these trends.

In one well-known instance (from 2007), a student was expelled from an Indiana university for reading the wrong book. This book was about how the KKK had its wings clipped during the 1920's. In other words, it was aimed at exposing and resisting tyranny.

Nonetheless, an onlooker objected to the book's cover, which showed robed Klan members, and on this basis alone accused its reader of being a bigot. Solely on these grounds, without so much as a hearing, the school refused to allow the accused to register for any further courses.

Lukianoff also documents cases where university residence halls asked incoming freshmen to reveal their sexual orientation. This was supposedly to facilitate offering special services to gays, but wound up as a device for clamping down on anyone who believed homosexuality is sinful.

Residence programs have also been in the forefront of the battle against racism. This might be applauded if it entailed treating students equally, but all too often "sensitivity" programs have required students to admit that whites are inherently racist, while blacks are incapable of racism.

Disturbingly, when such programs have been challenged in court, the administrators who created them have rallied to their defense. Even when these have been ruled illegal, they introduced subterfuges to keep them going.

In, for me, what was one of the more alarming sequences in Lukianoff's book, the professional organization to which residence hall officials belong, held a quasi-religious service during which they congratulated themselves on their intransigence.

They lit candles, much as one would in church, to celebrate their devotion to spreading wisdom—as they perceived it. For them, forcing vulnerable students to agree with their own ideological commitments was a sacred cause. That these practices were an affront to freedom of speech and thought never entered their heads.

But it should enter ours. Indeed, it should do more than that. It should arouse us to make certain that self-righteous academics do not confuse their personal beliefs with a liberal education. Higher education should be about examining multiple sides of controversial issues, not foreclosing discussion in the name of pre-determined virtues.

Book Burning: Liberal Style

Nowadays, given what liberalism has become, I frequently reminisce about what it was when I was in high school in the 1950's. The disparities are so glaring that it almost seems to be an entirely different belief system.

Back then, the ravages of World War II were fresh in the minds of my teachers. The Holocaust had touched the lives of many of those I knew and hence they were eager that we never repeat it. This meant that it was crucial we never emulate the Nazis.

One of the practices we students were specifically warned against was book burning. Hitler's bullyboys had seized materials contrary to their beliefs and tossed them into roaring infernos. This was to make it plain that ideas hostile to National Socialism would not be tolerated. Beliefs associated with Judaism were explicitly forbidden.

This ritual horrified my instructors. They considered themselves intellectuals and cautioned that suppressing marginal thoughts was the express path to tyranny. If we were ever to learn the truth, we had to tolerate philosophies contrary to our own. This was the only way to compare opinions and figure out which were correct.

Fast forward to today. I am sure that contemporary liberals would also condemn book burning. They too would tell us that this is an anti-intellectual travesty that would set us squarely on the road to medieval superstition. Only reactionary troglodytes condoned any such thing.

And yet liberals are in the forefront of exactly this sort of behavior. Not long ago the political scientist Charles Murray was scheduled to give a talk at Middlebury College. He was going to discuss his recent book *Coming Apart*, which explains why middle and lower class Americans are dividing into antagonistic camps.

In fact, Murray never got to give his address. He was shouted down. For over an hour, a room full of young people booed and hissed. They called him vile names and were impervious to appeals to hear him out. They even jostled him physically when he attempted to leave.

These mostly students would, I am sure, have described themselves as "protestors." They would also claim to be upholding their constitutional rights. The first amendment would subsequently be cited in support of this contention.

But let me quote from that amendment. "Congress shall make no law… abridging the freedom of speech…or the right of the people to peaceably assemble, and to petition the government for a redress of grievances." Is this what happened at Middlebury?

I submit that it was not peaceful protest. Nor were the perpetrators asking for a redress of grievances from the government. What occurred was that a mob abridged the freedom of speech of a scholar they loathed. Because they mistakenly believed him to be a racist, they refused to let him speak.

This was intimidation, not a defense of freedom. It was not intended to protect of a marketplace of ideas, but to engage in a fascist power play. Yes, I know that "fascist" has become an overused epithet. Those on the left are now remarkably fond of characterizing conservatives in this way.

Nonetheless, look at what took place. This was an updated version of book burning. It was an exercise in using violence to shut down free speech. We should all be terrified, not only of what occurred, but that it was justified in the name of moral principles.

Left wing activists claim to be compassionate. They tell us they are seeking to protect the downtrodden. But then again, Hitler told us he was protecting the much maligned German people from oppression. Was his, however, the best way to go about it?

Murray is pessimistic about what this trend portends. He has a right to be frightened. I am sure that those who hate him for the supposedly racist things he once wrote in the *Bell Curve* never read the book. It was over twenty chapters long, but they so fixated on one small piece of a single chapter that they rejected the whole out of hand.

Is this what intellectualism has become? Is this type of intolerance what we transmit to the young in what is euphemistically called "higher education?" If it is the new normal, our civilization is in grave jeopardy.

Unlearning What's Learned in College

Every now and then I discuss the state of the ideological skew at colleges and universities with one of the administrators at Kennesaw State University. He too is aware of how dominant the liberal perspective has become, but is more sanguine than I about the long-term implications.

He points to the fact that as people grow older their opinions tend to migrate from the left toward the right. In the end, he argues, it does not much matter that a biased view of the world is inculcated at school because this will eventually be corrected once graduates must deal with reality for themselves.

Recently the conservative economist Thomas Sowell made some useful suggestions about the sorts of books alumnae can be provided counteract the propaganda that flooded their minds in university classes. Indeed, I just finished reading a biography of Calvin Coolidge that helped dispel myths I learned in high school.

But my question is: why should students need to do this unlearning. Why are we so complacent about the misconceptions they are force-fed in the name of education? If what they are being taught is so one-sided that it distorts the truth, what is the point of exposing them to this in the first place?

Colleges remain good places to obtain technical skills. If the goal is to become a mechanical engineer or a registered nurse, there are few better venues to acquire the relevant skills. Yet what of learning about life or how to be a social leader? Shouldn't a higher education be helpful here too?

For the last several decades, undergraduates have been voting with their feet regarding these issues. Fewer and fewer decide to be English or history majors. The liberal arts, which were once considered the core of what every educated person should know, have fallen on hard times.

So have social sciences such as sociology and political science. As interesting as these subjects can be, they are avoided by first class minds because what they teach is already known by those familiar with the tenets of political correctness.

Long ago, upon graduating from college as a philosophy major, I faced the problem endemic to philosophy majors, namely what sort of employment could I obtain. Consequently, as an accomplished test-taker I decided to sit for the City of New York's welfare caseworker exam.

And indeed I did well. Without ever taking a single course in social work, I came in third among the hundreds of applicants testing along side me. The way I did this was by answering the questions how I thought social workers would want them answered. In other words, I pretended to be a goody-two-shoes.

A parallel strategy applies to contemporary colleges. Their bias is so predictable that an intelligent person can figure out what is expected without having to crack open a book. What then is their purpose? Why not skip the entire exercise and head straight for the job market?

It seems that I am not alone in this reasoning. College enrollments have begun to decline. Michael Barone has gone so far as to write that the college bubble has burst. If he is correct, perhaps the public has begun to figure out there is little "there, there" on campus.

Liberal faculty members would thus be wise to note these trends. For their own professional survival, they might consider moderating their biases. At the very least, it is in their interest to hire, and promote, colleagues who present the other side of the ideological picture.

Nonetheless, I am not holding my breath. In the hermetically sealed environment of the contemporary college campus, the atmosphere has become so stagnant that most of the oxygen has already been sucked out. Thus, my guess is that there will be few meaningful reforms until people begin to expire of intellectual asphyxiation.

Still we must try. There is too much as stake.

Academic Freedom Revisited

Am I a contrarian? In response to several of my recent columns in the *Marietta Daily Journal*, some readers have concluded that I am. In this, they are probably correct. I do tend to disagree fairly vociferously with opinions I believe to be wrong, even when I am in the minority.

As a consequence, I am very fond of academic freedom. My right to say out loud what others may not appreciate strikes me as an essential tool in pursuing the truth. While I know that I make mistakes, a constant fear of retribution would hamper my efforts to rectify where I have gone astray.

Much of this attitude derives from my childhood in Brooklyn, New York. To this day, I warmly remember my high school teachers quoting Voltaire as saying "I disapprove of what you say, but I will defend to the death your right to say it." This always struck me as the essence of fair-minded scholarship.

My teachers back then were all liberals, so I assumed that liberalism implied the encouragement of diverse ideas. It was only when I migrated to neo-conservatism that I discovered this was not the case. Previous allies suddenly became extraordinarily intolerant of disagreements emanating from my new direction.

In time, it became apparent that liberals are in favor of free speech—for liberals. When it comes to effective competitors, they are all too eager to suppress articulate dissent. While they fancy themselves contrarians, they are not nearly as approving of determined opposition.

This, sad to say, is the situation on most American college campuses. Dominated as they are by a liberal consensus, they do not welcome efforts to challenge what they take to be obvious truths. For many university professors, criticism of their views—in any form—is tantamount to an assault on academic freedom. So surrounded are they by like-minded colleagues that is does not occur to them that silencing those who dissent is an attack on the latter's academic freedom.

Yet if truth is to emerge, academic freedom must be even handed. Criticisms must be tolerated, not as evidence of a desire to stifle particular views, but as part of the process of testing what is correct. However convinced people are of the validity of their positions, if these cannot survive scrutiny from doubters, the odds are they are not well-founded.

These considerations apply to our college campuses, but also to a larger social context. Universities have acquired a vital role in our techno-commercial society. They prepare large numbers of individuals to perform difficult tasks, in the absence of which we would all suffer.

Put another way, ours is becoming a professionalized society. More people than ever must be self-motivated experts in what they do if they are to supply the goods and services upon which we rely for our survival and/or comfort. Furthermore, it is our universities that groom millions of people for these professionalized jobs.

This fact positions institutions of higher education as social gatekeepers. Like it or not, the degrees they confer have become tickets to socially responsible activities. As a result, for most people, if they hope to achieve social mobility, they must first obtain evidence of academic success.

This means that society as a whole has a fundamental interest in overseeing how universities perform their jobs. We, all of us—not just professors and students—are legitimately concerned with how effectively colleges train their graduates for the chores they must eventually execute.

Which brings us back to academic freedom. If what universities are teaching interferes with people becoming effectively professionalized, they deserve to be criticized. If, to be more specific, a pervasive neo-Marxism undermines the capacity of college graduates to participate in a market economy and democratic traditions, it is not just the right, but also the duty, of ordinary citizens to say so.

Academics accustomed to being ensconced in a bubble of impunity may recoil at this prospect. Nevertheless it is not their comfort that should determine social policy. There are larger issues at stake. One is social survival, and another is the truth itself.

The Fall of the Faculty

I have a new hero. He is Benjamin Ginsberg, a professor of political science at Johns Hopkins University. For many years now college professors, such as myself, have been under assault. Indeed, we have been accused of all manners of evil.

Now Ginsburg has come forward with a ringing defense of our virtues, while offering a new set of villains. They are the college administrators. In *The*

Fall of the Faculty: The Rise of the All-Administrative University and Why It Matters, he explains that things are not always what they seem.

But before I detail some of Ginsburg's claims, let me make it clear that we professors are not blameless. In the rush to effect "social justice," many of us have foisted political correctness on relatively defenseless undergraduates. Too often, the classroom has become a scene of indoctrination rather than education.

And yet, as Ginsburg asserts, we professors are not alone in this. Our bosses, the college presidents, provosts, and deans, have also been ardent fans of racial and gender agendas. Indeed, most are similarly left wing in their politics. Furthermore, they have utilized social issues to control an otherwise unruly faculty.

When race, gender, and social class are put center stage, they provide an excellent rationale for imposing strict standards on the faculty. The professors can be sent for sensitivity training and held to account for violating ideological dictates. Even though college professors are among the least biased persons in the nation, they can be intimidated for failing to comply with administrative mandates.

Much of this is done in the name of improved educational outcomes. Yet I am reminded of 110 Livingston Street. As the former headquarters of the New York City Board of Education, during the 1960's it became synonymous with bureaucracy run amok. Crammed with administrators who multiplied like rabbits, it spewed out regulations that paralyzed, rather than facilitated education.

Today we see the same pattern developing in higher education. It too is churning out administrators at a greater rate than needed. Indeed, the proportion of administrators is expanding at nearly twice the rate of the faculty. In other words, instead of keeping the ratio of professors to students low, it is the ratio of administrators to students that is declining.

Put another way, professors must now teach more students, whereas individual administrators are responsible for fewer learners. But how, one may ask, is this supposed to improve scholarship? After all, administrators don't do the teaching—professors do; hence the mystery.

And then there is the problem of cost. Many people rightfully complain about the escalating expense of a college degree. They assume that this is because the professors keep earning more for doing less, but this is mistaken. If anything, the administrative bloat is at fault.

Because there are now twice as many administrators per student, this demands additional dollars. But the situation is worse than this considering that administrators are paid far more than professors. In fact, they often earn two, three, four, five, or more times as much as their underlings.

Consider this. In order to be promoted from an assistant to an associate professor an academic has to run a challenging gauntlet. He or she has to accumulate excellent teaching evaluations, publish several articles or books, and engage in demonstrable services to the college and his/her discipline. Then, only if his/her colleagues, chairpersons, deans, and provosts are satisfied, will advancement be granted.

For this, the new associate professor will receive a raise of between two and three thousand dollars. Meanwhile, if this same person is appointed to an administrative post, the raise is generally twenty, thirty, or forty thousand dollars.

So where do the incentives lie? Is there any question about why so many professors covet an administrative role? Similarly, are there any doubts about why administrators engage in empire building by creating legions of loyal lieutenants?

And so the game of dismantling higher education goes on—with power, not learning, the central consideration.

The Hollowed-Out University

For years I have been reluctant to write about the problem of "compression" for fear of sounding like sour grapes. Recently, however, I heard a television commentator assert that our colleges are so expensive because professors get paid too much. This is a serious misunderstanding.

Before I proceed, let me make several things clear. I love college teaching. I also love the freedom it provides to pursue scholarship. Moreover, my wife and I live comfortably. While the issues I am about to discuss rankle, I am a big boy who freely chose to do what I am doing.

So what is compression? Over the last couple of decades the salary differential between newly hired and senior faculty has shrunk. It is currently almost at the vanishing point. Recent Ph.D.'s with no experience and few publications earn nearly as much as the most productive full professors.

Let me be specific. I earn scarcely more than $10,000 above my novice colleagues. Despite a quarter of a century at Kennesaw State, sixteen published books, many journal articles, hundreds of newspaper columns, editorship of a professional journal, and excellent teaching evaluations, my income has remained static. Raises, when they come, are trivial.

Why is this so? The answer is that if our university did not compete to attract competent junior faculty, our assistant professors would be a sorry lot. As a consequence, the funds to pay them are extracted from the budget that might pay me.

Although faculty at elite institutions do well financially, those at schools like Kennesaw do not. I literally make fifty thousand dollars less than is paid to high school teachers in places like Chicago. I actually make less than many police officers.

To make matters more degrading, college administrators are paid far more than professors. The presidents of large institutions, for instance, routinely make at least five to ten times what I do. Although many are good at their jobs and deserve to be adequately compensated—what about me?

It is an open secret at mid-level universities that if faculty members wish to earn more, they must switch to the administrative track. If they do, they will immediately be rewarded with twenty, thirty and even fifty thousand more.

Ordinary professors, on the other hand, are constantly pressured to "publish or perish." But if they do, their only recompense is to avoid being dismissed. Where then is the incentive to do one's best?

Readers may be saying to themselves; well, these folks made their bed: let them lie in it. Besides, they are crowd of left wing zealots who are corrupting our children. If they are suffering, their distress is richly deserved.

This, however, is shortsighted. It is not for nothing that we say: You get what you pay for. Consequently if we pay full professors chickenfeed, we should not be surprised to find colleges filled with chickens.

Reality has not yet caught up with this bald fact. College teaching is so attractive that we have maintained adequate recruitment into the faculty's lower ranks. Nonetheless, this cannot continue. Word will get out that there is no future in becoming a professor; hence the best and brightest will shy away.

Most conservatives already find superior respect and compensation beyond academe. Do we wish to continue this trend? If we do, the endpoint is predictable. We are in the process of creating hallowed out universities. The halls of ivy remain, but their intellectual eminence is swiftly becoming history.

With a college education more necessary than ever to produce the self-motivated experts needed by a mass techno-commercial society, this is a self-defeating policy. If we are no longer able to transmit wisdom to the younger generation because those who possess it have gone elsewhere, what is to become of us?

Still I am not going anywhere. I really do love KSU. But where are the competent educators who will replace me? Many, I am afraid, have decided to pursue more lucrative careers outside higher education.

Defensive Education

You've heard of defensive medicine. This is where physicians perform unnecessary medical tests in order to protect themselves from potential lawsuits. The consequence has been to drive up medical costs, while forcing a wedge between the doctor and patient. If anything, this has worsened medical outcomes.

Today we are experiencing something similar in higher education. Colleges too are threatened with lawsuits if they do not provide the desired benefits. As a result, they have adopted practices designed to thwart such legal actions. Here too the outcomes have been less than satisfactory.

The recent spate of college protests has exacerbated a long-term trend. Ever since the 1960's, college administrators have been capitulating to student demands. Fearful that angry students will close down their campuses, they accede to foolish policies.

During the safe spaces movement, demonstrators stipulated that unwelcome opinions be quashed. But more than this, they tied their requirements to the Black Lives Matter crusade. Some of the more strident demands have therefore concerned who can teach what, so as to preclude racism.

Once upon a time competence counted. Professors were asked to teach the courses where they possessed an expertise. Now, in this era of identity politics, the instructor's ethnic and ideological credentials are more salient. Academics with the wrong skin color, gender, or sexual orientation need not apply.

This is a serious development. People have been forced to resign their jobs; others were never hired. As importantly, many new positions have been created to accommodate the radicals. These were not instituted for academic reasons, but for political ones.

Kennesaw State University, along with colleges across the country, has witnessed an explosion in vice-presidents. Most of these are intended to demonstrate that the school cares. Their portfolios are generally oriented toward keeping problem students happy.

Mind you, the administrators who create these positions know that they are window-dressing. Nonetheless their hands are tied. They have learned from bitter experience that if they do not follow the lead of other schools, they will lose subsequent lawsuits.

Unless these administrators can point to programs similar to those of their competitors, this will be regarded as prima facie evidence of a dereliction in duty. They are thus forced to defend themselves by initiating useless policies ostensibly aimed at implementing justice, but achieving nothing.

Actually, they do accomplish something. They water down education and serve notice to all on campus that they must be politically correct or place their careers in jeopardy. In other words, this educational defensiveness spreads like kudzu into every corner of academe.

When this is combined with other programs such as Complete Georgia, the outcomes are disastrous. In order to make sure that every student is able to obtain a degree, standards are lowered and controversial subjects sidestepped. Instead of genuine learning, we get pabulum disguised as wisdom.

When I was younger, social promotions allowed students who could not read to graduate from high school. Today we permit students who cannot think to receive a college degree. Who this is supposed to help is another one of life's enduring mysteries.

As long a politicians continue to promise that everyone can get a college education and that no one should be offended by uncongenial ideas, this nonsense will prevail. The administrators have little choice. They realize either that they will be fired or that their schools will be deprived of millions of dollars.

Higher education is supposed to be on the cutting edge of scholarship. It has long been regarded as the custodian of our shared knowledge. This, however, is an ideal that is receding into history. Nowadays the objective seems to be reinforcing the pretense that everyone is genius-in-waiting.

This nonsense will not stop until more of us have the courage to demand that it does. Unless those who insist on higher standards also begin to intimidate the people who run our colleges, they will continue to cave into those who care not one bit about actual learning.

Academic Suicide

I have been writing about how we—as a society—have lost our way. Sadly, just the other day I was reminded of how far my own university has strayed from common sense and its historic mission. Instead of educating students for the world they are about to enter, the school has decided to commit suicide.

I have never been a fan of online education. In my experience—and that of my students—it is an inferior substitute for genuine learning. Now our administrators are threatening to convert this travesty into a total charade.

First let me share their vision. It is widely assumed that classroom-focused education is old fashioned. Face-to-face teaching is described as yesterday's technology. Anything involving the computer is supposed to be more effective than merely elucidating ideas for students.

The ultimate objective is full-blown distance scholarship. Students are to stay home and switch on their personal computers when it is convenient for them. This way they will not have to commute to a central location, nor will colleges require brick and mortar facilities.

Moreover, the lessons will be designed by the very best professors and then presided over by less highly trained adjuncts. This way the students will have access to superior instruction that is more flexible and less expensive.

In the end, everyone will be able to get a college education. That, at least, is the theory. The reality is different. It is a dumbed down ritual that imparts very little knowledge. Students may obtain a degree, but one that is less useful than toilet paper.

Let me explain the problem. In an ordinary classroom, students are motivated by human interaction. They not only hear their professor, they are able to look him or her in the eye and read their facial expressions. They can also ask questions that receive responsive answers.

In other words, face-to-face learning has a human dimension that facilitates thinking and makes complex materials comprehensible. The computer, however, is more remote. It is disembodied box that has serious limitations.

In an attempt to get around these, online courses feature chat rooms and videos. Students watch taped lectures and then post responses to which others reply. The trouble is that these videos feature poor production values and hence tend to be deadly dull, whereas the posts only allow for inadequate communication. These discussion boards are thus like extended tweets, only less clever.

What is worse, these methods are labor intensive. It takes time for the instructor to reply to every student via the keyboard. There is likewise less incentive to require written assignments that are arduous to grade.

Initially it was hoped that smaller classes coupled with extra faculty pay could avoid these difficulties. Accordingly, in my school, classes were capped at twenty and then thirty. Instructors also received an additional fifty dollars per head.

Now the proposal is to increase class size to between fifty and one hundred and twenty, while hiring non-Ph.D.'s to preside over them. This is a sham! In an effort to save money, learning is being thrown out the window. No lecturer, no matter how dedicated, can deal with five, one hundred and twenty student sessions—except in the most cursory manner.

Writing assignments will become a thing of the past and chat rooms a farce. Instructors, who have been converted into assembly line robots, will go through the motions—as will their students. Books will not be read, exams will be over-simplified, and no one will care because the exercise is so impersonal.

This so-called reform is not being driven by pedagogical necessity. Rather, it is being propelled forward by a misguided effort to provide affordable higher education for everyone.

Lastly, I guarantee that the politicians will depict these efforts as brilliant. You will be told about how well these innovations are succeeding, but don't believe it. We on the front lines know better. We see the casualties first hand!

Educational Indulgences

Almost five hundred years ago, the Catholic Church was in all its glory. Easily the foremost denomination in Europe, it was rich and powerful, and growing richer. In the midst of a building boom, it had recently started construction on the new St. Peter's Basilica, which was to be the largest cathedral in all of Christendom.

The problem was that the church's ambitions exceeded the assets at its disposal. More money was needed; hence a fund raising drive was in order. This entailed dispatching papal emissaries to distant outposts so that they could sell indulgences to the faithful.

Indulgences were writs that presumably allowed sinners to speed their journey from purgatory to heaven. In return for cash, the church promised that the souls of the departed would literally have to spend less time cooling their heels as they waited for eternal salvation.

Martin Luther, until then an obscure German monk, went ballistic. How could the Pope's legate, Johann Terzel, make such a claim? It made no sense to believe that one of the Lord's servants could commit the Creator to so significant a decision—and do so for something as crass as money.

As a result, Luther issued his Ninety-Five Theses. In these, he challenged the corrupt practices of the Church, thereby launching the Protestant Reformation.

Today another powerful institution has gone into the indulgence business. Not monolithic or spiritual like the medieval church, but nonetheless arrogant and over-ambitious, contemporary universities have entered the salvation business. And they too have done so for cash on the barrelhead.

What is being sold today is not entry to heaven, but the credentials to move ahead in the commercial marketplace. The instrument for doing so, however, is not a signed document from the Pope, but official credits that allow the bearer to graduate with a college degree.

The means whereby this fraud is perpetrated is the on-line college course. It is supposed to be the equivalent of a traditional college course, yet rarely is. Inferior in the materials taught and the information acquired, it often bears little resemblance to what it theoretically replaces.

Why, you ask, is this done? The answer is money. Colleges charge a premium for on-line courses. The schools get more per credit hour and their instructors are remunerated with additional dollars per head they teach. So conventional has this practice become that no individual school can afford to repudiate it lest its competitors leave it behind.

Nowadays one hears computer based learning lauded as the wave of the future. It is said to be innovative and efficient. No doubt it is convenient. But is it effective? Its partisans say yes, but most students concerned with learning say no—at least in the humanities and social sciences.

Almost everyone agrees that there is more cheating on-line, but the apologists for web-learning assure us they will soon have this weakness under control. By the same token, most acknowledge that the communication between the teacher and student is truncated, yet they counter that this is more than compensated for by the individual attention made possible.

In fact, quality suffers. Some insist that the for-profit schools, which specialize in on-line courses, will eventually be the model for higher education. Nonetheless, these folks must also admit that the diploma mills cater to vulnerable students, many of whom cannot hack it at a traditional college.

The truth is that easy answers did not work five hundred years ago and they will not work now. Back then shortcuts to heaven were an invitation to buy one's way out of trouble. Today they allow the lazy and unmotivated to obtain the simulation of a college education without having to invest the intellectual energy required by the real thing.

What we lack—that early modern Europe found—is someone to sound the alarm in a way that is heard. Without this, we too may wallow in corruption.

Online Loneliness

Have you ever been in a room filled with young people engrossed in their electronic devices? Have you noticed how oblivious they are of one another as they play their computer games or send messages to absent friends? This fact of modern life has, however, had dire consequences.

The Internet is, in many ways, a boon. But it has also been a curse. One of its worst side effects has been the coarsening, and degradation, of interpersonal communications. Many of us are familiar with how mean tweets can be. We have also witnessed the shallowness of FaceBook.

What we may not have realized is how seriously the electronic media eroded interpersonal skills. Millions of computer addicts use their machines as a buffer against the world. Because they can control what they see and hear, they are able to exclude unwanted contacts.

As a result, they never acquire the ability to deal with unpleasant messages. Nor do they become skilled in coping with strong emotions. For that matter, most are inexperienced in reading the subtle cues on the faces of the folks with whom they might have direct interactions.

This leaves many of the young unprepared to deal with the give and take of their subsequent occupations. They have difficulty evaluating personal character or standing up to vigorous competition. This is one of the reasons large numbers of college students cannot endure what they find offensive.

Indeed, it is why a college education is not worth what it once was. Unhappily, college administrators are conspiring to convert a bad situation into an unprecedented disaster. They are eagerly expanding their online offerings, irrespective of the consequences.

You've seen it on TV. You've been told a thousand times about how convenient distance learning is. The impression you are given is that this modality is superior to the old-fashioned classroom. Nonetheless, this is a grave error.

First, a caveat. I do not teach online. But I do teach at a university (KSU) that boasts of many online offerings. I also teach in a department that offers a fully online degree. I have even helped edit a journal issue dedicated to exploring the realities of online programs.

What is more, I frequently quiz my students about their online experiences. The better ones almost uniformly assert that these are an inferior form of learning. They tell me that what they absorbed was cursory and that cheating is rampant.

What they typically neglect to say is that college is about more than books and examinations. It also entails interacting with other students. In fact, the informal contacts that begin in class or arise from extracurricular activities are often more influential than the dealings with their professors.

This was certainly the case when I was an undergraduate. My friends and I routinely discussed the ideas to which we were exposed. Actually "discussed" is the wrong word. Oftentimes we argued, and in the process made novel ways of thinking our own.

Even Plato wrote about the way the young tussle over philosophies; much as puppies do over a bone. Are we now intent upon depriving learners of this opportunity by confining them to the solitude of their home screens? Is their world to be restricted to a computer display in the name of efficiency or modernity?

To be honest, online designers are aware of this pitfall. They therefore attempt to compensate in a variety of ways. One is to make graphics more stimulating. Another is to encourage instructors to create videos that emulate the classroom.

But the most important substitute for interpersonal connections are the chat room or electronic discussion board. These are often made mandatory in the expectation that they will stimulate student thought.

Too bad this is a vain hope. The stilted, and coerced, nature of these exchanges is no replacement for the real thing. In their artificiality, they cannot reproduce the spontaneity of face-to-face conversations. They thus cannot inspire the momentary flashes of insight that develop out of emotionally laden contacts.

Internet learning is improving. It may even be useful in teaching math and accounting. But when the humanities and social sciences are stripped of their human component, they cease preparing the young for social realities. This sort of enforced loneliness only creates isolated clones.

The Self-Directed University

Education matters. It matters so much that many of us have opinions about how it should be reformed. Certainly politicians have introduced a variety of measures designed to improve learning outcomes, while lowering costs.

As for me, I have been taking pot-shots at many of the programs promoted to overhaul higher education. Among the policies I have decried are Complete Georgia, fifteen to finish, and the e-core. All of these, I have argued, reduce quality without improving efficiency.

So what do I have to offer in their place? Just as opponents of ObamaCare are asked to provide a superior alternative, I can reasonably be requested to put forward a substitute.

As it happens, I have done exactly that. My latest book, *Redefining Higher Education: How Self-Direction Can Save College*, is now out. It explains what caused the recent "college bubble" and proposes a path to solve this dilemma.

I am therefore calling for a "self-directed university." What, you may ask, is that? The answer is that it is a way to reconceptualize the mission of higher education. Too often when we talk about fixing what is broken, we never inquire into what would constitute an advance.

My answer to this question is that a mass techno-commercial society, such as ours, requires a democratic and professionalized *elite* to provide the leadership for decentralized decision-making. We need more people who are capable of providing the self-motivated expertise a democracy and market economy demand.

The mention of an "elite" may be off-putting, but it does no more than recognize an ineluctable fact. No complex society has ever been all chiefs and no Indians. All have found it necessary to delegate leadership to some, rather than others.

Complex tasks require coordination. They also demand common objectives. Leadership, including decentralized leadership, provide these. What is not needed, is vesting authority in particular persons because of accidents of birth. Democratic societies have to provide opportunities for merit to rise to the top.

This is what self-directed universities are designed to facilitate. The goal is not to convert everyone into a manager, but to allow individuals to move up as far as their abilities and efforts will take them. They must not only want to succeed; they must demonstrate the skills and motivation to do so.

Nowadays many observers regard higher education as either meaningless or a glorified technical education. Colleges are equated with trade schools—with the exception that the trades they impart are more difficult that those taught by their predecessors.

In fact, while our colleges and universities provide training in engineering, business, and nursing, they also deliver more generalized proficiencies. Although they are sometimes described as instilling "critical thinking," at their best they teach "independent thinking."

Competent leaders need to be able to make competent choices, even in an environment of uncertainty. They must also have the courage to make mistakes and the flexibility to fix them. In short, they must be dedicated to getting the right answers and resilient enough to cope with failure.

But this is a matter of motivation. It does not depend on memorizing lists of facts. Or being incredibly smart. Or being appointed to supervise others. Competent leaders have to be able to produce, because they personally take the risks and assume the responsibility to do what's best.

It is these sorts of persons self-directed universities are designed to groom. Their ranks, however, will never include everyone. Nor ought they be filled exclusively by the sons and daughters of the wealthy and well placed.

Self-direction is not easy. Nor should it be. Our colleges must maintain high standards if they are to turn out independent thinkers and courageous leaders. As such, they must allow people to explore their strengths and to build upon their abilities.

Shortcuts designed to save money are a waste of scarce resources. Unless our tax dollars are spent wisely, i.e., in cultivating self-direction, they are being thrown down a bottomless pit.

The Corruption of Sociology

I am often asked by readers of my columns how I survive as a sociologist. They know that I am a conservative, whereas my discipline is extremely liberal. In fact, it is difficult. Most of my colleagues are neo-Marxists. Outside of my own department, many regard me as a traitor.

Some years ago, the husband of a close associate ordered me—point blank—to stop writing for the *Marietta Daily Journal*. He told me that my views did not represent sociology and therefore I should desist. My Ph.D. in the field was canceled out by my apostasy.

Similarly, when I attend conferences, I have literally been told to shut up. Instead of being heard out, I am treated to a lecture. Academics, who do not know me, take it upon themselves to reeducate me.

With the advent of President Donald Trump, things have gotten worse. My wife (who is also a sociologist) and I usually enjoy attending the Southern Sociology Society (SSS) meetings in New Orleans. We like the town, but are having second thoughts about going.

What triggered this decision was the "call for papers" put out by the organization. Professional societies, such as the SSS, are supposed to promote science. They are intended to be places where scholars get together to share their results. This cross-fertilization is meant to advance our collective understanding.

It should go without saying that a true science is empirical. Neutral observations of the real world are expected to be confirmed—or disconfirmed—by other neutral observations. Bias is supposed to be weeded out as a source of error and confusion. This way the truth can emerge.

But those days are gone. No longer does the SSS see this as it mission. Today the goal is to promote a political agenda. In addition, no one should be surprised that this is a left wing agenda. Political correctness has so corrupted the social sciences that even mainstream sociologists have become activists dedicated to destroying Trump.

If this sounds extreme, let me quote an extended passage from the SSS's call for papers. The reader can judge for him or herself the purpose of a conference entitled "Racial Theory, Analysis, and Politics in TrumpAmerica."

The call begins, "We want all Trump-related sociological analysis to be the focus as our nation…needs answers and explanations. How did a patently unqualified person like Trump get elected? Why did we not predict his election? Why did so many whites support him."

It should be evident that this statement is harshly judgmental. The outcomes of the desired studies have been predetermined. Conservative explanations are not welcome. Neither are dispassionate analyses.

But let me continue. "Is Trump's election a short-term development or a political egg that has been hatching for a long time? What is our analysis of Trump's core supporters? Were [they] just expressing their 'class anxieties'. What are the politics needed to undo TrumpAmerica?"

Bear in mind that these are southern sociologists. Bear in mind as well that the current president of the SSS is from Duke University. These are not a bunch of kooks from a marginal association. They epitomize the deep-seated attitudes of academics in one of the most conservative parts of the country.

One last line that stands out in this call for papers is, "Will Democrats cave into the idea that to get back to the White House they need to stop relying on 'identity politics'?" The import of this injunction is that sociologists must defend identity politics.

Identity politics, of course, stresses the special needs of "minorities" such as blacks, women, gays, and the poor. The idea is thus not to investigate the truth, but to find ways to help those our culture exploits. In other words, the truth is known; it is just a matter of applying it.

This, however, is standard Marxist thinking. Marx, having discovered what he believed to be the driving force of history, told capitalists they needed to stand aside or be run over. Furthermore, he, and his associates, would organize a proletarian revolution to see that they did.

The folks at the SSS have the identical mindset. Only now their archenemy is that capitalistic icon Donald Trump. He is clearly in their sights.

The Fate of Sociology

I am a sociologist. I make no bones about it. Despite the fact that I am part of a tiny conservative minority within my discipline, I am proud to be studying what makes human societies tick. The way we interact is so complicated that it is a challenge to unravel the intricacies.

Moreover, the details of how we deal with each other are far from trivial. Their impact on how we cooperate and what we can collectively achieve is profound. If we do not understand these, we are bound to veer off into egregious dead ends. Not only will things go wrong; they can go dangerously wrong.

Sadly, many contemporary sociologists are not social scientists. They are not so much interested in investigating social truths as in promoting the agendas they brought with them when they entered the field. Accordingly, if they do research, it is advocacy research. They employ the trappings of science to legitimize their prior commitments.

Who am I talking about? Why, it is those feminists who are out to smash the male hegemony. It is those class warriors who are set on toppling the economic elites. It is those minority members who see discrimination under every bush. Most of these folks are out for revenge.

Ask almost anyone what sociologists believe and the answer will be the same. A majority of these academics are thought to believe that society is permeated by oppression. Privileged individuals, whether they are male, wealthy, white, or straight, are allegedly conspiring to keep their victims in bondage.

What is more, most sociologists purportedly want every well-meaning person to join their crusade to overthrow these villains. Only then will we, as a group, achieve the equality that is our due. Only then will we effectively collaborate for our shared benefit.

Nonetheless, matters are not that simple. A cartoon universe, in which everyone is divided into good and bad guys, is belied by the complexity of the world we inhabit. As adults ought to discover, we humans are ménage of contradictory impulses. We are far from straightforward creatures.

Nor do we always wear our motives on our sleeves. Indeed, what we want and how we intend to get it is often invisible. Sometimes our desires are unconscious. We literally do not recognize them. At other times, they are disguised. We try to fool ourselves—and others—into believing we are better than we are.

In any event, despite our intelligence, we frequently do not see what is there to be seen. Even when reality is rubbed in our noses, we cling to socially acceptable rationalizations. At moments like this, genuine sociology can come into play. It can piece the veil that shields us from unpleasant facts.

Let me provide an example. For years Americans have sought to improve the quality of childhood education. We have also attempted to promote democratic values. To this end, trillions of dollars were poured into reforming the schools.

But has this worked? Did, for instance, spending more on impoverished school districts raise their achievement levels? Almost everyone assumed this had to provide improved results.

And yet social research, starting with James Coleman, demonstrated that there is no correlation between the dollars expended and the amount students learn. It seems as if there should be, yet there is not.

The strongest connection is actually between the attitudes of parents and the accomplishments of their youngsters. Not surprisingly, the greater the emphasis mom and dad place on learning, the greater the effort Johnny is apt to make.

But how do we compensate for parents who disparage education? How do we help their offspring get what is not available at home? The answer has been to ramp up school budgets.

All of this, however, has been of little avail. Learning has not improved. Why? Because teachers cannot substitute for parents. They cannot provide the love and security of a stable family. And yet the myth persists. Most people still believe that fancier educational facilities will have the desired effect.

Sociology could set them straight. Much could be learned if it returned to being a social science, as opposed to an ideological plaything. This, at least, is my hope!

Chapter IX

Forward-Looking Conservatism

Social Change

Societies change. They always have. Sometimes this is for the better; sometimes for the worse. No society, however, is perfect. All have their limitations and vices. An impulse to make improvements is therefore widespread. Which way is best is thus the real question. Liberals are essentially domesticated revolutionaries. As neo-Marxists, they intend to bring radical changes to our civilization. They want to get rid of capitalism and replace it with an idealized form of socialism. If they could, they would do this immediately. They would tear our economic and political institutions apart and substitute universal love and kindness. In the meantime, they place their faith in an enlightened bureaucracy. They assume that if the best and the brightest take charge of the federal government, they will create programs and regulations that benefit the entire community.

Conservatives are less sanguine. They look upon what the liberals have wrought with jaded eyes. Is this, they wonder, what is meant by progress? Is arrogant incompetence to be the shape of our future? Many observers assume that right-wing resistance is equivalent to wanting to reinstate the past. Isn't this what it means to be *conservative*? In fact, it is not! Political labels have a way of transmuting. They take on diametrically opposed meanings depending on the politics of the moment. The paradigm for this transformation is "liberalism." The term was initially used to designate views equivalent to contemporary conservatism. As a consequence, we now refer to nineteenth century conservatives as "classical liberals." In essence, the original conservatives began by agitating for change, not trying to hold it back.

Conservatives can still be forward-looking. They do not need to cede this stance to those who deceptively identify themselves as "progressives." We live in an increasingly middle class world. This demands that more of us become professionalized. Conservatives must—and can—recognize this development and seek modifications accordingly. They can sponsor what amounts to a new Great Awakening. What distinguishes them from liberals, however, is the sort of changes they advocate. Instead of promoting a neo-Marxist regime, they want smaller government. Rather than assume that one day we will become one huge loving family, they stress the importance of the free marketplace. They also believe in personal liberty, family values, and democracy. None of these are old-fashioned. All are capable of being updated. Indeed, that is happening.

So-called progressives, as it happens, are mired in the past. They have not escaped the nineteenth century fantasies of Karl Marx and consequently hope to revive the failed policies of Franklin Roosevelt. As a result, when confronted with unfamiliar conundrums, they resort to stereotypical solutions. This will not do! Forward-looking conservatives must provide opportunities that promote genuine advances. They need to encourage people be their best selves and to assume responsibility for solving problems that only they can resolve. Our mass-techno-commercial society has produced a host of unexpected changes. These must be recognized for what they are and, to repeat a by now familiar mantra, dealt with realistically.

One such unwelcome development is the explosion in unwed pregnancies. Millions of children are born to single parents who do not have the emotional or economic resources to raise them the way they deserve to be raised. An epidemic of divorce has also contributed to this dilemma. Some on the left respond to this occurrence by denigrating the institution of marriage. They complain that it is an instrument for holding women in bondage. This is a tragic error. We have no better means of providing emotional support for adults or the appropriate love and socialization for children than durable intimate relationships. Hillary Clinton and the radical feminists may have thought otherwise, but their collectivist aspirations have long since demonstrated their inadequacy. Change, nonetheless, remains necessary. The gender roles of our grandparents have to be revised. With most women today working outside the home, the traditional gender division of labor must be modified.

Nor can our attitudes toward the poor remain static. Although progressives insist on total equality, this is unattainable. We are a hierarchical species, which means that we always rank ourselves with respect to others. The answer, therefore, is not equality, but social mobility. We must provide everyone with an opportunity to move up. The best way to achieve this is not by artificially moving people around. Strategies, such as affirmative action, tend to blow up in our faces. It is more sensible to provide people with the tools for succeeding. Foremost among these is self-discipline. Unless people acquire the inner strength to control their behaviors, they will not be able to implement effective action.

If forward-looking conservatives are to hold society together, they must stand foursquare against retribalization. Liberals are committed to an identity politics in which favored groups receive special privileges. Those on the left are anything but fair. Accordingly, they tend to dismiss anyone not aligned with them. As a consequence, they totally miss the importance of "social individualism." They do not realize the increasing importance of personal decision-making that is based on an accurate understanding of how humans and societies operate. Because they seek only government solutions, they overlook what people can do for themselves. They thus fail to cultivate the strengths needed to make independent choices on the assumption that these do not exist. No wonder they downplay the significance of individual courage.

Earlier we discussed the three-cornered war between liberalism, spiritual conservatism, and libertarianism. None of these traditional ideologies are sufficient to deal with contemporary complexities. But neither are they going away. Social individualism may be emerging as an alternative; nonetheless it must acknowledge the continuing contributions of its predecessors. Instead of escalating the culture wars, we need social balance. Forward-looking conservatives should encourage this equilibrium. They ought, as a corollary, to promote an enlightened individualism that serves as a social fulcrum. Individuals, who are principled, emotionally mature, and aware of what is possible, can make sensible selections between competing points of view in accord with emerging circumstances. They can function as the pivot and arbiter between otherwise incompatible approaches to overcoming our problems. This is a dynamic conservatism. It is clear-eyed and muscular. It is decidedly not stuck in an outmoded past.

Progressive Conservatism

A Professionalized World

The world is changing around us. But it is moving in directions we do not always anticipate. Our society is so complex that is often difficult to fathom its machinations. Still, like it or not, we need to be aware of these changes, lest we be left behind. What we do not understand can hurt us. It may doom us to be less successful than we would wish.

As I have explained in my book, *The Great Middle Class Revolution* (published by the KSU Press), ours is the first fully middle class society in the history of the world. Not only was it the first in which the majority of people became middle class, it is the first in which the middle class sets the standards and the first in which middle class virtues are most closely linked to social success.

A middle class world is a professionalized one. It is a world in which a larger proportion of the population is required to be self-motivated experts in what they do. Not only doctor, lawyers and engineers, but also police officers, nurses, social workers, business mangers and financial administrators must know how to perform complex tasks and to do so based on internal motivations. They must, in essence, be self-starters who can supervise their own activities.

Even in their personal lives they must be self-motivated experts. Unless they know how to make voluntary intimacy work, and are mature enough to implement this knowledge, their marriages are unlikely to be successful. By the same token, if they do not know how to raise middle class children, their offspring are less likely to be successful when they grow up.

What this adds up to is that middle class successes must be both knowledgeable and self-directed. They must be able to make independent decisions and correct these when they go wrong. In other words, they must know the facts and how to apply them. It also helps if they have the courage to exercise responsible initiative. The world can be an unpredictable and unforgiving place for those who do not possess the daring to deal with it as it is. It can also be intimidating for those who have difficulty coping with its increasing human diversity.

This is where a college education fits in. It is not merely about obtaining a credential that will facilitate social mobility. Yes, it can be a ticket to a better job and greater financial security. More fundamentally it is about preparing students for middle class professionalization. Good grades are not enough. It is more important to grow into the sort of person who can exercise competent discretion.

Contemporary universities, including KSU, pride themselves in teaching critical thinking. This must not, however, be an empty phrase. It should become a deep-seated value. The theologian Paul Tillich once talked about acquiring "the courage to be." Today professors and students must collaborate in attaining the courage to be professionalized.

A Third Great Awakening?
Glenn Beck is a wonder!

Who else, on his own hook, could have attracted over a half million Americans to the Washington mall to celebrate the nation's heritage? Who else could have convinced so many people to travel so far to listen to message promoting honor and character?

And no wonder. Beck has done some of the best investigative reporting in recent memory. His exposes about Van Jones, Jeff Jones, and Acorn alerted many millions of television viewers to the radical fringe surrounding Barack Obama. Similarly, his defense of the American Constitution awakened a love of country in many more.

But Beck is wrong about one thing. He believes the nation is about to undergo a Third Great Awakening. During the 18th and 19th centuries, the United States was swept by two massive religious revivals. All up and down the East Coast, ordinary people renewed their faith by attending mass rallies led by inspirational preachers.

Beck may himself be inspirational, but the religious fires that fed these earlier conflagrations have long since died down. Thus, although efforts to renew our moral fiber are undoubtedly worthy, they cannot depend on restoring a comparable religious fervor.

Mind you, religious principles have been essential to creating our nation and maintaining its core values. No doubt too, they will continue to hold many of us to honest and virtuous standards.

Even so, religion cannot supplant the secular practices that have become the norm. It can supplement, but not displace them. I see evidence of this daily in my classrooms.

When I ask my students at Kennesaw State University if they believe in God, between ninety and ninety-five per cent assert they do. This is in line with surveys that show the same for the nation at large. Indeed, the United State is probably the most religious large country in the world.

But when I ask these same students to identify the first or last of the Ten Commandments, most cannot. The few who do are almost always among the oldest in the class. Nor when I ask how many of them are Protestant do any hands go up. Amazingly, though a majority are Baptists and Methodists, they have never heard the term "Protestant."

Meanwhile, if I ask how many students are on Facebook, every hand shoots up. Similarly, were I to spy on their laptops, they would likely be watching YouTube, not reading passages from the scriptures.

Like it or not, ours has become a secular country. Though most people have faith, few are seriously devout. They believe in a loving God who created the world. They are also sure He will eventually save them and that they personally will go to heaven. That, however, is about it. Ask them about the specific tenets of their own churches, and they are flummoxed.

None of this bodes well for another Great Awakening. Exhortations to do what is right may be met with enthusiastic applause, but this does not presage a return to an old time religion based on fire and brimstone.

Nevertheless, Americans are by and large good people. Most want to do right. They are merely less likely to seek direct guidance from theological sources.

If Beck himself is motivated by strong religious commitments, the rest of us are apt to benefit from his courageous integrity. Nonetheless, we are unlikely to join him. We too may be distressed by the low standards set by politicians, but our response will probably be less spiritual.

So what lies ahead? Maybe there will be a "conservative" awakening. Perhaps there will be a "democratic" restoration. People may even become better educated about the need to defend the Constitution or reign in astronomical budget deficits. Expecting more, however, is only a remote possibility.

The Liberals' Biggest Mistake

How well do you know Barack Obama? Do you know him as well as your father? Or your uncle Jack? Or your cousin Sue?

The answer to all of these questions is probably "not that well." A great many people were certainly surprised by the sort of president Obama has turned out to be. What they saw on television during the campaign has not accorded particularly well with what they currently see as he performs his office.

Think too of one of Obama's many promises. On more than one occasion he pledged to be his brother and sister's keeper. He would look after our personal welfare as if we were his very own siblings. But guess what? He is not my brother. Nor do I expect that he is one of yours.

And herein lies Obama's biggest mistake; one he shares with liberals in general. Obama thinks that society is—or should be—one big family. Moreover, he and his political allies perceive themselves, if not as our surrogate parents, then at least as our protective older siblings. They therefore intend to safeguard us from our personal follies.

This, of course, is the patent medicine they are now attempting to sell us with regard to health care. Unfortunately many of us refuse to see this reform as in our interest; hence it must be forced upon us much as cod liver oil was once forced down the throats of small children.

The trouble is that Obama is not, in fact, our well-meaning parent or brother. Nor are his congressional associates our altruistic elder siblings. They are politicians who merely claim to be the equivalent of our relatives. Indeed, if we listen carefully, they admit as much.

Thus, one of the arguments that has been used to persuade reluctant Democrats to vote for ObamaCare is that if they do not, the president's political capital will be irreparably damaged. In other words, they are being asked to care more about his interests than those of their constituents.

The point—and it is not a trivial one—is that we are not members of a single extended family. We—all three hundred million of us—are not biologically related. Nor do we usually behave as if we were. We may be human, and reside within the same boundaries, but this does not convert us into genetically linked intimates.

The fact is that we do not—and cannot—constitute a single family. There are simply too many of us. It is both physically and psychologically impossible to treat each other as actual kin.

First, we cannot literally meet, never mind know, hundreds of millions of others. We may depend upon these strangers for our livelihood, but that is not the same as distinguishing between them as individuals. This means that Obama cannot hope to address a host of diverse needs it is impossible for him to identify.

Second, we cannot literally care for hundreds of millions of others. Our biology is such that we human beings are capable of loving only a relatively few. Therefore, when politicians claim they love all their fellow citizens this is at best a figure of speech. They, including Obama, are essentially manipulating our need to be loved for their own purposes.

Speaking now as a sociologist, I must again point out that we are not, in fact, family. We are not biologically related. Ironically, that we must sometimes cooperate as if we were is perhaps the central problem of modern mass societies. We are, in reality, what sociologists call a Gesellschaft society, that is, a community of strangers who often act as if we were not.

To repeat we are not family, hence to pretend otherwise is a huge mistake. Moreover, assuming so can lead to horrendous errors. For instance, to imagine that faceless bureaucrats would administer government run health care as if we were members of their own families could prove ruinous.

Obama and company may mean well, but their assumption that we are one big family is more than silly. It is an intellectual fiction of which we must all be wary.

Looking Forward—Why Conservatives are Not Conservative

Conservatives are supposedly against change. According to liberals, they haven't had a new idea since Calvin Coolidge proclaimed that the business of America is business. Why, if it were up to these right-wing fuddy-duddies, we would still be wearing high-button shoes.

This, however, is complete nonsense. Whatever the conventional wisdom may say, most modern conservatives are actually forward looking. If "conservative" means being opposed to change, then American conservatives are not conservative. In fact, they are more progressive than most progressives.

Contemporary conservatives may honor tradition, but they do not stand pat on it. To the contrary, they believe in building upon the best of the past. They perceive the valuable contributions of our ancestors as a foundation upon which to construct further improvements.

Let us see what this adds up to. The four pillars of conservatism, i.e., the four principles upon which conservatives agree, are these. They believe in freedom, in democracy, in market economics and in family values; none of which is mired in the past. All, in fact, look toward the future.

Consider the case of democracy. Conservatives favor decentralized government. They universally support institutions that allow individuals to make decisions for themselves. Instead of delegating more power to Washington, they prefer that authority to be exercised closer to home. This, they assert, permits a flexibility that better suits the needs of ordinary people. How then is this a conservative idea? Doesn't it actually foster novelty and responsive-ness?

Then there is market economics. Conservatives are alleged to be friends of big business. But they also support small business. What they truly favor is not bigness, but the opportunities and creativity inherent in capitalism. They remember (in a way most liberals do not) that this system has produced greater wealth, and distributed it more broadly, than any other economic arrangement in the history of the world. In what way is prosperity a conservative phenomenon? Maybe it isn't.

Next come family values. Conservatives do have a warm spot in their hearts for families. They believe in stable marriages. They also encourage parents to commit to raising their own children. Far from endorsing a patriarchal dictatorship in which men exploit women, most "conservatives" realize that the modern family is a companionate affair, where husbands and wives cooperate in establishing "a haven in a heartless world." They know that loving families protect the interests of all concerned. There is nothing conservative in this except the conservation of human happiness.

Finally, we come to the most important conservative principle of all. If equality is the *master value* for liberals, freedom is the *master value* for conservatives. They insist that ordinary people be allowed the room to control their personal destinies. As such, conservatives are pleased to live in a nation that guarantees liberty for all. They are happy to honor a two hundred year old constitution that incorporated a Bill of Rights from the outset.

Is freedom a conservative idea? Does it prevent people from changing? Far from it! Freedom gives us the room to make changes. Freedom allows people to experiment in all sorts of directions; directions that may not have been contemplated by their forebears.

To be blunt, freedom is a progressive idea. Indeed, it may be the most progressive idea extant. Freedom allows people to innovate and to adjust. Coupled with democracy, market economics, and family values, it liberates the human soul to expand and to embrace an ever better future.

If the notion that liberals are progressive is one of the greatest frauds perpetrated on humankind, then the canard that conservatives oppose progress has got to be the second greatest fraud. Sometimes language misleads us. We get fooled into believing that a word characterizes that to which it is applied. This, unfortunately, has been the fate of the label "conservative."

Marching Backwards—Why Progressives are not Progressive

During last year's primary campaign, Hillary Clinton confessed that she preferred to be considered a progressive rather than a liberal. In this, she is not alone. Many liberals feel the same way. They think of themselves as enlightened advocates of a new and more socially rewarding epoch that is just around the corner.

As the direct descendants of Karl Marx, most liberals are convinced that they are on the right side of history. They assume that their policies must inevitably prevail and that when they do we will all share in a more just, more satisfying, and more productive future. In their less guarded moments, they even conceive of this future in utopian terms, with total equality and universal love having become the norm.

There is only one thing wrong with this vision. It has nothing to do with reality. Liberals are not progressive; they are regressive. Liberalism is reactionary and seeks to return us to a romanticized past, not to cope with the actual challenges of the techno-commercial world we are destined to occupy.

Consider the evidence. President Obama tells us that he intends to relieve our current economic distress, but where does he find his inspiration? As most of us know, he finds it in Franklin Delano Roosevelt's administration. For him, The Great Depression was a halcyon period when big-time spending and government control were the prescription for what ailed us. Of course, those days were the better part of a century ago.

Then there is the liberal Democrat mantra about how our worst problems were created by greedy capitalists. They, not over-reaching federal regulators, intentionally precipitated the present housing crisis. This attitude, however, harks back even farther in time. Marx would have been proud of the accusation. He too believed that greedy business people were at the base of almost every social problem. He too wished to see them overthrown

But the looking backwards is not finished. As the Middle Ages came to an end, monarchs across Europe sought to extend their control over the nations they ruled. This was the era of absolutism when Louis XIV of France famously proclaimed that he was the state. He, and his peers, thought of themselves parental figures who had the right—indeed the duty—to manage everything they possibly could. They knew best, and it was therefore up to the governed to obey.

Among other things, these absolutists distributed monopolies to their favorites. Only a friend of the king could import herring or acquire land in Virginia. Now Obama is the one distributing government favors. Despite claiming that he didn't want to control the automobile industry, he is currently prompting his minions to turn over controlling interests in GM and Chrysler to his buddies in the UAW. He has similarly encouraged Timothy Geithner to extend his tentacles into every crevasse of the financial industry, whether invited or not.

Come to think of it, hasn't Obama appointed Czars to control everything from the environment to drug enforcement? Imagine what he will be able to do if he gets his hands on the health care industry or the energy sector of the economy.

But there is still more of this liberal marching to the rear. How many people remember Obama's acceptance speech at the Democratic nominating convention where he said, "we must…rise or fall as one nation; [our] fundamental belief [must be] that I am my brother's keeper; I am my sister's keeper." In other words, Obama and his colleagues want to be our keepers. This, of course, brings us back to Biblical times. Perhaps he thinks of himself as the new Moses.

Actually, it takes us back even farther to hunter-gatherer times. Liberal leaders seem to think of themselves as village elders who are responsible for protecting us from ourselves. In their view, they have the expertise and the maturity, whereas the rest of us are like children who need to be led by our betters.

Liberals have told us many lies, but perhaps none is bigger than the canard that they are progressive. They are nothing of the sort. They do not have new ideas, but merely very old one's that they have skillfully repackaging as innovative.

A Progressive Time Warp

It has become a science fiction cliché. Sooner or later the plot is apt to boast an excursion into the past or the distant future. As it happens, my wife and I recently experienced an episode of the former when we attended the annual conference of the Society for the Study of Social Problems (SSSP) in New York City.

Virtually all of the attendees would happily have described themselves as "progressive," or maybe "radical," in their political orientations. An odd collection of aging hippies and earnest young disciples, their principal objective was to develop exciting new ways to cure the ills of our society.

And yet, if a visitor from outer space paid attention to what was said in many of the sessions, she could not avoid feeling caught in a time warp. Here were the 1960's (and sometimes earlier) brought back to life with gusto. Nuggets of "wisdom," I heard as a young man, were breathlessly re-uttered as if freshly discovered.

One of the favorite topics was "victimhood." Thus in a session devoted to drug use, we were told that women addicted to methamphetamines were losing their identities because of misguided government programs. Instead of having their status as mothers affirmed, this was undermined by taking their children away.

These women were therefore double victims; victims of a frightful drug and of professional insensitivity. Even though they loved their children and found comfort in their roles as mothers, the officials did not care and callously separated families that should be kept intact.

While this exposition was well received by the audience, it was a bit too much for me to bear and so I rose to tell two stories from when I worked as a methadone counselor. The first concerned a woman I helped get her children back after they had been placed in protective services.

My heart had gone out to her when she tearfully explained how her children were all she lived for. Then when she subsequently came to see me with her youngsters in tow, almost the first thing that happened was that she rapped her little girl across the face with the back of her hand when the child plaintively expressed a desire for candy.

This woman was sincere in expressing her love, but that did not mean she was a good parent. Nor were the social workers that sought to protect her children entirely mistaken in their concern for their welfare.

In another instance, a woman whose children had been removed from her care bore a fourth baby by a different man and then moved in with a third. Soon thereafter, he, in a fit of pique, threw this infant against the wall when he could not get it to cease crying. The child in question shortly died.

Upon concluding these tales, I made the point that morality mattered. These women were not merely victims; they were agents who needed to be held accountable for their actions. To do less was to invite dire consequences.

To this an audience member responded by suggesting that my comments were ill-advised. I was told that I should not be invoking "*morality*" because the concept was too contentious. We needed to find another word that would not invite the authorities to act as self-righteous busybodies.

So here we were with tired relativistic platitudes being used to justify failing to protect the innocent from abuse. The alleged victimhood of the mothers was to prevent us from intervening for the sake of their children. Because the investigator felt sympathy for the women she interviewed, we were to ignore the plight of sufferers she never meet.

All of this is defended in the name of compassion. Somehow it is supposed to be "progressive" to jettison moral standards. Social discipline is to be thrown out the window because those forced to behave in ways they do not like might be offended.

Were this to become the conventional attitude, chaos would surely reign.

Conservatives Cannot Afford to Be Conservative

Football fans will know the strategy. It is called a prevent defense. When you are leading toward the end of the game, instead of trying to score more points you have your defenders drop back in an effort to make sure that the other team does not score. The trouble is this often backfires and allows them to move ahead.

By now many commentators have suggested this was a major reason Mitt Romney lost the election. He could not believe that the country would vote for a man who was both dishonest and a terrible steward of the economy. Why, after all, would anyone want a nation that was both poor and weak?

But people did vote for Obama—because they did not perceive that they were given a dynamic alternative. Mitt was a technocrat. He was an honest man with demonstrable economic skills. I still believe this is exactly what we needed; nevertheless it was not what the voters thought.

As commentators such as the economist Thomas Sowell and the newly seated Texas senator Ted Cruz have counseled, now is not the time to go "moderate." The electoral problem was not that Republicans failed to resemble Democrats; it was that they were ashamed of being full-blooded Republicans.

Conservatives believe in freedom. Conservatives support a free marketplace. They also favor a smaller government. To these ends, they have rightly defended the constitution and sought to lower the deficit. These are noble objectives, but they are not inspirational.

Remember how Ronald Reagan called us to "greatness." Remember how during his second presidential campaign he told us that it was "morning in America." These are not conservative themes. They did not look backwards, but forward. They offered visions of a better world, not a return to an old one.

Freedom isn't an outmoded concept! Nor is a market-based economy! These are the keys to unleashing the energies and genius of ordinary people. This, therefore, is what erstwhile "conservatives" need to stress; it is what will give the young and moderate a reason to vote Republican.

What I am about to say will offend many people, but I must say it anyway because I believe it is the truth. During this last election cycle Republicans put too many eggs into the evangelical basket. They expected religious conservatives to come out in huge numbers, whereas they did not.

This false assumption prompted the party to select candidates, who sounded as if they favored rape, to shape its image. As a result, social issues, rather than the economy or our future, came to the fore and persuaded moderates that Republicans had nothing new to offer.

This must change. Cruz suggests that conservatives pivot and champion an "opportunity" society. Over a decade ago Newt Gingrich came to a similar conclusion. Unfortunately, Bill Clinton, who evidently believed the same, quickly preempted this strategy.

So opportunity is a good starting point. It speaks to the aspirations of constituencies who have been drifting Democratic, such as the Hispanics and young women, and promises them a better future. Moreover, it tells them this future is in their own hands.

But we need more. We need a renewed call to greatness. Obama has been playing "small ball" and this should be used against him. He keeps on picking at small-scale grievances so as to gather a coalition of those who feel as if they are on the outside looking in.

Republicans consequently have an opening to appeal to Americans as Americans. How can ordinary people take pride in a country that is limping a long, barely keeping its head above water? How can they feel good about having an ambassador shot or about Iran acquiring nuclear weapons?

Reagan drew on the best in the American people. He told them they would succeed if they helped themselves. More than this, he assured them that they had the stuff to do so. Have we somehow grown feebler since then?

Why Not a "Responsibility Agenda"?

The game has changed!

Ever since the election of Scott Brown, everyone—with the possible exception of Nancy Pelosi—understands that it may be impossible for Democrats to enact comprehensive medical reform or cap-and trade legislation. Brown's extra senate vote seems to have barred the way to the Obama administration's fondest liberal dreams.

It has not, however, diminished the president's budgetary ambitions. He still plans to spend trillions of dollars the nation does not possess. While he claims to understand that there must be fiscal restraint, he essentially hopes to shut the barn door only after the horse has long departed.

As a consequence, the Republicans must be the party of No. While they have put forward many proposals for improving health care and energy consumption, as of now their primary objective has to be to prevent the majority from tearing down what generations of Americans have built.

Nevertheless, in the long run this will not be enough. An opposition party that intends to become the governing party must also have a positive agenda. As George Bush the elder learned, it needs to offer a "vision," i.e., a far-reaching proposal for enhancing the national well-being.

Most Republicans understand this. Even so, they have had difficulty articulating an inspirational program. Some have suggested resurrecting a version of Newt Gingrich's Contract with America, while others have recommended a revision of Obama's proposals. George W. Bush, of course, mistakenly believed that an appeal to freedom would do the job.

Unfortunately none of these approaches has demonstrated the candle-power to elicit voter excitement. It may, therefore, be necessary to rethink the party's fundamental agenda. Although the underlying conservative goals of *freedom*, *democracy*, a *market economy* and *family values* remain valid, how these are implemented, and as importantly how they are packaged, can use tweaking.

One possibility is for Republicans to support a *personal responsibility* agenda. As the party that believes in decentralized governance, it should more forcefully advocate the individual competences that make for improved personal decisions. Reshaping the national focus away from what the government can do for its citizens, to what they can do for themselves, will ultimately make for a happier and more productive populace.

Like it or not—quite in opposition to the movie *Avatar*—ours is a mass techno-commercial society. As such, if it is to function more productively, it must foster a host of knowledgeable choices at the local level. Indeed, were these to be supplanted by a bevy of government dictates—as was the case in the late lamented Soviet Union—it too would die of terminal stupidity.

Although Barack Obama does not appreciate this truth, he is politically shrewd enough to recognize that most Americans value personal responsibility. As a result, he says he does too, while, in fact, pursuing the opposite. Time and again, he proposes government programs intended to rob others of private initiative.

The supreme irony here is that in concentrating ever more responsibility in the hands of the federal government, he and his minions have been utterly irresponsible. They have been sloppy planners, corrupt delegators, and reckless fiscal stewards. In short, they have been driving us all—at breathtaking speed—to the poor house. And doing it with our money,

The alternative must, therefore, be an appeal to voters to take back control over their destinies. They must be encouraged—which is to say, given the courage—to face life more reliant on their personal abilities and decisions.

This is something politicians can do. They cannot provide the all-inclusive protections that Democrats promise, but they can nurture an awareness of our shared need to become better custodians of our respective futures. Personal responsibility has to be more than a cliché. It must become a commitment to which each of us, including our political leaders, are dedicated.

Our Greatest Social Problem: Unwed Parenthood

Few would deny that we confront significant political problems. The current impasse between liberals and conservatives has become so extreme that almost everyone is aware something is radically wrong. What is amiss may be in dispute, but that something is seems clear.

In fact, so passionate have arguments about the proper role government become that they have sucked most of the oxygen out of the public arena. As a result, there is little energy left over to discuss anything other than ObamaCare, energy policy, or potential federal deficits.

This, however, does not mean that all is well on other fronts. To be more specific, we are mired is a "social" problem the dimensions of which are at least as terrifying as the likelihood of national bankruptcy. This issue is none other than the tsunami of unwed parenthood that has broken over our shores.

Almost unnoticed, the number of children born to unmarried couples has risen from less than one in twenty to about two out of every five births. That's right, as of now nearly forty percent of all children are what used to be called "illegitimate."

Many folks—mostly liberals—profess to being unconcerned by this development. They tell us that there are all sorts of ways to raise children; that no particular way—such as the traditional two-parent family—is better than any other. This is often described as "multiculturalism" and is hailed as evidence of our growing social tolerance.

Nevertheless, there is a problem. Indeed, we are being engulfed by a catastrophe of unprecedented proportions. Never before have so many children been abandoned to an undeserved fate. Never before has a nation entrusted its future to a generation, this many of whom, have not been provided the protection of two devoted parents.

Before we go any further, let us get something straight. Being raised by a single parent, either because of an unwed birth or divorce, is typically a severe disadvantage. Despite the exceptions (and there are exceptions) more often than not the innocent victims come up on the short end of the social stick.

Let us review some of these burdens. Those who grow up in single parent households are more likely to:

- Have lower incomes
- Obtain lesser educations
- Have poorer health, including mental health
- Become involved in crime
- Be swept up in drug and alcohol abuse
- Participate in unstable relationships of their own

In other words, children born to unwed parents are apt to be less successful, including less happy, than those blessed with two loving parents who remain committed to each other and their offspring.

President Obama and his allies tell us that they have promoted health care reform in large part because they intend to redistribute social resources. They believe it is unfair that some people have fewer advantages than others and are determined to rectify this injustice.

But if "illegitimacy" has the effects outlined above, then merely shoveling money and/or services to the underclass will have few lasting benefits. In the end, the poor will still be poor and unhappy.

So why haven't politicians been falling all over themselves to correct this inequity? The reason is deceptively simple. It is because they haven't got a clue as to how to fix things. They just don't have the programs to turn them around.

And the reason they don't is that successful families depend on "responsible" behavior by the participants. Only prospective mothers and fathers can control themselves such that they remain dedicated to each other and their children.

Politicians may talk a lot about "personal responsibility," but guess what—personal responsibility is personal. It is something that people have to do for themselves.

The Divorce Crisis: The Second Wave
Two decades ago, when I began teaching introductory sociology at Kennesaw State University, I knew I had to include a module on the family. I also knew I had to include information about divorce. These were standard materials in every introductory sociology course nationwide.

But I was not optimistic. Since most of the students in my classes were fairly young I reasoned that few of them had ever been married—never mind divorced. This was a subject to which they had to be exposed, yet one they would probably find boring.

Almost immediately, however, I realized I was profoundly wrong. A majority of my students—especially the younger ones—found divorce a fascinating subject. They sat up and paid attention. They even asked more penetrating questions than usual.

At first I was confused. But then it hit me. I decided to ask how many were the children of divorce. Much to my astonishment, time after time, more than half raised their hands. This was clearly why they were so interested. It was a problem with which they had personally grappled.

In fact, the number of divorces occurring in the United States, having peaked in the early 1990's, has rolled back somewhat. Despite the early enthusiasm many people felt for an opportunity to escape bad relationships, large numbers soon discovered that this was easier in theory than practice.

Now it is their children who are discovering another legacy of divorce. What we in sociology have learned is that the children of divorce are less likely to marry than those brought up in intact families. Worse still, should they marry, they are twice as likely to divorce as their peers.

Nor should this be surprising. Having experienced, up-close and personal, how fragile intimate relations can be, they worry that they may not be able to make them work for themselves. After all, if Mom and Dad, both of whom were adults, could not keep their vows, how could they, as their children, expect to do better?

By the same token, how could they be expected to trust members of the opposite sex? Having witnessed the undependability of one parent or another, the lesson that men or women are inherently undependable was easy to incorporate. Clearly, although people may say they love one another, this does not mean they keep their word.

Add to this the anger of having been betrayed by their parents and their own adult relationships are apt to be fraught with insecurity. Ironically, as desperately as they desire reliable love, to this same degree they suspect love is never reliable. And because they are apprehensive, they contribute to its fragility.

So where does this leave us as a society? The lesson is this: precisely because modern marriage has become voluntary, it remains vulnerable to our human limitations. Likewise, because divorce has become so common, there are many more people whose personal experiences predispose them to undermining their own desires.

What then are we to do? The answer seems simple. Surely we must be personally responsible for our own marriages. No government program is going to come to our rescue here. In fact, strong marriages result from partners who are individually committed to making them work. Strong marriages also depend on two people who know what they are doing; which is to say, how to live intimately with another imperfect human being.

And so, despite what I have just said, the answer is not really simple. Hillary Clinton told us that it takes a village to raise a child. Well, it takes something beyond a village to save a marriage. Rather, it takes two people who are dedicated to making it work. And that is never easy.

The bottom line is that the government cannot guarantee our happiness in all areas. Only we can. Only we can assure interpersonal success; but only if we are individually, and collectively, dedicated to being accountable. Once more personal responsibility makes all the difference.

Why Marriage?

What is the purpose of marriage? Why do we have the institution? Now that the pressure to legalize gay marriages has reached the boiling point, what is so important about allowing homosexuals to partake in the same tradition as straights?

The sociologist Andrew Cherlin has argued that contemporary marriages are individualistic. People embark upon them because they want to be happy. Couples assume, correctly so in the case of good marriages, that tying the knot will lead to greater personal fulfillment.

From this perspective, if making a matrimonial commitment does not enhance one's personal well being, a divorce is in order. More than this, if a person is uncomfortable with promising to be faithful forever, then engaging in cohabitation is a viable alternative.

Given this background, why are gays so insistent on participating in what many people have described as a dying convention?

I submit that it is because homosexuals also want to be happy. As human beings, they too seek love that they can depend upon. Since they too assume that marriage is a bond they can trust, they crave access to its benefits.

But is this what marriage is about? Why, since at least hunter-gatherer times, have all societies established some form of permanent heterosexual union? Why have they all insisted that couples pledge to remain together—no matter what?

The evidence is compelling. It is because marriage is not about personal happiness, but about providing security for the children a man and woman may produce. Were it just about obtaining a compliant sexual partner, shacking up would serve quite as well.

Way back when our ancestors roamed the countryside pursing game and picking berries, it was impossible for a mother to raise her offspring without assistance. She could scarcely have tracked prey animals with toddlers trailing close behind. No, she needed a husband to do the hunting and to bring home the fruits of his labors.

Times have obviously changed. For most people, meat is no longer obtained by stalking buffalo, but comes pre-packaged in the supermarket. There is no reason for a woman, or her children, to be protein deficient, that is, as long as she has money in her purse.

Moreover, now that most women are out in the marketplace earning their own dollars, they do not need a man to do this for them. Even if they are unemployed, they can rely on the government to provide a welfare check and food stamps.

So why the need for marriage? As it happens, the research shows that children do much better when raised by two parents. Unwed parents sometimes succeed, but the results are far from uniformly positive.

All right then, so why not sponsor gay marriages on the grounds that they too are superior compared with single parenthood? The answer here is not clear. First of all, far fewer gay alliances produce children than do heterosexual ones.

This is especially true with respect to gay men whose unions are notoriously insecure.

As to lesbian couples, these are rearing fewer offspring than media accounts might leave one to surmise. Nonetheless, if they do as good a job of parenting as do a traditional husband and wife, does this matter?

According to the studies that have been produced, being raised by a gay couple is no worse than being raised by a straight one. The trouble is that this research is largely anecdotal and, because it is recent, is not long-term.

The bottom line is that we do not know if homosexual marriages are as good at raising children as the conventional sort. They may be. But then again, perhaps they are not.

With all of the contemporary agitation in favor of gay marriage, we probably need more time to figure out what works before committing to an entirely new form of interpersonal commitment. While gays deserve as much happiness as straights, the real concern here is what happens to their children.

Why Marriage II

Whenever I assert that the central purpose of marriage is to protect children, someone usually objects that not all marriages are blessed with children. How, they ask, can an institution be about something that is not always present?

This is a fair question, to which there is a good answer. Consider the rules of the road. American drivers know that when they get into their automobiles they are required to drive on the right side of the street. They also understand that without this rule, the gridlock would be so bad that no one could ever get anywhere.

Nonetheless, there are times we have the roads exclusively to ourselves. At four o'clock in the morning we might be the only vehicle for miles around. Even so, we are required to keep to the proper lane. And we do.

But why do we do? Why don't we simply throw caution to the wind and aim our machines anywhere we desire? If it sounds silly that we do not, there is actually a very good reason that we don't—and it does not involve the fear that we may get a ticket.

The reason is habit. The need to keep to the appropriate side of the road is so compelling that doing so must be reflexive. It needs to be something we do not think about, but take for granted. Only in this way can we ensure that people—and not just us—do what is necessary most of the time.

This same social strategy applies to marriage. Some social institutions are so deeply ingrained in our hearts and minds that they seem natural. They have to be because there are times when we might be tempted to violate them that are so egregious we must prevent this from occurring.

Mind you, social rules are broken with tedious regularity. Every society has an injunction against murder, nonetheless murders occur everywhere. Yet there would be far more murders if we did not take these proscriptions seriously. If we ignored them, then whenever we felt insulted there might be blood on the floor.

It is the same with marriage. Marriages are supposed to be lifelong commitments. When people agree to wed, they publically vow to remain together until death does them part. Not all do, but the fact that they take these promises seriously enhances the prospects that they will.

This is of particular importance to children because the benefit of having two parents is so great. A mother and father dedicated to remaining a couple are likely to be dedicated to protecting their offspring. There are exceptions, but emotional loyalties improve the odds.

These attitudes are embedded in people when they are very young. They derive in part from the importance that society attaches to marriage. The reason that nuptial ceremonies are public affairs is so that the community can add external pressures to personal desires.

If this is so, then tampering with time-honored marital traditions may be more dangerous than many people suppose. If traditional marriages strengthen the bonds between individuals, then scoffing at this custom may loosen attachments upon which we all rely—especially children.

Which brings me to the subject of gay marriage. Gay marriages may be a good idea—but then again they may not. If in imposing this recent innovation people become convinced that marriage is arbitrary, the sense of sanctity with which it has been surrounded may be reduced.

Then where will we be? Will we feel free to drive on whichever side of the road we please? Will we decide that multiple spouses are okay? Or that cohabitation is just as good as the old-fashioned kind of marriage?

But if we do: what about the children? Will we also decide that a commitment to them is also arbitrary? I hope not, because if this transpires the amount of personal unhappiness will be staggering.

Why I am Not a Feminist

As a sociologist, before I begin teaching most of my classes I make a confession. Because a majority of my students expect sociologists to be liberal, I explain that I am not. Moreover, because much of what I teach involves gender relations, I have to explain that I am not a feminist; that I am indeed an anti-feminist.

Before I continue, I must make something else very clear. I am not against women. I have no desire to see them returned to being "barefoot, pregnant and in the kitchen." If women wish to become the CEO's of major corporations, that is perfectly okay with me. If they want to join the military, that is also fine.

No, I am not anti-feminist because I hate women, but because I love children. It is a desire to protect the young that initially impelled me to suffer the wrath of the politically correct. The problem, as I see it, it not the ambition of many women to be vocationally successful, but the implications of radical feminism per se.

Radical feminists paint a dire picture of heterosexual relationships. They regularly portray women has innocent victims and men as cruel exploiters. Although women are said to be every bit as powerful as men, they are simultaneously depicted as in need of protection from constant threats of rape.

Once upon a time, according to the feminists, the genders were on a par. If anything, women had more power than men. Then the advent of agriculture changed everything. The need for upper-body strength to propel a plow vaulted men into the lead. Subsequently, in order to maintain their advantage, men bullied women into submission.

Now, say the feminists, this male hegemony must be challenged. The rules have to be changed so that everything is fifty/fifty. Because the differences between men and women are sustained primarily by raising boys and girls differently, once this disparity is eliminated, the male advantage will disappear.

For the radical feminists, the ideal state is androgyny. All gender differences, except for the physiological ones, have to disappear. People must essentially become genderless. Individuals need to be judged as people, not men or women. The goal is thus absolute equality.

If this sounds fair, and perhaps democratic, it is anything but. It assumes that the differences between men and women are artificial. As a result, it demands that these be completely expunged. Women are required to become more like men and men more like women. Anything less is depicted as unfair.

Nevertheless, what is unfair is what has happened to many marriages. The voluntary intimacy necessary to sustain long-term heterosexual relationships is put in jeopardy when men and women are assumed to be the same. They are further endangered when women are regularly portrayed as the good guys and men the bad ones.

If men and women are to collaborate on developing strong relationships, they must be allowed to be who they are. More than this, if the parties to a marriage are to tolerate their inherent differences, they must accept these for what they are.

And there are differences, many of which are grounded in biology. Most men are more aggressive than most women, while most women are more emotionally sensitive than most men. There are, to be sure, exceptions but the trends are demonstrable in the different ways male and female brains function.

Mind you, these differences are not better or worse; they are merely different. If anything, they permit men and women to work together synergistically, so that the two can be stronger as a couple than they are individually.

Where children come in is that a strong relationship between their parents is to their advantage. It permits them to rely on two dependable parents who contribute different strengths to raising them. And this in turn makes them stronger and happier than they otherwise would be.

But the feminists interfere with this by turning men and women into enemies. They make marriages more fragile and therefore put children in jeopardy, for utterly imaginary purposes. There is no good reason men cannot be men and women, women, and the two still get along. As a result, I say, let them be themselves. In the end, everyone will be better off.

50/50 Nonsense

The family is in trouble. Divorce and single parenthood are proliferating. Much of this owes to the rubbish that has been disseminated by radical feminists. In the name of equality, they have done their best to poison the relationships between husbands and wives.

One of the worst pieces of nonsense they spout is that intimate unions should be 50/50. Everything that spouses do must therefore be exactly equal.

This goes for their jobs outside the home, as well as the tasks they perform within it.

Thus, the man should diaper the baby as often as his wife. He should also wash the dishes as frequently as she does and cook just as many meals. Anything less than complete uniformity is regarded as exploitation. It is considered evidence that men are irredeemably selfish and why liberated women must resist becoming domestic slaves.

In any event, with Christmas coming, the emphasis on family harmony is on the rise. Romanticized love fills the airwaves and makes many people feel that they should be more starry-eyed than they are. Because they know that they don't live up to the idealized role models, they assume they are doing things wrong.

But guess what, it is the idealized equality that is wrong. Within our separate households, the goal ought not be cookie-cutter equality. The real objective must be fairness, rather than androgyny.

Nowadays, with both men and women well educated, and with most wives holding down demanding jobs, the traditional domestic division of labor is largely obsolete. The notion that he is the sole breadwinner and she the single homemaker is belied by on-the-ground arrangements.

Today, most spouses must come to a private agreement about how they will divide up household responsibilities. They don't necessarily do things the way their parents did—or, for that matter, the way their friends do. Instead, they find a solution that is unique to them and their circumstances.

People may not advertise these private arrangements, but they develop out of their personal inclinations and opportunities. First off, because men and women differ, their choices often reflect their genders. Women, for instance, are generally more comfortable interacting with babies than men.

Men, on the other hand, are commonly more mechanically inclined. They like tinkering with automobile engines. But that does not mean there cannot be a role reversal. Indeed such turnarounds have become commonplace. Many a husband now cooks dinner, while his wife deals with the smoke alarms.

Other factors also influence the choices couples make. Their work schedules, for example, might make it sensible for him to do the grocery shopping, while she picks up the laundry. Or if one becomes handicapped, this might dictate a modification in their assignments.

In short, contemporary couples negotiate their domestic roles. They make idiosyncratic deals about who will do what. Moreover, to repeat, in doing so what counts is fairness, not equality. People, whatever their gender, do not enjoy being used. As result, they demand parity, not uniformity.

As a sociologist, I often bring up the subject of the domestic division of labor in informal conversations. The mostly middle class people with whom I converse are then happy to rattle off their unique understandings. And so I am told about how he likes to do the ironing, while she is in charge of the washing machine. Or that she mows the lawn, while he does the vacuuming.

Furthermore, I do not hear many recriminations. People seldom accuse a spouse of being completely insensitive. Instead, they chuckle about a way of dividing tasks they assumed were exclusive to them. They may even feel a bit self-conscious at being "different."

As it happens, in my home I do more of the cooking than my wife. I also do most of the vegetable chopping because knives make her uncomfortable. Yet she does all of the baking—because she is good at it and fond of it. By the way, I am glad of this. Her oatmeal cookies are to die for.

The point of these observations is that modern families differ from the traditional models, but that does not signify they are broken. Nor do husbands and wives have to become androgynous clones in order to be happy. Nowadays we have the freedom to do what works. Shouldn't we enjoy this?

Concern for the Poor

Many years ago I worked as a reporter for the *Hudson Dispatch*. The paper was located in Union City, New Jersey, just across the river from New York. As a result, the area it served was very urban and, in many cases, very poor.

This was also at the height of Lyndon Johnson's war on poverty; hence it came as no surprise when I was assigned to cover a meeting called by poverty workers to organize the poor. The goal was to empower the downtrodden so that they could demand the benefits that were rightly theirs.

The theory upon which this intervention was based assumed that the poor are poor because the rich keep them that way. It was therefore up to members of the underclass to force this uncaring elite to share their undeserved affluence. Only if the wealthy had their arms twisted, would they disgorge their ill-gotten gains.

Once I got to the meeting, I found the hall packed. There was standing room only, with perhaps a hundred and fifty persons present. Then, the meeting was called to order by its governmentally sponsored organizers. They wanted to know what these poor people needed in order to improve their situation.

At this, pandemonium broke out. It seemed that everyone in the room had an answer that required an immediate hearing. From front to back, virtually everyone stood up to shout out what they believed. So vociferous was this cacophony that no one was able to hear what anyone else said.

These folks were not from the middle class, therefore, they were not accustomed to turn taking. As a consequence, the meeting never did settle down. Indeed, so raucous did it become that it had to be canceled.

Now we are hearing Mitt Romney condemned because he said he did not care about the poor. It did not matter that he quickly amended his words to say that his concentration was on the middle class, but that he would make certain he maintained, and repaired, the current social safety net.

Meanwhile, Newt Gingrich, sensing an opportunity, asserted that he most certainly did care about the poor and would provide them, not with a safety net, but a trampoline, so that they could rise in society.

Gingrich's words, however, were no more than policy by way of metaphor. What, after all, was the trampoline of which he spoke? The safety net consists of welfare, food stamps, Medicaid, and so forth. It may not be deserve rave reviews, but what it is, is known.

If by the trampoline, Gingrich meant jobs, how was he going to supply them? And did he really believe that Romney—who has promised to revive the economy—was going to prevent the poor from getting jobs thereby created? Both clearly intend to increase the middle class by lifting millions out of poverty.

The problem is that it is difficult to help the poor. Caring alone has never been enough. Even the war on poverty, despite expending trillions of dollars, was unable to get the job done. Like it or not, the poor have a way of undermining their own life chances.

We, in sociology, have been fighting over these issues for over a century. Having worked with the poor, I am among those who believe that a *culture of poverty* is one of the reasons why many people do not do for themselves what they could do if they put their minds to it. Many of my colleagues, however, condemn this attitude as "blaming the victim." They claim that I am without compassion.

But I say (along with Mitt?) that there are some things only people can do for themselves. I believe, that no matter how many kind words, or trillions of dollars in transfer payments, are on offer, if they don't help themselves, no one else can.

As a college professor, I see this in action in my classrooms. Many of my students come from disadvantaged backgrounds. But many of these have committed themselves to using a college education to provide them with an economic leg up.

Nonetheless, some don't take advantage of this opportunity. They don't study! What of them? Who is responsible if they don't get out of poverty? Me? Or Mitt? Or rich people in general?

Human Hierarchies

I am a sociologist. I love being a sociologist. It gives me the opportunity to study how people live and why they do the things they do. Furthermore, because I regard myself as a social scientist, my goal has been to utilize the tools of science to expand our knowledge of the social world.

In this quest, I have had many allies. Talented sociologists, past and present, have contributed to building a wealth of unexpected insights. Nevertheless, a large proportion of contemporary sociologists function more as moralists than social scientists.

These latter folks are more concerned with promoting pre-established moral agendas than unearthing new facts. An example of this tendency has been provided by a shift in how they conceive of their subject matter. Thus, where once they talked about social strat-ification (i.e., social class differences), today they study inequalities.

"Inequality" is, of course, a loaded term. It is tendentious, that is, it incorporates an unstated moral judgment. We in the United States, given our Jeffersonian heritage, cannot but assume that inequality is bad. Having been told, from our tenderest years, that equality is an unalienable right, we believe it is.

Now whether it is, or isn't, is not my current concern. The issue I wish to address is whether pursuing an unexpressed moral agenda is inimical to good science. When one's moral goals take precedence over the search for truth, is it possible to discover the truth?

One of my professional idols, Max Weber, insisted that sociology should be value-neutral. He contended that whatever our personal commitments, we must leave them at the door when we put on our scientific hats. Yes, we can have moral convictions, but these should not blind us to unwelcome realities.

For me, this is the bedrock of genuine science; hence I try to utilize it as a beacon while navigating the shoals of unexplored knowledge. As a result, instead of studying "inequalities," I have investigated the ins and outs of human hierarchies.

In particular, I have studied how social hierarchies are created and maintained. Rather than assume that equality is the normal human condition—as many sociologists do—I have explored what people do when they engage in ranking themselves relative to others.

As a consequence, I have come to the conclusion that we are hierarchical animals. All of us, the elites and the underclasses, seek to improve our status in comparison with others. We want to be winners and not losers. Indeed, so important do we find this, that we some-times put our lives on the line in its pursuit.

My conclusions have recently been published in a book entitled *Human Hierarchies: A General Theory* (Transaction Publishing). Much to my amazement, this title seems not to have previously been utilized. Apparently the idea that we are an in-herently hierarchical species has had limited appeal.

Yet, if I am correct, it is impossible to understand why we behave the ways we do without placing our conduct in a hierarchical perspective. Thus, we today find ourselves in the midst of class warfare. This could not happen if we did not divide ourselves according to differences in social power.

Are the wealthy bad people? Are the poor sainted victims? Why do some people come to these conclusions? And are the lessons they draw valid? Without disinterestedly examining what is taking place, it is doubtful that the truth can be reached.

For my own part, I have concluded that ranking systems are inevitable and that everyone, from the top to the bottom, participates in perpetuating them. What is open to change is how they are constructed—not whether they will exist.

This is not to say that hierarchy is always fair. Clearly, it frequently is not. But neither is it to suggest that we can totally eliminate unfairness. We cannot. Moral improvements can be effect-ively pursued, but only if we recognize the limits of what is possible.

Social Discipline

We have become a middle class society, but in the process we have inadvertently corrupted our lower classes. Because the rules that apply to middle class folks don't always apply to the poor, treating everyone the same has resulted in a host of tragedies.

Let me explain. I have been reading Charles Murray's new book *Coming Apart* as well as an article about Melvin Kohn's ideas on social values, and putting the pieces together. What they suggest is something that at first blush sounds antithetic to the American Dream.

Murray richly documents the diverging fates of those at the upper and lower ends of our social class system. While members of the upper middle class are doing very nicely, the lowest thirty percent are trapped in a cycle of crime, unemployment, and disintegrating marriages. Moreover, they are unhappy.

Meanwhile, Kohn has provided evidence that middle class parents teach their children to be self-directed, whereas lower class parents demand conformity. The latter insist on obedience and if it is not forthcoming have no compunctions about imposing physical discipline.

What this results in are upper middle class children who are capable of self-discipline and lower class children who have difficulty with self-control. The former internalize social standards such as morality, while the latter become oppositional and seek to get away with what they can.

The difference in these orientations is on display in the sports they favor. Thus, the middle classes enjoy golf, an activity that is notorious for the personal concentration it requires. The lower classes, however, are enraptured by pro-wrestling, a spectacle in which large-bodied paladins often cheat in order to defeat their opponents.

This disparity may seem amusing, yet is anything but. When it is translated onto the larger social scene, it means that middle class persons are more worthy of trust than their lower class peers. Because they monitor their own behaviors and control their selfish impulses, they can be allowed to function without external controls. Indeed, as social leaders they often control others.

Meanwhile, those belonging to the lower strata more often seek to elude social constraints. They hate being bound by rules, thus if they believe their activities are not being monitored, they over-step the lines. I saw this when I worked at a methadone clinic where the attitude was that law breaking was okay—as long as you didn't get caught.

Put this together with the fact that our society today believes in "tolerance" and the consequences are alarming. We are now supposed to offer everyone "unconditional positive regard" and refrain from being "judgmental." This stance appears humane, yet is fraught with danger.

We can indeed take a hands-off approach with people who are self-directed. Because they discipline themselves, they can be allowed to make independent choices. On the other hand, those who are not self-directed cannot be extended a similar independence.

The Perils of Affirmative Action

Most fair-minded people believe that everyone deserves an equal chance—irrespective of race, gender, or religion. Nowadays this frequently boils down to providing everyone with an opportunity to acquire a good education.

The question, however, is how best to achieve this? Many people, especially liberals, assume that this must entail what has been called "affirmative action." They want to make sure that minorities are not excluded from higher education and therefore they support balanced admission "objectives."

According to the advocates of this policy, colleges should set admission targets for African-Americans—but not quotas. In practice, of course, these come down to exactly the same thing. They also say that race should serve only as a tiebreaker when candidates' credentials are fairly close.

In fact, affirmative action has been used to admit minorities to elite colleges for which their academic preparation is wholly inadequate. The effects of this strategy have recently been chronicled by Richard Sander and Stuart Taylor in their book, *Mismatch: How Affirmative Action Hurts Students It's Intended To Help, and Why Universities Won't Admit It*.

As this work's title suggests, the lead author's research demonstrates that students who are admitted to colleges for which they are unprepared suffer serious injury. Many do not graduate, or if they do, they do so poorly that they have difficulty entering the job market.

Good intentions do not always produce good results. For a long time critics have been asking how it benefits a student to be admitted to a school, but then fail out? Now the data is in and it confirms the worst fears of the doubters. The supposed beneficiaries of affirmative action do less well than their peers who do not receive this presumed assistance.

Sander, who is a law professor at UCLA, has spent over a decade and a half studying the admissions policies of law schools. He finds, and this has been confirmed by other researchers, that students with low grades and test scores cannot keep up with the demands of the more rigorous schools.

He also finds that they become discouraged and drop out. Or if they graduate, they cannot pass the bar exam and therefore do not become lawyers. Meanwhile, students who are better matched with lower ranking schools get better grades and do pass the bar.

The point is that what matters is how well a student's academic grounding fits the standards of a particular school. The better the fit; the better the outcome. Efforts to vault people into programs they cannot handle does them no good. It only leads to frustration and bitterness.

To me, one of the worst aspects of this discovery is how it has been dealt with by academics. For the most part, they are in denial. So committed are they to affirmative action that they refuse to alter their programs.

Thus, when California, by law, forbade its university system from using race to determine college admission, the professors and administrators were up in arms. They predicted complete disaster, with African-American students totally excluded for top-tier schools.

And indeed, the number of blacks admitted to Berkeley fell substantially. But the surprise was that the number who graduated increased. Since only well-prepared students were accepted, these could, and did, keep up.

So what was the lesson that the academics learned? Well, they didn't learn. They were so determined to keep affirmative action in place; they changed their admission policies. Instead of relying on grades and test scores, their practices became more "holistic" and hence subjective.

In other words, the university officials cheated. They stacked the deck to bring back minorities in the desired numbers. As an academic, I was mortified that scholars who supposedly believe in empirical facts rejected these in favor of touchy-feely moral sentiments.

So where does this leave us? Will our colleges institute reforms that actually make things better, or will they remain in the same anti-intellectual rut? In short, members of the lower classes require a greater variety of external constraints. If they are to behave in a disciplined manner, they must be subject to exterior sanctions when they violate social standards.

Nonetheless, we as a society have decided that imposing standards on people violates their rights. This tactic, while it works perfectly well with most middle class folks, invites irresponsibility and lethargy from lower class folks.

Once upon a time, most people understood this. They realized that social discipline was required if we were to have an orderly society. The founding fathers recognized this when they endorsed religion as a means of keeping people socially accountable.

Most ordinary people endorsed it when they subscribed to a legal system that punished the guilty. They also approved it when they scorned those who broke their marriage vows.

Regretfully, we too must uphold social discipline. The fact is that there are some folks who need it and others who suffer when it is absent.

Holding Our Society Together

Once upon a time, our ancestors were hunter-gatherers. They lived in small groups of little more than a hundred souls who wandered their territories in search of sustenance. These folks cooperated with one another because they had too. They were also tied together with bands of affection.

Hunter-gathers knew everyone in their tiny clans. They had interacted all of their lives and worked face-to-face daily. This, moreover, was the world for which they were genetically primed. It felt natural because it was.

How different things are with us. We are surrounded by millions of strangers, most of whom we never meet. Although we depend upon these people, we don't have an opportunity to develop a personal relationship with more than a few. We are not emotionally attached for want of the interactions that enable these to happen.

Nowadays, the impact of this lack of bonding is making itself felt. Our society is retribalizing. We are breaking down into smaller, mutually hostile, groups. Not only do liberals hate conservatives, but blacks do not trust whites, women are skeptical of men, and gays look askance at straights.

Despite repeated calls for universal love, we don't love everyone—because we can't. Genuine love is contingent upon in-timacy, which is impossible when so many folks are involved.

So what are we to do? We see people fighting with each other in the streets. We witness angry diatribes on television. We worry about the effects of increasing diversity. With all of these centrifugal forces, how can we strengthen the attachments upon which we depend?

There are, in fact, a number of ways. Love may not be enough, but it can be supplemented by other means. One of these is morality. All societies have moral rules. These enable us to reduce the conflicts between people who have competing interests. They tamp down disagreements—even between strangers.

The problem is that as societies grow larger, the rules they impose must be modified. To illustrate, what constitutes theft among hunter-gatherers is not the same as what does in an industrial society. In the former, for instance, there is no intellectual property to steal.

In any event, our mass techno-commercial society is in the midst of a gigantic renegotiation of our shared values. What are we to decide about abortion, gay rights, or the sanctity of marriage? Opinions not only differ, they ferociously differ. Even whether free medical treatment is a "right" is up for grabs.

What then are we to do? How can we develop a consensus that permits us to live comfortably with a multitude of strangers? To which communal rules can we give allegiance, despite our disparate backgrounds and interests? If we are to trust one another, a set of core principles is essential.

I suggest five. They are: honesty, personal responsibility, fairness-defined as universality, individual freedom, and family commitment. All are grounded in our history, but must be modified to deal with emerging challenges. Only then can they form a nucleus around which agreement is feasible.

To cite one area in which modifications are necessary; the family is not what it was. The roles of men and women have changed, so, therefore, must the ways in which they maintain intimate commitments. This is, in fact, occurring in households across the nation.

Once we reestablish what we believe is moral, we can use our collective allegiances to settle differences. We may not love each other, but we can be truthful, mutually supportive, and abide by the same standards. Under these conditions, we will know what to expect from one another, including those we never previously encountered.

Yes, we must judge one another. We have to if we are to enforce agreed upon principles. But, in the process, we also learn how we are apt to be evaluated. This facilitates choosing the appropriate conduct.

Shared principles provide shared goals. When these point in directions from which most of us benefit, they can coordinate complex activities. They are able to hold us together because they lead down common pathways.

Strangers, because most seldom interact, cannot always be motivated by emotional ties. They can, however, be moved by internalized moral commitments. And if they are, they can operate conjointly despite their differences.

Social Individualism: Texas Style

When Texas was first being settled by Anglos, they had a problem. There was plenty of free land available on the frontier, but the Comanches were contesting it. What is more, this tribe had a fearsome reputation. Its warriors were rightly regarded as the scourge of the southern plains.

Families that ventured out to lonely homesteads were essentially on their own. Raiding parties could attack them at any time to steal their horses and collect their scalps. It took extreme courage—and tenacity—to take such a chance. Nonetheless, the original Texans prided themselves on their rugged individualism.

One of the things that social scientists have learned is that cultural adaptations tend to persist. The same willingness to take risks, without complaining about setbacks that characterized their state's pioneers was still visible in the reaction of Texans to the devastation wrought by hurricane Harvey.

Instead of crying about how cruel nature had been, they immediately got out and started helping their neighbors. Rather than sit on their hands and wait to be rescued, they did the rescuing. Many of these folks placed their lives in jeopardy, despite the destruction done to their own homes.

It has become customary for millions of Americans to scream out for government assistance whenever they encounter a difficulty. Uncle Sam is supposed to provide the money and the expertise to extract them from whatever situation makes them unhappy.

While it is true that the Trump administration has effectively organized federal support, FEMA and the National Guard found enthusiastic partners already on the ground. Ordinary citizens had taken the initiative to climb into their boats and trucks to brave the elements. Mere floods were not going to stop them.

The rest of the nation looked upon this bravado with awe. It clearly took courage to defy the unknown. It also took pluck to begin the process of rebuilding before the waters receded. There was no complaining. There was just good old-fashioned hard work and cooperative effort.

Texan individualism demonstrated something else. People who take personal responsibility are better able to utilize assistance from others. They can join forces with, let us say the police, because they are standing on their own two feet.

Responsible individuals think for themselves. This makes it easier to figure out how best to collaborate with officials. Responsible individuals can also make adjustments. They are able to modify their responses because they are not terrified by the unexpected.

Most importantly, people who are individualists have a strong sense of self. They are comfortable with who they are and consequently are comfortable with people who differ from themselves. Individualism does not equal selfishness. Indeed, it frequently signifies the reverse.

I have recently been arguing that our post-industrial society requires a new ideal. The squishy calls for social justice coming from the left are insufficient. So are the demands for liberty emanating from the right. These are all well and good, yet they are not enough.

What we need now is social individualism. We need more people who are willing to be themselves and to save themselves, while at the same time collaborating with their neighbors. In other words, more of us must both be for ourselves and for others.

The Texans has shown us how this can be achieved. There is no contradiction between being personally strong and concerned with the welfare of our fellow citizens. People can make independent choices that benefit themselves, while pulling up their sleeves to help the guy next door.

Social individualism is the opposite of collective dependence. Instead of abdicating what we can do for ourselves, it takes satisfaction in personal achievement. Instead of clamoring for a bigger piece of the federal pie, it seeks to bake it's own pie.

Social individualism is aware of the limitations placed upon us by inhabiting a mass society, but it is also aware of the opportunities made available when strong people team up with other strong people. They do not whine. They do not point fingers as supposedly oppressive enemies. They just get down to business!

Dodge Ball and Me

Once dodge ball was ubiquitous. Almost every middle school in the nation expected students to play this game. In gym classes, two teams would be organized to throw soccer balls at one another, with the last student who remained untouched declared the winner.

This diversion was regarded as great exercise and an excellent way to encourage competition. But, with the rise of liberalism, this activity came to be regarded as barbaric. Instead of promoting cooperation, it urged teenagers to inflict symbolic injuries. This would not do.

I, however, loved dodge ball. One reason was that I was good at it. Because I was neither very big nor strong, I wasn't going to be a star in football or basketball. I was nonetheless quick and agile, and hence well equipped to get out of the way of a ball aimed at me.

Still, it was another ability that ensured I was generally one of the last players standing. It was my strategy. I did not play the game the way most of my peers did. Almost all of them gathered together in a defensive cluster. Their idea was to protect themselves behind a wall of others.

As for me, I stood alone. My aim was to be as far away as I could. This was judged foolish in that it apparently defied the other side to take me out. After all, I was a well-defined target. Why not show me I was vulnerable?

But that is not usually how it worked out. The opposition habitually aimed at the target rich scrum. They calculated that if they missed one person, there was a good chance of hitting another. In this, they were correct.

Moreover, the crowd made it more difficult for individual players to recognize when they were targeted. Because others obscured their view, they might not see the ball coming. This made it difficult to react appropriately.

With me, it was different. Because I stood alone, it was absolutely clear when someone aimed at me. Furthermore, I had the room to get away. With no one standing next to me, there was no one hindering my lateral movement. This permitted me to take advantage of my agility.

Why do I bring this up? My teenage days are far behind me. Besides, no one has directed a dodge ball at me in decades. Nor do I expect kudos for modest achievements that occurred ages ago. So what is the point?

As I ponder the changes that have come upon our society, like others I have contemplated what the future holds. My conclusion is that liberalism is about to expire and will be replaced by "social individualism." Since our society is becoming more complex, it will be necessary for more people to be self-motivated experts.

Yet those who are self-directed need the courage to make independent decisions. If they are to make full use of their skills, they must be willing to take risks. Although their autonomous choices could be wrong, they cannot otherwise bring their abilities to bear.

If so, more people need to be capable of operating as individuals. They will require the personal fortitude to stand alone, even though they might be blamed for their mistakes. Just like me, when I played dodge ball, they will often have to separate themselves from the crowd.

Rugged individualism was once a hallmark of what it meant to be an American. The pioneers of yore took amazing chances to bring our nation's potential to fruition. But the same is true of us. If our country is not to fall into decline, we must be the one's to save it.

Nonetheless, many people find individualism frightening. They are afraid that if they stand out, they will become a target. In fact, they may. But this need not make them defenseless. If they remain alert, and know what they are doing, they too can get out of the way.

As for myself, I enjoy the idea of being a sturdy individual. I want some of my triumphs to be my own. That, however, does not mean I am unwilling to work with others. To the contrary, I am pleased to contribute to common causes. Why, indeed, can't our nation be a tapestry of hardy individuals dedicated to their own and each other's welfare?

Toward a Balanced Society

The meanness and vituperation of the contemporary scene show no signs of abating. Despite alarming instances of violence, politicians are still at each other's throats, while the media remains as vulgar and ill tempered as ever. Is there no way to end the vicious partisanship?

Recently I suggested a "social individualism" solution to our ideological logjam. If we learn to be emotionally mature individuals who make decisions based on "principled realism," we may be able to reconcile many of our competing interests.

Nonetheless, I fear that some of my recommendations may be misunderstood. I have contended that not only liberalism, but conservatism and libertarianism are obsolete. They, on their own, cannot help us overcome the partisan rancor.

But this does not mean that they can no longer contribute to our collective welfare. Although they may not answer all of our needs, they can answer some of them. Together, if they are balanced against each other, and if they respect our social and personal limitations, they can make life easier.

Let us start with religion. We are an increasingly secular society, but belief in a deity remains widespread. Spiritualism has been part of the human condition for as long as we have any records. It is therefore safe to say that it is not going away.

Furthermore, religion provides warmth and reassurance to many lives. It comforts people in the face of a frightening universe and furnishes a reason for living. These benefits are too useful to be jettisoned. As a result, religion should be preserved and protected.

Next we must deal with our market economy. The freedom to buy and sell goods in the marketplace has enabled us to become wealthier and more secure than any previous generation. We eat better, are more comfortably sheltered, and are even more extensively entertained.

Capitalism has not, irrespective of socialist complaints, enslaved people. It actually provided the resources for democracy, thereby enabling people to enhance the quality of their lives. And so, the free market too ought not be discarded. It also deserves to be preserved and protected.

Then there is the welfare state. The federal bureaucracy may have grown arrogant and sclerotic, but it continues to supply a safety net for millions who might otherwise suffer. They too eat better, sleep better, and are better educated than they would be without these services.

If religion and the marketplace have added our security, so have the programs administered by the government. While these may sometimes be inefficient and overbearing, most of us would not want to do without them. Thus, they also merit being preserved and protected.

It is accordingly not a question of getting rid of any one of these. None ought to be eliminated so that the sole survivor can dominate everything we touch and do. Not only would this be overly restrictive, but it would soon demonstrate that a dogmatic monopoly was unworkable.

What is thus necessary is not the complete victory of one set of partisans over the others. If a crucial balance is to be achieved, a reciprocated appreciation that no collection of ideas has all of the answers is indispensable. Mutual respect is consequently in order.

Human life is complicated and our societies are even more complicated. As a result, there can be no simple solutions to our metastasizing problems. A bit more humility, accompanied by huge doses of realism and principled behavior are essential if we are to flourish.

This is supposedly the best-educated generation ever, but it is not very well informed if it does not respect the limitations inherent in our situation. We can never have all we want or be all we want. Sometimes we need to settle for what the universe makes available.

This must begin by accepting the fact that none of us has a corner on truth and goodness. From time to time, we all need to make room for the other guy's insights. These need to offset our own so that solutions can come from multiple directions.

It used to be said that politics is the art of the possible. Americans likewise once understood that compromise was central to our national institutions. Unless we reclaim these truisms, we may never achieve the balance to prosper.

The Symphony and Tradition

With Christmas coming up tomorrow, I was recently reminded of the importance of traditions. About a week ago, my wife and I attended a performance of the Atlanta Symphony at Kennesaw State University. As usual, their holiday selections were a pleasure to hear.

But as I sat watching these talented musicians play, I became aware of how remarkable the concert was. Here were dozens of separate individuals collaborating on creating musical magic.

Most of the time, we take orchestras for granted. Even if we do not attend their performances, we know they exist. We have heard them on the radio, on movie soundtracks, and from our i-pads. Their music is, as it were, the wallpaper of our lives.

Nonetheless, orchestras are made up of dedicated performers, who spend years honing their craft. Had they not cared, they would not have made the effort. Nor would they take pride in attaining skills most of us never approach.

How then can these folks, who must have strong egos, submerge themselves in a group endeavor? All of those involved take bows at the end of the performance, but during it, they are often regarded as cogs in a well-oiled machine.

What I realized, in listening to their joint effort, was how minutely it was orchestrated. Different instruments contributed distinctive sounds that were exquisitely coordinated. If only one came in at the wrong time, the impact might have been jarring.

Next I wondered how this combination came to be. The compositions played, the instruments used, and the way these were synchronized had obviously evolved over many centuries. They were not the product of an identifiable individual who dreamed them up in a modern living room.

What I was listening to owed to a continuously developing tradition. Many people contributed to refining the instruments and compositions I was enjoying. These were so complex that no single person could have ever have put all of the pieces together.

These musicians were part of a much larger tapestry. They could not have learned their parts nor mastered their instruments had these not preceded them into existence.

Then I realized that the same applies to Christmas. It too is a remarkably intricate tradition. It too has many pieces we inherited from our ancestors. They bequeathed us the Christmas tree, Santa Claus, Christmas carols, turkey dinners and streets decked out in colored lights.

Many people denigrate the holiday because they feel it imposes a particular religious system upon us. They believe that erecting crèches in our town squares is a violation of the First Amendment. As for me, despite my Jewish heritage, I consider this nonsense.

Christmas is both a religious and a secular holiday. Nowadays, in addition to celebrating the birth of Christ, it celebrates the family and love. What is wrong with that? What is wrong in marking the winter solstice with an evocation of the new life that will erupt once spring returns?

Nowadays music is all too often a solitary event. People are plugged in to performances that only they hear. Even when they go to hip-hop concerts, they jump up and down in private ecstasy. Our sense of community has long since eroded. Why then not retain a holiday dedicated to renewing it?

Many Americans are also consumed with the new. Novelty for its own sake has become a modern icon. But this does not mean that what is up-to-date is always best. The melodies of old are frequently more satisfying than the jarring rhythms of screaming super-stars.

Traditions can be comforting. They can also lay a foundation upon which we add improvements. Indeed, without tradition we would be adrift. We would be thrown into the world without a compass and deprived of fellow travelers engaged in understandable activities.

So as for me, I will continue to say Merry Christmas. What is more, my wife and I erect a Christmas tree and light a Hanukah menorah. Here's hoping you also have nourishing traditions.

The Fulcrum of a Balanced Society

As I have previously written, we are in the midst of an ideological crisis. There amounts to a three cornered war between liberalism, conservatism, and libertarianism. Adherents of each side are convinced that they are in the right and that the only way for society to be saved is for them to win.

Unfortunately all of their conceptual frameworks derive from times very different than our own. None furnish answers to problems significantly unlike the ones their dogmas were designed to solve. Their ideas developed in less complex times, whereas we live in a mass techno-commercial civilization.

Thus, religious conservatism traces back two thousand years to the agricultural empires, libertarianism arose during the enlightenment when commerce began to flourish, and liberalism, better described as bureaucratic collectivism, arrived on the scene concurrent with industrialization.

Their mismatch with post-modernism is therefore striking. None supply the tools needed to maintain social integrity in extremely populous states where millions of people are dependent upon strangers for survival. Neither love, nor social justice, nor prosperity can do the job alone.

This is not to say, however, that each cannot make valuable contributions. The world would be in desperate shape if any one of these ideologies completely vanquished the others. In fact, if they collaborate—much to the distress of their sponsors—they can complement each other.

The question then remains as to how we can achieve this balance. What is the fulcrum upon which these idea systems might find an equilibrium? As I have previously suggested, I believe we are moving toward "social individualism." Each of us must become personally strong enough, and realistic enough, to make choices as circumstances transform.

There may be times when government interventions are necessary, but there may be others where the free marketplace requires greater latitude. Similarly, for some, their religious convictions provide the guidance to endure what seems unendurable.

The best solutions vary with the time, the players, and the challenges. So how are strong individuals to decide? What qualities do they need in order to choose wisely? These radically diverge from those required of our ancestors. Moreover, they are not easy to cultivate.

First, social individualists must be emotionally mature. They need to be adults who can deal with powerful emotions without falling apart. More specifically, their passions cannot be so intense that they cloud their judgment. Whether they are afraid, or angry, or sad, they must not revert to the primitive impulses of children. In other words, they need self-control.

Second, they must be principled realists. They require a moral compass that enables strangers to resolve their inevitably clashing interests. This entails a commitment to honesty, personal responsibility, fairness as defined by universality, liberty, and family values. Without these trust is impossible.

But they must also be realists. Their idealism must be temper-ed by the constraints placed on us by nature and social imperatives. They have to understand, for instance, that universal love is impossible, as is complete equality. For humans, love is always circumscribed, whereas we all want to be winners, which ensures that some will be losers. What counts is unobstructed social mobility, not exact parity.

Third, more of us must become professionalized. Both at home and at work, we need to be self-motivated experts at what we do. If we cannot make competent decisions in environments of uncertainty, others will make these for us. When this is the case, they control our destinies.

All of this is a tall order. Social individualism is not automatic. It must be cultivated and protected. For us to achieve it, whether for ourselves or society, we have to begin by understanding what is needed and recognizing that it will not be attained unless we tenaciously pursue it.

We are today better educated than our ancestors. We also live more comfortably. As a consequence, we have the time and the resources to nurture our best selves. But this is up to us. No one can do it for us.

Happily, this means there is a way out of our ideological predicament. Yet it entails seeing what we may want to see and doing what we may not want to do. Nonetheless, our salvation is in our own hands.

Chapter X

Some Final Thoughts

Cutting the Gordian Knot
There can be little doubt that we are collectively enduring a period of turmoil and despair. Despite our unprecedented wealth, America's historic optimism has been questioned. Anger stalks our nation, with folks of differing opinions refusing to talk to one another. The blame for our anguish is usually assigned to our political adversaries. Nevertheless, I have argued that its primary cause is an ideological crisis. The conventional ways in which we understand the world have let us down. Liberalism, in particular, has not delivered on its promises. But then, neither are religious conservatism or libertarianism, on their own, up to the job. A new set of conceptual tools is therefore essential.

Our country's founders were on the right track. The checks and balances they built into the constitution have served us well. Today these must be extended to cover our philosophical differences. Balance is vital. Given our mass techno-commercial society, we need to embrace *social individualism.* If we are to make sensible choices about what is appropriate to deal with our unprecedented trials, we must be up to the task. Instead of relying on government experts, we need to understand our selves, our social circumstances, and the realm of the possible. To this end, we must become principled realists, who are professionalized, courageous, and emotionally mature. Only then we can save ourselves from the perils threatening us.

An updated version of conservatism can cut the Gordian knot. By pursuing smaller government, a free market, democracy, personal liberty, and family values, but doing so flexibly, we can solve a host of contemporary dilemmas. Tradition ought to be respected. But we must also make suitable adjustments. Most of us—especially the young—want to make the world a better place. We are inspired by the prospect genuine improvements. Only a forward-looking program can achieve this. In other words, conservatism must not be strictly conservative. Although it needs to resist the blandishments of neo-Marxism, it has to do so in accord with our abilities and social facts. At the moment, we are renegotiating what we want our future to be. The social individualism agenda offers an alternative to failed ideologies derived from the past. I hope the preceding columns have contributed to explicating why this is the case.

Made in United States
Orlando, FL
04 March 2023